THE HIDDEN JANE AUSTEN

In this major study, leading Austen scholar John Wiltshire offers new interpretations of Jane Austen's six novels, *Sense and Sensibility* (1811), *Pride and Prejudice* (1813), *Mansfield Park* (1814), *Emma* (1816), *Northanger Abbey* and *Persuasion* (1818). Much recent criticism of Austen has concentrated on the social, historical and intellectual context of her work, but Wiltshire turns attention back to Austen's prose techniques. Arguing that each of Austen's works has its own distinct focus and underlying agenda, he shows how Austen's interest in psychology, and especially her treatment of attention and the various forms of memory, helped shape her narratives. Through a series of compelling close readings of key passages in each novel, Wiltshire underscores Austen's unique ability to penetrate the hidden inner motives and impulses of her characters, and reveals some of the secrets of her narrative art.

JOHN WILTSHIRE is Adjunct Professor at La Trobe University, Melbourne. He is author of *Jane Austen and the Body: 'The Picture of Health'* (Cambridge, 1992) and *Recreating Jane Austen* (Cambridge, 2001), and editor of *Mansfield Park* (Cambridge, 2005) in The Cambridge Edition of the Works of Jane Austen.

D1453853

THE HIDDEN JANE AUSTEN

JOHN WILTSHIRE

La Trobe University, Melbourne

CAMBRIDGE
UNIVERSITY PRESS

CAMBRIDGE
UNIVERSITY PRESS

University Printing House, Cambridge CB2 8BS, United Kingdom

Cambridge University Press is part of the University of Cambridge.

It furthers the University's mission by disseminating knowledge in the pursuit of education, learning and research at the highest international levels of excellence.

www.cambridge.org
Information on this title: www.cambridge.org/9781107061873

© John Wiltshire 2014

First published 2014
Reprinted 2015

A catalogue record for this publication is available from the British Library

Library of Congress Cataloging in Publication data
Wiltshire, John.
The Hidden Jane Austen / John Wiltshire.
pages   cm
Includes bibliographical references.
ISBN 978-1-107-06187-3 (Hardback)
1. Austen, Jane, 1775–1817–Criticism and interpretation.   I. Title.
PR4037.W53 2003
823′.7–dc23   2014000292

ISBN 978-1-107-06187-3 Hardback
ISBN 978-1-107-64364-2 Paperback

For my grandsons, Angus and Oscar

Contents

Preface

Austen studies for the last few decades have often been concerned with Jane Austen's place in history. A book called *The Hidden Jane Austen* might well belong to this genre, since exploring the historical circumstances and written sources to which Austen's work may refer can certainly throw light on previously missed or misunderstood aspects of her novels. No one writing seriously now about Austen can ignore this historicist approach or its very fruitful results, but on the whole this volume belongs to another genre. It seeks – as far as possible – to read Jane Austen as our contemporary, and so to offer new readings of the novels to some extent inspired by twenty-first-century preoccupations, while keeping closely attentive to her texts.

The topic of attention in fact is central to this book in two ways. I'm going to suggest that it is a key issue for Austen readers because in all of her published novels the heroine's attention or inattention is coupled with and sometimes played against our own engagement. Memory, which is dependent on attention in the first place, is just as important a feature. This book seeks to explore how attention and memory are dramatised, but at the same time to illuminate the reading experience of attention, and often to distinguish between reading and re-reading, as well as practising careful attention itself. The heroines are treated as psychological realities because I believe that imagining characters as actual beings is the primary, natural act of reading the realist novel, and that re-reading is a poor thing if this is lost sight of.

I take my orientation in each chapter from within the space of each novel, rather than co-opting each into an overmastering argument. The word 'hidden' in this book thus has a wide range of meanings. It appears in all of these chapters, but it does not always point to the same aspect of the texts, for to explore the inner workings of each novel is to recognise, equally, that each one has its own unique atmosphere and agenda. Nevertheless, in all of them I hope to show how astonishing is Austen's penetration of the hidden inner motives and impulses of her imagined characters.

This book does not enter one realm that its title might seem to promise. *The Hidden Jane Austen* has nothing to reveal about Jane Austen's personal life. I have, however, been constantly reminded of the phrase – extraordinary in itself – that Austen's family included on her tombstone in Winchester Cathedral: among the familiar pieties is a line in praise of 'the extraordinary endowments of her mind'.

All references to Jane Austen's novels are to the Cambridge Edition of the Works of Jane Austen, 2005–8, and take the form: abbreviated title (where this is not clear from the context) in italics, volume number in roman, followed by a colon, chapter number, and page number in this edition. Thus (*P&P* II: 14, 235). Most references take the form (1: 2, 21). Deirdre Le Faye's edition of *Jane Austen's Letters* (Oxford University Press, 1995) is cited as *Letters*.

Acknowledgements

I thank Dr Linda Bree for her initial encouragement and continual mentoring of this book. Her questions and suggestions throughout its development have been invaluable. My colleague Laura Carroll has also read the book in its penultimate draft and made suggestions about its structure I have found especially helpful. I thank too, the anonymous readers for Cambridge University Press. I'm indebted to my friends Ann Blake, Ira Raja, Max Richards and Bill Spence for their help and encouragement, in all sorts of ways. I would also like to thank Louis Le Vaillant and the staff at the Johnston Collection in Melbourne where I have been giving talks on the eighteenth century for the past five years, as well as the successive presidents of the Jane Austen Society of Melbourne, Andrea Richards and Mercia Chapman. My principal debt, however, is to a friend on the other side of the world, Professor Marcia McClintock Folsom, with whom I have collaborated on a volume about Jane Austen for many years and who has read and commented in perceptive detail on almost all the chapters of this book as they were drafted. I cannot thank Marcia enough for her continual kindness and support.

Chapter 3, 'Elizabeth's Memory and Mr Darcy's Smile', has had several previous incarnations. In this book I draw on some of the material in my chapter, 'Mr Darcy's Smile', in a volume on which I collaborated with David Monaghan and Ariane Hudelet, *The Cinematic Jane Austen: Essays on the Filmic Sensibility of the Novels* (Jefferson, NC: McFarland and Company, 2009). Since the project of that book was to consider the novels in relation to the cinema, the essay here has a quite different focus. I gave a paper under the same title at the 'New Directions in Austen Studies' conference, Chawton House Library, 9–11 July 2009, and subsequently to the Massachusetts branch of JASNA in Boston later that year. At the 'Celebrating *Pride and Prejudice*' conference in Cambridge, June 2013, I presented a paper called '*Pride and Prejudice*: Memory and Smiles' which was a redaction, in part, of the chapter in this book. I thank the organisers of these conferences, Dr Gillian Dow and Professor Janet Todd, respectively, for inviting me to speak. I would also like to thank my friend Paul A. Komesaroff, whose concept of micro-ethics has been a powerful influence on my reading.

An earlier version of Chapter 2 was given as 'Concealments' at a one-day conference celebrating *Sense and Sensibility* while I was a Visiting Fellow at the Chawton House Library, in September 2011, and subsequently at the '*Sense and Sensibility* after 200 Years' conference that Laura Carroll convened in Melbourne, in October 2011. During my Fellowship I worked on this book and would like to thank Dr Dow and the staff at Chawton for making my stay so enjoyable. I gave a talk based on Chapter 5 to the Jane Austen Society of Melbourne in 2012, and thank the members for their appreciative suggestions.

I have collaborated with Professor Folsom on an edited collection of essays for the Modern Language Association, to be published as *Approaches to Teaching Jane Austen's Mansfield Park*. I learned a great deal about the novel from our contributors, and would like to thank them all for their willingness to work with our suggestions. As I acknowledge in the chapters on *Mansfield Park*, I have found inspiration especially from the essays in the volume by Julia Prewitt Brown, 'Questions of Interiority: From *Pride and Prejudice* to *Mansfield Park*'; Monica Cohen, 'The Price of a Maxim: Plausibility in Fanny's Happy Ending'; Dorice Williams Elliot, 'Gifts Always Come with Strings Attached: Teaching *Mansfield Park* in the Context of Gift Theory'; and Kay Souter, '*Mansfield Park* and Families'. I have drawn also on the volume's jointly authored Introduction. My chapter, 'Jane Austen: Sight and Sound' in *The Cinematic Jane Austen* (pp. 17–37) mentioned above, is an earlier version of the argument in Chapter 7 of this book.

Introduction

In December 1813, nearly a year after *Pride and Prejudice* was published, Sarah Harriet Burney, half-sister of the more famous Frances, wrote to a friend:

> Yes, I *have* read the book you speak of, 'Pride & Prejudice', and I could quite rave about it! How well you define one of its characteristics when you say of it, that it breathes a spirit of 'careless originality.' – It is charming. – Nothing was ever better conducted than the fable; nothing can be more *piquant* than its dialogues; more distinct than its characters.

Burney then adds, 'I have the three vols now in the house, and know not how to part with them. I have only just finished, and could begin them all over again with pleasure.'[1] Sarah Harriet may have been one of the first readers to feel that the freshness of Jane Austen's novel would not fade with re-reading and that the second time round it might be even more rewarding. A like-minded contemporary of hers was William Gifford, the editor of the *Quarterly Review* and right-hand man of the most prestigious publisher of the time, John Murray. He first tells Murray in November 1814 that having 'for the first time, looked into *Pride & Prejudice*' he finds it 'really a very pretty thing', and then in September or October 1815 he writes that 'I have lately read it again – tis very good'.[2] He is saying that this novel is certainly something other than a genteel romance aimed at the circulating library market, and encouraging Murray to add Jane Austen to his list – which he did.

Since then, Austen readers tend to identify themselves as re-readers. Much later, in 1838, when Sarah Harriet found that Sir Walter Scott 'thought so highly of my prime favorite Miss Austen – he read her "Pride & Prejudice" three times', she trumped him, saying '*I* have read it as bumper toasts are given – *three times three.*'[3] Even Mark Twain, despite being 'maddened' by Austen's work, seems to admit to reading it more than once.[4] In the middle of the century, George Henry Lewes, the partner of George Eliot, who had been writing about Jane Austen's artistry in the journals for over a decade, published a long and eloquent tribute to her work in which he included a personal, even domestic, note:

> We have re-read them all four times; or rather, to speak more accurately, they have been read aloud to us, one after the other; and when it is considered what a severe test that is, how the reading aloud permits no skipping, no evasion of weariness, but brings both merits and defects into stronger relief by forcing the mind to dwell on them, there is surely something significant of genuine excellence when both reader and listener finish their fourth reading with increase of admiration.[5]

Later in the century the note of fandom is sounded. Agnes Repplier gushingly confesses that Austen's novels are her 'midnight friends': 'We have known them well for years. There is no fresh nook to be explored, no forgotten page to be revisited. But we will take them down, and re-read for the fiftieth time'; and a sterner critic, Reginald Farrer, in a famous centenary article in the 1917 issue of the *Quarterly Review*, could declare even more hyperbolically that her work 'is so packed with such minute and far-reaching felicities that the thousandth reading of "Emma" or "Persuasion" will be certain to reveal to you a handful of such brilliant jewels unnoticed before'.[6] A. C. Bradley, famous for his work on Shakespeare, referred to himself, in an important lecture, as one of 'the faithful', as if he re-read Jane Austen as regularly as he went to church.[7]

David Lodge re-echoed such comments in the late twentieth century. Austen's novels, he wrote, were so 'permeated with irony' that they 'can sustain an infinite number of readings'.[8] It is established, then, that to best enjoy Jane Austen one should re-read the novels. Each reading makes one even more convinced of Austen's greatness, as Lewes insisted, or of what so many critics following in his wake celebrate as Austen's 'art'. The corollary of re-reading is not only, as Gifford understood, that Austen's comic and romantic novels were serious publications, but that they are so constructed as to invite, perhaps to require, re-reading. This is certainly the case with *Emma*, as Richard Cronin and Dorothy McMillan argue. 'It was in her writing of *Emma*, and in particular her bold decision to write a novel that demanded repeated re-readings, that Austen made the most striking claim for her profession', they write.[9] Re-readability, they suggest, was becoming the key distinction between literary work that one might want to purchase and the circulating library trash that one borrowed by the volume and returned quickly in order to pick up the next. Cronin and McMillan go on to suggest further that in writing

Emma Jane Austen was prepared 'to sacrifice readability' to re-readability, in order to make good her claim to serious professional status.[10]

But what re-reading consists of is a trickier question. John Mullan's *What Matters in Jane Austen?* (2012) offers a start towards answering it. Citing their 'minute interconnectedness', he suggests that this 'is the reason why, when you re-read her novels, you have the experience of suddenly noticing some crucial detail that you have never noticed before, and realising how demanding she is of your attention'.[11] (Perhaps this is what Repplier had in mind when she wrote of 'nooks'.) Mullan often suggests that first-time readers absorb such effects of detail unconsciously. It is only when the novels are returned to with alert (and possibly more informed) attention that one understands how these effects are gained. One of the objects of this book is to focus on the way the writer shapes and manages her readers' – and her re-readers' – attention as they peruse her novels. It also investigates Austen's interest in attention as a psychological facility, and how it relates to memory, to remembering and to misremembering. After all, one difference between reading and re-reading is that the subsequent reading is informed by at least some memory of the first.

It is the role of criticism and scholarship to equip the modern, the twenty-first century, re-reader with the information and understanding that enables him or her to give Austen's novels the attention they ask for. 'Readers today need to recognize that *Mansfield Park* is consciously set in the post-abolition period', Peter Knox-Shaw states correctly, for example, though, as he also notes, enduring commentary on the novel has been written in ignorance of this.[12] For many years now there has been a concerted critical project to recover the historical and literary circumstances in which Jane Austen's novels were composed and published. This has involved consideration of publication and printing practices in Jane Austen's London, as well as study of the novels and plays that form the context for her writing. Increasingly it has been understood that Austen's writing engages in a form of conversation, if not debate, not only with some of the canonical novelists she knew, but with the fictions pumped out by the circulating libraries (on which, to be sure, she partially depended for the sale of her own novels). At the same time, much attention has been given to the political, legal and social setting in which she wrote, with the result that the earlier assumption that the novels are isolated or sequestered from the historical circumstances of Austen's time has been thoroughly displaced. Thus a critic could write in 2000 that *Mansfield Park*, for instance, which is mostly set in an isolated country house in the English provinces, is 'now often read as a novel engaged with the events of its day – the abolition of the slave trade, the French revolution, political upheaval in the Caribbean',[13] and the Napoleonic 'war at a distance' has been shown to echo throughout at least her later works.[14] Austen is thus re-created as a novelist who is intellectually abreast of her literary and philosophical inheritance and well aware of the contemporary context, but who, having chosen merely to allude to this material, to imply her knowledge rather than to display it, requires modern scholarship to recover what might have been taken for granted by her first readers.

This would certainly then be one way of conceiving what is hidden in Jane Austen. This book engages with and draws on this common project and sometimes, as in the chapters on *Northanger Abbey* and *Mansfield Park*, seeks to contribute to it. But in the main this book focuses less on the allusive and referential aspects of Austen's novels, or on her indebtedness to other writers, than on facets of her writing that might elude the attention of the first-time reader, but that are, as Mullan suggests, the condition and source of her greatness – the reason for which readers are drawn back to her novels again and again. It also proposes that while Austen's work does reference important political, social – and religious – matters, the novels can best be read as single, stand-alone works, each of which has its own shape and agenda. The assumption of this book's structure is that each novel has its own distinct ethos or imaginative co-ordinates, that each develops its own terms, and therefore requires and licenses a different approach and distinct array of critical materials. What is alluded to in Austen's novels is less important here than the implicit suggestions about human motive and behaviour that are conveyed in the pauses and implications of her prose.

My main concern then is with the silences in the novels, not with the silences of the novels, though this cannot be a hard and fast distinction. 'Charming Miss Woodhouse! allow me to interpret this interesting silence', Mr Elton insinuates in the carriage taking them home from the Westons', Austen here allowing the reader to interpret Emma's silence in quite a different way from his (*E* I: 15, 142). The more famous silence that follows Sir Thomas Bertram's response to Fanny Price's question on the slave trade (*MP* II: 3, 231–2) is both a silence represented or spoken of in the novel, and a silence of the novel itself, since what Sir Thomas says is not reported, and what the novelist means by raising the issue of the trade is left to the reader to decide. As a silence *in* the novel it suggests the ambiguities of Fanny's reticence: 'It would have pleased your uncle to be inquired of farther', Edmund suggests. She excuses herself by saying that she did not want to put herself forward, but that involves a reflection on her cousins at the same time. She is thus not merely shy. As a silence *of* the novel, which can readily be translated into a silence of the novelist, it has prompted critical investigations of a very different order. But for the most part the silences of the novels, for example about what Sir Thomas Bertram did in Antigua, or in Parliament, or, to give a more egregious instance, what Frank Churchill may have been up to in London when he went to order a piano for Jane, though intriguing, and in the first case productive of much controversy, do not concern me here.[15]

There is, however, much that is specifically hidden from the reader by Jane Austen's plotting. Far more intricately, deviously and amusingly, but in common with the eighteenth-century playwrights, like Sheridan, and novelists she admired, like Burney, Jane Austen's novels often deceive and play with the first reader's attention. This is most obvious in *Emma*, but the concealment of information, or the delayed disclosure of motive, is a feature of all of them. The reason for Frank Churchill's visit to London, for example, is eventually revealed, but that information is kept back for many chapters; the reason for Colonel Brandon's abrupt departure from the picnic party in an early chapter of *Sense and Sensibility* is that he is rushing to the aid of Eliza. Both events are made the occasion for character commentary: when he hears about it, Knightley thinks that heading off to London for a haircut is just the sort of thing a 'trifling silly fellow' like Frank would do – and at this point neither he nor a reader is conscious of his jealousy; Willoughby whispers spitefully to Marianne that Brandon has probably forged the letter that calls him away, a response whose full nastiness is only apparent much later in the novel.[16] As on so many occasions in Austen's writing, the way people talk about unexpected events reveals their characters, but their speculations divert the first-time reader from guessing the truth, and divert the re-reader who knows it.

Even more interesting to the re-reader of her novels than the secrets of Austen's plotting are what one might name their secretions. This book attempts to probe the inner life of Austen's novels, which she once called, encouraging her niece's own writing, 'the heart & beauty of your book'.[17] In biology or physiology secretions are scarcely perceptible substances extracted or released from a cell or gland which then perform other, benign and useful functions within the entire plant or body. These chapters aim to locate qualities of Austen's writing that perform, without a reader's being necessarily aware of it, the essential functions that generate the serious power of her art. Some of these are minute or local effects; others, drawing on them, are latent structural or conceptual designs that exert their influence more pervasively. These secretions will not be apparent to the first-time reader, but coming back to the novel one might certainly become more conscious of their presence and power.

Throughout these chapters, then, passages of Austen's writing, sometimes quite lengthy, are displayed and subjected to careful analytic attention. This allows the reader of this book to bring their own reading to a focus, and to agree or disagree with the reading presented here. Austen employs a vocabulary more restricted than many other novelists', and when she uses metaphoric language it is usually to register its banality. Instead she gets her results, and controls her meanings, largely through the precise exercise of syntax: grammatical construction, punctuation, emphasis and rhythm. Her writing therefore rewards the kind of close consideration that poetry requires: a considering attentiveness, both focused on the immediate words and able, if one is a re-reader, to recall or bring into play memories of other passages or episodes in the novel as one responds to the current page.[18] And as in poetry, the pauses, spaces and silences in the writing contribute essentially to its meaning, and to some extent, as in poetry, make it unparaphrasable. The analyses in these chapters all attend carefully to Austen's handling of cadences and movement, and especially to those passages of confessional speech or introspective brooding in which the structure of her sentences, as I argue, traces meanings unacknowledged by the character.

Jane Austen could use the standard or formal phrasing and punctuation that she inherited from mostly masculine writers in the eighteenth century to telling and elegant effect, as every reader knows. But when her characters speak she very frequently employs a distinct register of syntactic markers as signals for the informality of conversational utterance. Moreover, when she glances at, or represents, their private thoughts and reasonings, she employs still more of the stylistic devices she inherited from Richardson and Sterne and the sentimental novelists who followed them, and which are absent from the discursive male writers, like Johnson, whom she admired, and whose influence on her authorial or narrative prose is undeniable. Among such mimetic markers were dashes of varying lengths, exclamation marks, incomplete sentences, italics and repetition. One sure sign that the narrative is moving away from the narrator or author and into a character's inner speech is the presence of dashes in company with repeated words and phrases. 'He must — yes, he certainly must, as a friend — an anxious friend — give Emma some hint, ask her some question' (*E* III: 5, 379). In representing even Mr Knightley's struggle with his conscience Austen is the beneficiary of the sentimental tradition. Here, as elsewhere in her writing, dashes are among 'these discursive cracks where emotion lies', as Ariane Hudelet puts it.[19]

There may be risks, however, in assuming that the punctuation of the novels as we have them is Jane Austen's own.[20] The manuscripts that survive look very different from the texts of the novels in print. They are full of contractions, random or nearly random capitals, and mostly have no paragraphing. The last chapter of *Persuasion* in manuscript form is sprinkled with underlined words, as in '*she* had a *future* to look forward to', that were not italicised when they were included in the published version.[21] Printers, working to the house-rules of publishers, also seem to have understood that it was part of their job to bring more order and formality to the author's writing, to add to or alter her punctuation, to change dashes into semi-colons, for instance, or semi-colons into colons. This may be especially the case when John Murray, who was aiming at a more educated market, took over the publishing of Austen's novels.

Austen's employment of the dash is especially interesting. The 'fair copy' she apparently made around 1805 of 'Lady Susan', the short novel that remained unpublished in her lifetime, only uses dashes to indicate sentence or paragraph endings, a habit that persisted throughout Austen's writing life.[22] But the manuscript of 'The Watsons', written in the same period in which 'Lady Susan' was copied out, features no fewer than 850 dashes.[23] Many of these again are simply indications of sentence endings, but dashes also appear in the midst of character speech. Most interestingly, the dash starts to be used as a dramatic means. In the presence of Emma Watson, the heroine, Mr Edwards observes that 'elderly ladies should be careful how they make a second choice' of partner; and his wife corrects this: 'Carefulness — discretion — should not be confined to elderly ladies.'[24] Here the dash is developed as a plausible imitation of the hesitations of natural speech. When Mr Edwards goes on to add that young women should certainly be careful whom they choose, since they may suffer from a bad choice for more years than their elders, 'Emma drew her hand across her eyes — and Mrs. Edwards, on perceiving it, changed the subject to one of less anxiety to all.'[25] This uses the dash as a retardant intensifier, a space which the reader is invited to fill with feeling.

Either in Austen's preparation of her manuscripts for printing or in the printing house itself, most of Austen's dashes, it is reasonable to believe, were replaced with conventional punctuation.[26] But those retained are usually essential to her narrative effects. As with the repeated word, or the loosely analogous phrase, the dash as it appears in the published novels can only be the author's own. In her interesting comparison between *Pride and Prejudice* and its first translation into French in 1813 as *Orgueil et Préjugé*, the Swiss critic Valérie Cossy shows how crucial such effects in Austen's novels are. Elizabeth Bennet at Pemberley, for example, searches for 'the only face whose features would be known to her' (though this in the French becomes merely his 'portrait': 'le seul portrait qui l'intéressât'). Then Austen writes, 'At last it arrested her — and she beheld a striking resemblance of Mr Darcy.' 'It "arrests" her', as Cossy comments, 'in the same way as, in the text, a dash arrests the narrator and the reader.'[27] The French omits this sentence with its dash and thereby loses what it intimates: that Elizabeth is already primed to feel something strongly about a picture of Darcy. Such minute, but original, mimetic effects of syntax are means by which Austen extracts meaning from language that in itself is little more than commonplace.

Jane Austen's novels were able to convey not only a sense of natural speech and conversation but also, as in these examples, to actively lock in the attention, to feed the narrative greed, of the reader. In her later novels, and in *Emma* especially, the dash is put to even more daring uses, as when Emma's unwilling overhearing of Mrs Elton's talk is rendered as a series of mere topics separated by dashes so as to display its inconsequentiality (III: 6, 389–90). Perhaps Gifford, or John Murray's printers, recognised the dynamics of Austen's punctuation, for they kept such effects as those in Emma's wondering whether she dare use Frank Churchill's name in public: 'Now, how am I going to introduce him? — Am I unequal to speaking his name at once before all these people? Is it necessary for me to use any roundabout phrase? — Your Yorkshire friend — your correspondent in Yorkshire; — that would be the way, I suppose, if I were very bad. — No, I can pronounce his name without the smallest distress' (II: 16, 321). Since Emma thinks she is in love with Frank, but isn't, the repeated dashes – the false hesitations – convey a hilarious performative parody of what she imagines to be the inner conflicts of a true romantic heroine.

But it is in the realm of genuine inner conflict, or in eliciting the complexities of motive, that Jane Austen's ability to extract the maximum of meaning from the smallest devices comes into its own. In his earliest commentary on Austen, published when he was 30 in 1847, George Lewes was already claiming that she was greater than the then more famous Walter Scott, who, he declares, is certainly not comparable to Shakespeare: 'He had not that singular faculty of penetrating into the most secret recesses of the heart, and of shewing us a character in its inward and outward workings, in its involuntary self-betrayals and subtle self-sophistications.'[28] By implication, though he does not say as much, what is true of Shakespeare would be true of Jane Austen too. This is not today such an extraordinary claim to make for Austen's novels as it was then. (Throughout this book,

Shakespeare is a presence in the wings, and makes brief appearances in the chapters on *Sense and Sensibility*, *Emma* and *Persuasion*.) Through her capacity to write sentences that are both elegantly shaped and carry implicit suggestion – sentences that are both Augustan and romantic – Jane Austen certainly, as I shall argue, displayed the involuntary self-betrayals and traced the intricate, devious and even unconscious ways her characters protect themselves from knowing themselves and their motives. Largely dispensing with the poetic language of feeling, Austen can nevertheless lodge emotion in other discursive gaps besides dashes – in the silences or pauses that the prose dramatises, in what the narrator understates, and in what she simply elides by shifting the reader's focus. All of these strategies are germane to the project of this book.

But the remit of the hidden is certainly not confined to such local textual effects. What is hidden in Austen's novels is equally the conceptual structure or organisation that gives coherence and its specific focus to each of the books. What is hidden in all of them is this structure (one might almost say this topic), but it is distinct in each. Taken-for-granted aspects of human experience and behaviour, however, are typically mined for their salience and operative power as structural components of Jane Austen's texts. 'Elizabeth turned away to hide a smile' (*P&P* I: II, 63): her response to a pompous remark by Darcy early in *Pride and Prejudice* both draws the reader into her orbit and features an ongoing motif of the novel. Such an apparently everyday act of social life as the smile becomes much more than an incidental feature of company behaviour. Easy to pass over, too, are the many moments in the text in which characters recall previous events, but remembering, and misremembering, good and bad memory, cumulatively becomes the groundwork not only of the novel's psychological under-standing, but also of its ethical structure. Memory in its various forms, including the reader's, then actively operates as a controlling mechanism in *Pride and Prejudice*'s onward development. In *Emma*, the only one of Austen's novels to which the description of 'three or four families in a country village' accurately applies, another apparent accident of quotidian life, the overhearing of others' conversations, is developed into a means by which the reticulations of such a closed community can be communicated, and eventually supports and underscores its most telling moments. *Persuasion* deploys the same phenomena of overhearing others' speech, but here it serves, among other things, as I argue, the quite different project of illuminating and contesting the stereotypes of gender. What at first seems inconsequential in this novel about contingency and accidents is thus revealed to be the cornerstone of its structure.

The Hidden Jane Austen, then, offers re-readings of the six completed novels. There are many aspects of Jane Austen's art that are common to all of her published works, but the notion of a homogeneous 'Jane Austen novel' (frequent among those who do not read them) is quite misleading. So that while there is certainly a common focus on the 'hidden' here, the mode in which the hidden is addressed varies with the novel under consideration. The two chapters on *Mansfield Park* thus consider two further aspects of the hidden. They have in common a focus on the recesses of the characters' psychological life, as rendered in the various techniques at the mature Austen's command. Mrs Norris, the primary focus of the first, is Austen's most egregious example of a personality able to bury truths about herself, truths that the writer, very rarely venturing to touch on her inner life, nevertheless proposes through the novel's conceptual structure. The chapter approaches this through attending to Mrs Norris' speech and its distorted relation to Anglican religion. In contrast, the focus of the second chapter on *Mansfield Park* is on the dexterity, subtlety and persuasiveness with which the psychological damage done to the young heroine by her abrupt removal from her home to the quite different world of the Bertrams is communicated. It challenges the re-reader of this text to recognise what Austen conveys by her most indirect and subtle means. To write of the hidden in *Mansfield Park* is thus to invoke not only what the heroine conceals by her demeanour and behaviour, but also what she conceals from herself. In this chapter I suggest moreover that important truths about Fanny's predicament have in effect been hidden from too many of its critics.

This book begins with chapters on the two early novels, the first of which Jane Austen decided not to publish. *Northanger Abbey* is a frankly open text. Its plot sets out to reveal that there is nothing to be excited about in the secret places its heroine explores, nor is there anything mysterious about its two dominant characters, Isabella Thorpe and General Tilney, whose pretensions it consistently lays bare. Nor is there anything the reader might need to discover in Isabella's brother, or in Captain Tilney, or in Catherine herself. The novel's narrative content is reflected in a style which, like its heroine, is explicit, frank and open. Thus while *Northanger Abbey* displays what the novelist later learned to hide, the book's characterisation, plot and style all cohere together. I suggest also that *Northanger Abbey* amusingly initiates that enquiry into attention and memory which is taken up in Austen's later works. Quite different is the troubled world Jane Austen conjures up in *Sense and Sensibility*, a milieu in which all the gentlemen keep information about themselves secret, and in which the necessity of duplicity, or at the very least concealment, hovers persistently over the conversations and behaviour of the ladies. Concealment, in its many forms, is necessary to survival in the mercenary and competitive environment of Regency London, the novelist seems to say, but the narrative strains against this demand. Both in its caustic commentary, confronting the reader with the feelings Elinor does not express, and in its vindication of frankness in the man who has practised deception most assiduously, the novel exposes the problematics of the hidden rather than resolves them. One early novel is largely a counter-example to the premise of a hidden Jane Austen, the other an attempt to confront the hidden head on. Together these two chapters form a prelude to the analyses of novels in which Jane Austen is fully aware and in control, and where the minute particulars of characters' performance and inner life cohere with the implicit structure that gives each of them meaning.

The cover of this book shows a detail from a group portrait by the painter Joseph Wright (1737–94). It is customary in eighteenth-century English pictures of a gentleman and lady to have the wife look admiringly at the husband. But in this picture, the husband's gaze is on his wife, who is depicted as a strong-featured, independent woman. Quite often, too, as in Gainsborough's well-known picture of Mr and Mrs Andrews, in eighteenth-century paintings of genteel or aristocratic families the estate that they own is shown as an appropriate background to the couple who live there. But in this portrait, they are looking towards the land, pointing out its features, but what they are pointing to, apart from a small glimpse, is out of the picture. The expanse of the estate (or is it the countryside?) is not seen. Austen, like Wright in this picture, practises an art of suggestion, implication, evoking much that she does not represent.

CHAPTER I

Into the open with Catherine Morland

In Volume II of *Northanger Abbey* Isabella Thorpe presses her brother's suit on Catherine Morland, but she gets a surprising reception. John Thorpe has informed her in a letter, Isabella asserts, that he has 'as good as made you an offer'; and she can give circumstantial evidence that this is true. It happened, she adds, at their lodgings in Edgar's Buildings, on the morning immediately before Thorpe left Bath. Catherine is taken aback. She vehemently denies that any such conversation took place. 'As to any attentions on his side, I do declare, upon my honour, I never was sensible of them for a moment', she exclaims. Moreover, she declares, they were never together that morning. 'The last half hour before he went away! — It must be all and completely a mistake' (*NA* II: 7, 147). Catherine has been established as the soul of innocent integrity, a young lady too who has 'an unaffected openness to experience',[1] but if a reader turns back only three chapters, they will find that Catherine, for whatever reason, is here quite in the wrong.

There Jane Austen stages the farce of a man making a proposal so clumsily that the young woman hasn't the slightest idea of what he is about. The narrator, in the confidently ironic commentary that is Austen's mode in this novel, points up the comedy. Catherine hurries away, she writes, leaving Thorpe to 'the undivided consciousness of his own happy address, and her explicit encouragement' (I: 15, 127). Though Thorpe is generally so unreliable about facts as to be delusional, there is manifest textual evidence in this instance that he does make advances – sidelong, bumbling and roundabout as they are. What is surprising, though, is not that Catherine failed to catch his meaning, as that she has apparently totally forgotten the whole exchange took place. 'I did not see him once that whole morning', she asserts. Isabella instantly corrects her. 'You spent the whole morning in Edgar's Buildings — it was the day your father's consent came ... you and John were alone in the parlour, some time before you left the house.' Catherine is perturbed: 'For the life of me,

I cannot recollect it. – I *do* remember now being with you, and seeing him as well as the rest – but that we were ever alone for five minutes —.'

Jane Austen seems to have constructed here an egregious instance of the dependence of recollection on previous attention. A first-time reader of the novel may well credit Catherine's failure to remember Thorpe earlier that morning, because, in writing the scene, she has avoided calling any specific attention to his presence. He is mentioned, and his speaking is referred to, but nothing he says is quoted. (And though it is only a couple of chapters earlier, the exchange takes place at the end of Volume I, and the volume division might, especially for early readers of the novel, encourage them also to forget what has taken place, and thus put them in the same position as Catherine.) During the conversation there she responds to his inept attempts to advance his case as briefly as her innate kindness allows, though she is evidently preoccupied. As a way of getting rid of him, she twice wishes Thorpe goodbye, and makes clear that she is herself anxious to be off: 'Well, I wish you a good journey. I dine with Miss Tilney today, and must now be going home' (1: 15, 125). In fact she first rushes to the Allens to tell them the exciting news of James's engagement. So one might imagine she is full of this, but also that she is anticipating the pleasures awaiting her at Miss Tilney's, where she expects to see Henry Tilney again. This is not suggested in the narration; it is left to the reader to deduce, and perhaps deduce retrospectively, from her flat denial that the interview ever took place.

This seemingly incidental sequence is, however, germane to *Northanger Abbey's* continual interest in memory, or rather in the role memory plays in motivation and consciousness. The most obvious aspect of this is the influence that her memories of Gothic novels have over Catherine's adventures at the Abbey, but in the first of these adventures, when she is alone on that first night in her bedroom, the fictions themselves are less important than the fact that their terrifying features have been recently revived and impressed on her by Henry Tilney. Two chapters after the conversation with Isabella, she is on her way to Northanger, sharing his curricle with him. If inattention (or rather perhaps ardent interest in another man) precludes the formation of any memory of John Thorpe's presence or speeches, the opposite turns out to be true of her journey sitting next to Henry, which, as she reflects, is almost as good as dancing with him.

Prompted by Catherine's excitement at the prospect of staying in a real abbey, Henry entertains himself, and teases her, by spinning a facetious yarn about what she might expect to find if she really were the heroine of the thrilling novels she has been reading. (He has already been shown exercising his impromptu fiction-making gifts when he frightens his sister with a sketch of the real horrors in London that Catherine's innocent remark about something 'really shocking indeed' about to come out there might mean (1: 14, 113).) As he warms to his theme, the 'young lady' within his story becomes 'you', and a 'you' insistently planted in his sentences and in the midst of the narrative. 'Will not your mind misgive you, when you find yourself in this gloomy chamber — too lofty and extensive for you', he confides, for instance. 'Will not your heart sink within you ... How fearfully will you examine the furniture of your apartment!' (11: 5, 161–2). Catherine is drawn in, stimulated and excited by her presence at the centre of this drama, and Henry in turn is stimulated to greater and greater heights of comic inventiveness. There is undoubtedly a mutually excited rapport between them.

When Edmund Bertram watches the progress of Fanny's 'attention' to Henry Crawford's reading of Shakespeare in *Mansfield Park*, her face and movements are eloquent testimony to her engagement in the listening experience (*MP* 111: 3, 390). No such description is given of Catherine's features, but it is plain from her interjections to Henry's story that it holds her spell-bound. 'Oh, Mr Tilney, how frightful! — This is just like a book! — But it cannot really happen to me. I am sure your housekeeper is not really Dorothy. — Well, what then?' While she is struggling to resist him, her protests that 'She was not at all afraid' (11: 5, 162) convey the sense that she is all too caught up in the thrilling scenario Henry has invented, and imagining herself within it.[2] Eventually, enjoying himself no end, 'amused by the interest he had raised', but presumably unable to keep a straight face, he breaks off, and Catherine then 'began earnestly to assure him that her attention had been fixed without the smallest apprehension of really meeting with what he related' (11: 5, 164). Be that as it may, it is Catherine's mesmerised attention (perhaps shared by the reader, since Henry really is a compelling raconteur) that is to count later.

Jane Austen's delineation of Catherine's state of mind here presages the dexterity with which in subsequent works she traces the contesting impulses within her character's minds. Later, at the Abbey, Catherine again has thoughts and fears that she simultaneously disavows. As she makes her way to her room, she reflects that '*She* had nothing to dread from midnight assassins or drunken gallants. Henry had certainly been only in jest in what he had told her that morning. In a house so furnished, and so guarded, she ... might go to her own bedroom as securely as if it had been her own chamber at Fullerton' (11: 6, 171). The reader may be allowed to believe that these other self-addressed assurances conceal a little doubt. '*She* had nothing to dread', well, no; but her telling herself this (for Jane Austen represents her thoughts as inner speech) anticipates the moments when later characters brush aside, or deny, aspects of their own feelings. Maria Bertram knows that she ought not to encourage Crawford's advances, but she excuses herself from acting on that knowledge; Emma knows that Mr Knightley thinks well of the Martins, but so bent is she on taking up Harriet that this awkward impediment to her pleasing scheme of marrying her to Elton must be quickly whisked away. As in such instances, Austen decries and is able to represent an emotional driver behind the thought sequence that conscious rationalisation cannot quite put aside.

Henry's invention has blended elements from *The Mysteries of Udolpho* (1794), which Catherine has been reading at every spare moment in Bath, and which he too has read, he has told her, with his hair 'standing on end the whole time' (1: 14, 108), with another 'Gothic' tale by Ann Radcliffe, *The Romance of the Forest* (1791). In this earlier romance, the heroine, Adeline, led to a remote apartment in a ruined abbey in the south of France, finds, hidden behind the arras, a secret door leading down to an inner room.[3] Catherine is reassured when she surveys her comfortable chamber at Northanger, but later, when she retires to bed, having let the fire die down, and with her candle only partially lifting the darkness, she spies a 'high old-fashioned black cabinet' which she has previously (courtesy of her author) not seen. She remembers Henry's words: 'Your eyes will be attracted towards a large, old-fashioned cabinet of ebony and gold,' he has told her, 'which, though narrowly examining the furniture before, you had passed unnoticed. Impelled by an irresistible presentiment, you will eagerly advance to it . . .' (11: 5, 163).

In *The Romance of the Forest*, Adeline finds the door held by a bolt, but she gets it open, and having 'brought the light, she descended by a few steps into another chamber'. At this moment, she recalls a sequence of nightmares she had the previous night. 'She instantly remembered her dreams. The chamber was not much like that in which she had seen the dying Chevalier, and afterwards the bier; but it gave her a confused remembrance of one through which she had passed.'[4] Reality merges with Adeline's memory of the dreams in which she has 'seen' a sequence of rooms that resemble the suite of hidden chambers she now explores. In the first she has found a man 'convulsed in the agonies of death' who seizes her hand; in the third, even more terrifying, when she advances into 'very ancient apartments', she finds a coffin, in which a dead man lies, but from whose side gushes a stream of blood.[5] Then, when she explores the next evening, she finds a room 'exactly like that where her dream had represented the dying person; the resemblance struck so forcibly upon her imagination, that she was in danger of fainting'.

The 'irresistible presentment' that Henry mockingly foretells Catherine she will experience is his version of Adeline's recall of her dreams. But the presentiment that Catherine now experiences is not last night's terrors but what Henry has recounted that very morning. 'Henry's words, his description of the ebony cabinet which was to escape her observation at first, immediately rushed across her' (II: 6, 172). Adeline's experience is anticipated by her dreams, Catherine's – as it appears to her – by what Henry has foretold she will find. What in Radcliffe's fiction is the mysterious, supernatural anticipation of the dreamwork is transformed, and psychological plausibility based on memory replaces romantic fantasy as the ground for Catherine's heightened imaginative state.

Her imagination kindled by his narrative, Catherine's excitement as she explores the room and its contents in the semi-darkness is fuelled and repeatedly accompanied by her recall of the sequence in which Henry had placed her. She approaches the cabinet with intense curiosity: 'The key was in the door, and she had a strange fancy to look into it, not however with the smallest expectation of finding any thing, but it was so very odd, after what Henry had said.' If Catherine has been so inattentive to Thorpe's proposal that she does not even remember being in the room with him, here her previously intense fascination with Henry's speech is working the opposite effect, and his words become the influence, the motive force that drives her explorations.

Henry Tilney, evidently enough, is often a mouthpiece for the writer's own amused irony. Austen's tone in these pages, though, is quite unlike his habitual, critically inflected amusement. The focus of the narration is on Catherine's actions and her state of mind, though embedded in one sentence that describes them are hints that the reader need not take her excitement too seriously:

> Again therefore she applied herself to the key, and after moving it in every possible way for some instants with the determined celerity of hope's last effort, the door suddenly yielded to her hand: her heart leaped with exultation at such a victory, and having thrown open each folding door, the second being secured only by bolts of less wonderful construction than the lock, though in that her eye could not discern any thing unusual, a double range of small drawers appeared in view, with some larger drawers above and below them; and in the centre, a small door, closed also with a lock and key, secured in all probability a cavity of importance. (II: 6, 173)[6]

This long, awkward and convoluted sentence captures the reader's own attention to the process by which the barriers and difficulties are one by one presented and overcome. The reader is led through – perhaps gripped by – an intricate series of narrative impediments or delays, a syntactical journey corresponding to Catherine's baffled efforts to reach her goal. At the very same time, though, Austen slips in phrases like 'the determined celerity of hope's last effort' and 'her heart leaped with exultation' that recall the clichés and over-heightened emotions of a Gothic heroine. The reader is at once inside Catherine's fevered and excited emotions and made wary, or amused, by the extravagance of language that is both the genuine medium of her thoughts and recognisably derivative. Compressed too into one writerly performance are hints at the absurdity of that recurrent trope of the Gothic – the sequence of locked rooms or chambers, the series of doors that lead into hidden vestibules in the depths of an ancient abbey or castle. Primed to imagine that every enclosed space or 'cavity' must hide a secret, Catherine 'grasped the handle of a drawer and drew it forth. It was entirely empty.'

In *The Romance of the Forest*, Adeline finds among the debris on the floor of the hidden room she is exploring 'a small roll of paper, tied with a string, and covered with dust'. She sees it is a manuscript, and the few words she can decipher, though not yet revealed to the reader, impress her 'with curiosity and terror'. And sure enough, having managed the inner lock, Catherine finds in the cabinet 'apparently for concealment', 'a roll of paper pushed back to the furthest part of the cavity'. 'Her heart fluttered, her knees trembled, and her cheeks grew pale' (II: 4, 174). The reader might read this as farce, but might rather identify with the palpitating heart of the heroine. In the dim light of her candle, Catherine sees that there is indeed writing on the paper, a 'striking exemplification', she thinks, now completely in the thrall of his story, 'of what Henry had foretold'. Henry has indeed foretold that Catherine will find papers addressed to her, and, at the climax of his story, his calculated pauses play upon and arouse her breathless excitement:

> 'At last, however, by touching a secret spring, an inner compartment will open — a roll of paper appears: — you seize it — it contains many sheets of manuscript — you hasten with the precious treasure into your own chamber, but scarcely have you been able to decipher "Oh! thou — whomsoever thou mayst be, into whose hands these memoirs of the wretched Matilda may fall" — when your lamp suddenly expires in the socket, and leaves you in total darkness.'
> 'Oh! no, no, — do not say so. Well, go on.' (II: 5, 163–4)

Adeline's manuscript reads 'O! ye, whoever you are whom chance, or misfortune may hereafter conduct to this spot.'[7] In Radcliffe's novel, the papers turn out to contain the last testament of Adeline's real father, long a captive and left to die in that room — an essential element of the plot. In *Northanger Abbey*, the roll of paper, 'the manuscript so wonderfully found, so wonderfully accomplishing the morning's prediction' (II: 6, 175), as Catherine reflects, but which turns out to be a commonplace laundry list, is the climax or anticlimax of a series of concealments that conceal material with little or no significance at all. There is nothing much hidden in the black cabinet, even though it seems to Catherine's fevered imagination that the barriers to her search themselves signal a mystery within. Yet this discovery is (paradoxically) a key to the novel's whole design.

It seems then that Austen might have created the remarkable sequence in which Catherine cannot even remember being in the same room with John Thorpe as a deliberate counterpart to this episode in which Henry Tilney's enthralling story stays with her, prompting, and seemingly validating, her discovery. With her mind preoccupied with her brother's engagement and with the expectation of seeing Henry, Catherine does not notice what is happening; but the memory of Henry's very words, merging with her memories of *The Mysteries of Udolpho*, have the power, when combined with the howling wind and the darkness, to impel her to abandon her native good sense (for, after all, finding that what he has foretold has come true in her experience would be tantamount, in the unconscious, to imaginative union with him). Memory, in this almost exemplary instance, is dependent on attentiveness, which in turn depends upon young Catherine's attraction to a man whose willing display of overtly masculine intellectual authority Austen is suggesting she has found deeply appealing. The psychological coherence of this sequence does the work of making it apparent that Catherine is in love with Henry. Her constant recollection of his words anticipates the more subtle suggestions of Emma Woodhouse's inadvertent and unconscious attentions to Knightley's physical presence.

Catherine is ashamed at her discovery: 'How could she have so imposed on herself? — Heaven forbid that Henry Tilney should ever know her folly! And it was in great measure his own doing, for had not the cabinet appeared so exactly to agree with his description of her adventures, she should never have felt the smallest curiosity about it' (II: 7, 177). Yet while she is chastising herself, she is wavering: there is still something, apparently, that remains compelling about Henry's speech. But soon

Tilney is called away from Northanger to visit his parish, and it is his absence over two days, both physically and psychologically, that creates the conditions for the second phase of Catherine's Gothic explorations. In this sequence her instinctive aversion to General Tilney substitutes for Henry's words as the motive or instigation for her renewed confusion of reality with Gothic fiction. But this second phase is much less plausible and compelling, partly because of its comedic treatment.

The second adventure is essentially an extended reprise of the first. At night in her chamber Catherine has been seized by the notion that the locked cabinet, with its folding door within, must enclose some mysterious secret; in daylight, as she is shown over the Abbey, she forms the idea that beyond the folding doors that terminate the gallery, and behind the door behind them, must lie another fearful secret. But the psychological conviction, the plausible prompting, generating environment and excitement of the first is missing. There the repeated invocations of Henry's words push Catherine's actions along, but there is no equivalent here. Instead of the narrative momentum keeping pace with Catherine's excitement, and registering her thoughts as they succeed to each other, in Chapter 8 of this second volume the writer tends to stand back from the character. The reference points of her imagination become clichés of the Gothic novels she has read, rather than Henry's vivid recreation. The fusion of identification with the heroine's terrors and amusement at them which Jane Austen's writing achieved through the first adventure is lost.

Taken on a tour of the Abbey by the General, Catherine sees Eleanor Tilney throw open the folding doors at the end of the gallery, stepping forward beyond them to open another door, only to be reprimanded by her father. 'Miss Tilney drew back directly, and the heavy doors were closed upon the mortified Catherine.' She has seen 'in a momentary glance beyond them, a narrower passage, more numerous openings, and symptoms of a winding stair-case', all of which remind her of the intricate geography of ancient edifices in Gothic fiction. 'Something was certainly to be concealed', she concludes (II: 8, 191). As at this moment, the reader is prompted to see 'the mortified Catherine', sceptically, ironically, as the narrator withdraws from the figure, and such a word as 'symptoms' comically deflates her expectations.

The distinguished nineteenth-century novelist Margaret Oliphant was pleased to find that 'the machinery of the story' of *Northanger Abbey* 'is wonderfully bad', and when reading the passages in which Catherine snoops about the Abbey possessed by the belief that General Tilney has murdered his wife or is starving her in a secret room, it is difficult to disagree.[8] 'The well-read Catherine', as the narrator in another moment of uneasy half-mockery calls her, becomes a Female Quixote here, a figure from fiction in a book that mocks fictions, and that has up till now succeeded in making her ingenuous and good-hearted heroine perfectly credible. As in Charlotte Lennox's novel of 1752, in which Arabella takes medieval French romances as reliable guides to middle-class life in eighteenth-century England, Catherine now simply assumes that the world of Gothic fiction set in medieval France or Italy reflects modern reality, and this after she has already convicted herself of her earlier folly. The narrator treats her imaginings with broad irony: 'Nine years, Catherine knew was a trifle of time, compared with what generally elapsed after the death of an injured wife, before her room was put to rights' (ii: 8, 192); 'Catherine's blood ran cold with the horrid suggestions which naturally sprang from these words.' 'What could more plainly speak the gloomy workings' of a mind reviewing its guilt, she thinks as she watches the General pace the drawing room; 'Catherine had read too much not to be perfectly aware of the ease with which a waxen figure might be introduced, and a suppositious funeral carried on' (ii: 9, 196). 'Knew', 'naturally', 'perfectly aware': the reader is pulled away from Catherine's feelings when the writer herself can hardly represent them without these mischievous touches of mockery, touches that pretend, falsely, to take her seriously.

Catherine finds once again, when she unlocks the door, that nothing answering to her imaginings is there: a perfectly modern bedroom is before her, 'on which the warm beams of a western sun gaily poured through two sash windows!' (ii: 9, 199). Then she hears footsteps on the stairs, surprising her in a place where she has no business to be. Her terror now becomes plausible and real. The subsequent conversation with Henry Tilney when he comes upon her there is in a quite different register from the novel's earlier play with Gothic fictions and brings the two figures together in another phase of physical and emotional intimacy. His enquiries about her interest in his mother's bedroom are conducted with intense earnestness. He soon guesses that Catherine has imagined that his mother has been locked away there or starved like the victim of a Gothic villain, and he is shocked. His being shocked bestows upon the previous chapters a kind of retrospective reality, because it does take Catherine's imaginings seriously, as the previous narrative has not quite been able to do. While Henry scutinises her face closely, Catherine looks down in shame, hesitatingly and stumblingly explaining why she is there, hoping perhaps not wholly to discredit herself in his eyes. The moment when she confesses her suspicions brings them together. 'His quick eye fixed on hers', she is held by the intensity of his gaze. 'She raised her eyes towards him more fully than she had ever done before' (ii: 9, 202). This moment of mutual exposure creates the condition for the solemn inquisition that follows, as Henry, earnestly regarding her, presses Catherine for an explanation of her behaviour.

His culminating speech, opening with 'If I understand you rightly, you had formed a surmise of such horror as I have hardly words to ——' employs Austen's long dash as a means of communicating the pressure of conflicting feelings that cannot readily be sorted out and expressed. But then turning to her with 'Dear Miss Morland', he finds a way of being her mentor without ironic superiority and speaks to her from the depths of his dismay. His speech cannot be read by many modern critics, however, without disbelief:

> 'Consult your own understanding, your own sense of the probable, your own observation of what is passing around you — Does our education prepare us for such atrocities? Do our laws connive at them? Could they be perpetrated without being known, in a country like this, where social and literary intercourse is on such a footing; where every man is surrounded by a neighbourhood of voluntary spies, and where roads and newspapers lay every thing open? Dearest Miss Morland, what ideas have you been admitting?' (ii: 9, 203)

Sceptical readers point out that this is the 1790s, and probably in the aftermath of the French Revolution when certainly many 'atrocities' took place just over the Channel, and that, as one famous historian wrote, if with some rhetorical exaggeration, 'The indignation excited by the savage excesses of the French Terror produced in England by reaction an "anti-Jacobin" terror.'[9] Can Jane Austen possibly be presenting this panegyric to English liberty without irony? Henry, who has been a virtual stand-in for the author in so many earlier conversations in the novel, is surely now being exposed as a conservative patrician, blind to the condition of his own country. Perhaps it is a moment when the truths hidden in the Gothic that the novel seeks to deny emerge, by default, uncalled for. Surely Austenian irony must be in play, in other words, throughout this earnest reprimand that sends Catherine running off in shame.

But there is no such irony. Tilney's speech should carry its impact because it is completely without the inventive, perhaps supercilious, teasing quality of his habitual style. Strong evidence for reading it as 'straight', without subversive authorial intention, is the obvious fact that here, broadly speaking, is the England that Jane Austen describes or rather assumes in all her other novels, a place of freedom, peace and security, a world taken for granted by a reviewer of her work in *The Edinburgh Magazine* of May 1818, who commented that 'we could conceive, without the slightest strain of imagination, any one of her fictions to be realized in any town or village in England'.[10] Even stronger evidence for authorial endorsement of the unequivocal earnestness of Henry's speech is that here Austen marshals the authority of the eighteenth-century writer who most passionately warned against the dangers lurking within the imagination, a writer whom she never makes fun of.[11] A 'neighbourhood of voluntary spies', for example, echoes his description of a spa in *The Idler* 78 where 'each is known to be a spy upon the rest', it being the gossip of another tight circle, the local genteel 'neighbourhood', that is the point. 'For what do we live,' asks Mr Bennet, 'but to make sport for our neighbours, and laugh at them in our turn?' (*P&P* III: 15, 403)

Samuel Johnson, as Isabel Grundy remarks, 'is a special case in Austen's letters and novels. Opinions shared with him pervade her fiction at a deep level vital to structure and meaning.'[12] In this passage of *Northanger Abbey*, that bedrock of Johnsonian ethics underlying all Austen's work is for once exposed. Henry's dismay voices his adherence to Johnson's passionately held conviction of 'The dangerous prevalence of imagination', which is the title of a compelling chapter in his *Rasselas* (1759), the novel that in *Mansfield Park* (III: 8, 454) Austen assumes her readers will know. There the writer depicts a lonely astronomer who amuses his leisure so continually with daydreams or fantasies that ultimately, as Johnson puts it, 'fictions begin to operate as realities' and the figure becomes delusional, if not mad. The astronomer begins to believe that the capacities he has fantasised about – that he might be able to control the world's weather – are really his. 'All power of fancy over reason', Johnson then pronounces through the mouthpiece of the philosopher Imlac, 'is a degree of insanity.' Catherine's obsessive hunting through the house for evidence of General Tilney's crimes is a demonstration of someone who has allowed fictions 'to operate as realities', her mind to become hostage to her reading, severing its anchorage within reality; and that is why Tilney is so appalled.

Throughout his essays Johnson insistently depicts the human mind as a citadel that must be guarded against the various assaults of life that may unhinge or unbalance it. The metaphor of the mind as a place may ultimately derive from John Locke, but Henry's word 'admitted' implicitly reproduces Johnson's fear that this place may be invaded by dangerous ideas. His speech, moving because it is intimate as well as reproachful, because it conveys his love and concern for Catherine as well as the need to correct her, because she becomes his 'Dearest' at the same moment as he expresses his shock at her imaginative licence, insists that England, like Catherine herself, is 'open'. When he asks her to 'consider', to 'remember' to 'consult', he is vindicating that conversation of the self with itself and with actuality that would be essential to her formation as an adult modern being. He says later that her 'feelings ought to be investigated, that they may know themselves' (II: 10, 213), thus suggesting the future ethical development which he might foster and grow from Catherine's present innocent goodwill.

Something of the urgent autobiographical anguish with which Johnson treats the temptations of fantasy is reflected in the castigation that Catherine, unqualified by any hint of dissent from the narrator, later inflicts upon herself:

> Her thoughts being still chiefly fixed on what she had with causeless terror felt and done, nothing could shortly be clearer, than that it had all been a voluntary, self-created delusion, each trifling circumstance receiving importance from an imagination resolved on alarm, and every thing forced to bend to one purpose by a mind which, before she entered the Abbey, had been craving to be frightened. (II: 10, 205)

'Craving' strikes the true Johnsonian note (he writes, for example, that the visitors at the watering place 'gratify their cravings' by spying on each other). When Catherine goes on to rephrase the view of English society that Henry has put to her, the sentences in which her tentative refusal of fictional stereotypes is made pick up Johnson's early critique of 'romantick absurdities', the foundational gesture of his work that affirms reality over the distortions of fictional representation.[13] His assertion that 'wherever human nature is to be found, there is a mixture of vice and virtue, a contest of passion and reason' is comically restyled when Catherine confines her confidence merely to 'the midland counties of England'. Then, as Tony Tanner noted, the cadences with which the narrator restores Catherine to equanimity – 'The anxieties of common life began soon to succeed to the alarms of romance' – 'sound like a Johnsonian distinction'.[14] If Jane Austen's Johnsonian convictions emerge most openly in this novel, that explicitness is perfectly congruent with the aesthetic values that govern *Northanger Abbey*'s fictional world.

Tilney's adherence to the Johnsonian belief that the mind should be guarded is paradoxically all the more notable for its exceptional status in a

novel otherwise devoted, as in this speech itself, to the frank, clear and
enlightened. He celebrates a civil society, where nothing can be kept secret,
where 'roads and newspapers lay every thing open'. This of course is only
one of the multiple meanings of the word, and in *Northanger* openness in
fact has several modes. Jocelyn Harris has demonstrated that the novel
continually draws contrasts between light and darkness.[15] The light
flooding Mrs Tilney's bedroom that contradicts Catherine's supposition
she must be held among a 'range of cells' in a 'prison' is 'prefigured', as
Harris writes, by several other instances. 'The housemaid's folding back
the window shutters at eight o'clock the next day' has awakened Catherine
after her thrilling search the previous night, 'and she opened her eyes,
wondering that they could ever have been closed, on objects of cheerful-
ness' and a 'bright morning' (II: 7, 176). Another telling instance is when
Catherine, who has expected 'dirt and cobwebs', is disappointed that the
windows of the Abbey are 'so clear, so light!' (II: 5, 165–6). The light and
the clear, linked with discovery, are also repeatedly associated with the
open, and the open contrasted with the dark, the closed, the debarred,
the possibly hidden, concealed or secret. In another range of meaning, the
open as a moral quality – clear, unpretending, honest, direct – is vindicated
against pretence, hypocrisy and hidden motives. The concealed, mysterious and Gothic is exposed by the novel's plot, while concurrently the
novelist practises the ironic exposure of verbal deceit.

Like the folding doors that hide nothing, or rather which lead into the
ordinary and banal, the concealments or hypocrisies of the two characters
who initially deceive Catherine conceal little. The novel is premised upon
the demonstration that there is nothing mysterious about the motives of
Isabella in Volume I, or General Tilney in Volume II, though Catherine,
for the amusement of the reader, is often oblivious to what is immediately
made plain to him or her. *Northanger Abbey*'s comedy turns on the
contradiction between these figures' self-presentation or social performance and their transparently obvious motives, as in the early instance when
Isabella is much more interested in the men she claims to be avoiding than
they are in her, so that when they leave the scene, she and Catherine, 'to
shew the independence of Miss Thorpe, and her resolution of humbling
the sex', set off 'as fast as they could walk, in pursuit of the two young men'
(I: 6, 37), or when 'with smiles of most exquisite misery, and the laughing
eye of utter despondency, she bade her friend adieu' (I: 9, 64). (The same
trick of simultaneous pretence and exposure is performed repeatedly with
the General: 'He is a happy man!' said the General, with a look of very
happy contempt' (II: 7, 183).) Like the black cabinet, Isabella Thorpe's

protestations of affection and deep feeling are empty, as empty as her brother's boasts. A wonderful variation on Isabella's pretences comes when, disappointed at James's father's provisions for their establishment, she claims that she hates money – 'if our union should take place now upon only fifty pounds a year, I should not have a wish unsatisfied' – and her mother, oblivious to her daughter's obvious chagrin, responds with 'Yes, yes, my darling Isabella . . . we perfectly see into your heart. You have no disguise' (II: 1, 139). It comes as no surprise when Henry uses the same phrase about Catherine.

The novel's transparency means that citation here is redundant. The pretensions of these figures, one dominating the first, the other the second volume, however insistently kept up, do not conceal their commonplace motives and ambitions. General Tilney's self-presentation as chivalrous, unworldly, caring nothing about money, 'perfectly without vanity' (he declares it himself) is contradicted by everything he says and does. Catherine, realising that she has been wrongly accusing him, allows herself nevertheless to see 'some actual specks' in his character, acknowledging him 'upon serious consideration, to be not perfectly aimiable', and the comedy turns on the fact that he has been shown to be a bully and control freak from his very first appearance in the novel. The joke is a little more subtle, though, than its earlier outing, when Catherine 'could not entirely repress a doubt, while she bore with the effusions of [Thorpe's] endless conceit, of his being altogether completely agreeable' (I: 9, 63). That the collision of damning authorial phrasing against apparent dramatic rendering of character is turned to different, and more problematic, effect in *Sense and Sensibility* only makes the gay ease of its use here the more notable.

One of the novel's major achievements is that Catherine's credulity and ingenuousness (though hard to believe when she convinces herself that General Tilney is a Gothic monster) are rarely ridiculous. The sweetness of her nature is demonstrated in the most convincing way by her assuming that other people's motives must be good ones – and what the reader observes is then made explicit by Henry Tilney himself. 'Your attributing my brother's wish of dancing with Miss Thorpe to good-nature alone, convinced me of your being superior in good-nature yourself to all the rest of the world', he says to her face (II: 1, 135). Once again, when Isabella Thorpe's letter is being discussed, Tilney, apparently speaking of Isabella to his sister, says 'Prepare for your sister-in-law, Eleanor, and such a sister-in-law as you must delight in! — Open, candid, artless, guileless, with affections strong but simple, forming no pretentions and knowing no disguise.' Eleanor catches his meaning and replies smilingly, 'Such a sister-in-law, Henry, I should delight in' (II: 10, 211–12). Catherine, utterly without personal conceit, untuned to such indirect communications, picks up only his ironic reference to Isabella, thus showing again how open and guileless she still actually is.

One aspect of *Northanger Abbey*'s commitment to the many modes of the open is more problematic. This is the frequent display within the text of a lively and amused narrator (sometimes more like a compère) mastering the entertainment, whose opinions are outright, and whose presence is distinct from the world she depicts. This forthright voice – not difficult to associate with the youthful author – interrupts the narrative, especially in the earlier chapters, to offer her opinions as to men's interest in women's finery, or to advise women to keep their intelligence to themselves, or, most famously, to take up an opportunity to deliver a passionate defence of the novel as a literary genre. This extended passage includes a lively little vignette exposing the hypocrisy surrounding novel reading: '"I am no novel reader — I seldom look into novels — Do not imagine that *I* often read novels — it is really very well for a novel." — Such is the common cant. "And what are you reading, Miss ——? " "Oh!, it is only a novel!" replies the young lady' (I: 5, 31). Warming to her cause, the voice hyperbolically instances 'Cecilia, or Camilla, or Belinda' as works 'in which the greatest powers of the mind are displayed, in which the most thorough knowledge of human nature, the happiest delineation of its varieties, the liveliest effusions of wit and humour are conveyed to the world in the best chosen language'. (Usually in Austen such inflated claims, as in other parts of this novel, are balloons ready to collapse.) Though vigorous, witty and thrillingly forthright, plainly the work of a youthful genius, this declaration by the compère is paradoxically at odds with Austen's later achievement. Precisely this kind of extra-diegetic commentary is what her later published novels eschew, dissolving or sublimating their author's opinions into scarcely perceptible shifts of inflection or the subtle merging of points of view.

At other points in *Northanger Abbey*, the authorial 'I', and the directing of the reader to mark what has already been shown, as when the Morlands are contrasted with the Thorpes – 'they were not in the habit . . . of telling lies to increase their importance, or of asserting one moment what they would contradict the next' (I: 9, 62), the facetious references to 'my heroine' and to the author as her 'biographer' all identify this text as quite distinct from the works that Austen later wrote and published. In these the 'world' of the novel is water-tight, homogeneous, coherent unto itself. Focused largely on different communal locales – Regency London, a big house in rural England, a village in the home counties – each novel is itself a specific textual space with its own distinct ethical questions and atmosphere, and the disappearance of the authorial presence, as of a voice outside that milieu, was to prove essential to their narrative originality and greatness. In *Northanger Abbey* the open activity of the author/narrator is of a piece with the 'miraculous lightness'[16] of the novel's own conceptual world, but this makes it distinct from Austen's later and more seriously meditated work. Famously, in 1817 she decided to put 'Miss Catherine' back 'on the Shelve', declaring that 'I do not know that she will ever come out.'[17]

Northanger Abbey, then, is not a good example of the hidden Jane Austen. Straightforwardly accessible, it is, as Margaret Oliphant wrote, 'clear and vivid as the daylight'. Its focus on the mysteriously concealed in the Gothic novel contributes to vindicate the clarity, straightforwardness and good sense that is demonstrated in its own transparently comic style. Not that *Northanger Abbey* is not in many respects a harbinger of what was to come. For in secreting the reasons for Catherine's total amnesia regarding her interview with Thorpe, Austen anticipates that reliance on her reader's divination which is so much part of the fabric of her later texts, and the demonstration there of memory's dependence on attention, or more precisely on emotional investment, is taken up and developed in *Pride and Prejudice*. The vicissitudes of the heroine's attention are tracked carefully and intricately in *Emma* and *Persuasion*, too, and the technique by which Catherine's confused emotions are captured anticipates many passages in these later novels and carried to remarkable psychological depths in *Mansfield Park*. More problematically, the device by which the polite idioms of the genteel world are thrown against the narrator's acerbic phrasing is employed again in *Sense and Sensibility*.

The atmosphere of Austen's first published novel, though, is far from the daylight of *Northanger Abbey*. Here moral and ethical issues seem much less clear, and the world that is created far tougher, more threatening than Bath or Northanger itself, where, after all, some plainly kind and good people do reside. In Northanger there really are no secrets of any account. But in the world of *Sense and Sensibility* the men have hidden lives and the women are condemned to concealments.

CHAPTER 2

Elinor Dashwood and concealment

Marianne Dashwood has looked forward to coming to London because there, as she expects, she will see again the man she loves, John Willoughby. But though he leaves his card, he doesn't visit, he doesn't answer her letters, he's nowhere to be found. After a few days she has worked herself up into a nearly hysterical state, so her sister Elinor drags her off on a shopping expedition to one of the smartest streets of the West End:

> Wherever they went, she was evidently always on the watch. In Bond-street especially, where much of their business lay, her eyes were in constant inquiry; and in whatever shop the party were engaged, her mind was equally abstracted from every thing actually before them, from all that interested and occupied the others. Restless and dissatisfied every where, her sister could never obtain her opinion of any article of purchase, however it might equally concern them both; she received no pleasure from any thing; was only impatient to be at home again. (*S&S* II: 4, 187)

Like much of the writing in *Sense and Sensibility*, this is hyperbolic and exaggerated, but perhaps it gives a fair approximation of Marianne's feverish, restless state. Rather than just telling the reader that Marianne was constantly on the lookout for Willoughby, the narrator seems to enact an odd collusion with her character. The rhythms of the prose partake of her hectic emotions, though the judgements are those of her calm and staider sister.

Much later in the novel, when Marianne is still recovering from the fever that might have killed her, Willoughby, in a famous scene, arrives at Cleveland at night. He attempts to explain his behaviour to Elinor. He knew they were in London, he tells her, but also that he was, against his better feelings, determined to avoid them. He says that he even hung around till they left the house, and only then left his name:

> 'Watched us out of the house!'
> 'Even so. You would be surprised to hear how often I watched you, how often I was on the point of falling in with you. I have entered many a shop to

avoid your sight, as the carriage drove by. Lodging as I did in Bond-street, there was hardly a day in which I did not catch a glimpse of one or other of you; and nothing but the most constant watchfulness on my side, a most invariably prevailing desire to keep out of your sight, could have separated us so long.' (III: 8, 369–70)

There is clearly a match between these two passages, and readers who recall that Marianne spent some time in Bond Street might appreciate Austen's skilful plotting when they come across the second one, over 200 pages later. While Marianne has been on the lookout for Willoughby, he has been as consistently dodging her. Marianne is restless, Willoughby is continuously on the move. 'Her eyes were in constant inquiry', he is constantly watchful: he is as anxious to avoid her as she is anxious to find him. A game of hide-and-seek (or seek-and-hide) has been played. So, while the emotions of the characters themselves are agitated and painful, the narrative might reward the reader with an amusement that is hardly distinguishable from satisfaction at Austen's ingenuity.

Sense and Sensibility is full of secrets; and this contrivance might just count as one of them. Willoughby keeps secret his liaison with Eliza Williams, and Brandon must keep secret his knowledge of Willoughby's secret. Brandon, once he learns of the great likelihood that Marianne will marry Willoughby, must also keep secret his own love for her. Edward Ferrars does not disclose that he is engaged to Lucy Steele. Lucy has kept her engagement to him a secret, lest it lead to his disinheritance, and Elinor Dashwood, once she has learned from Lucy 'what was always meant to be a great secret' stays true to her word and keeps Lucy's secret. She must also then keep her own feelings for Edward a secret. Marianne, who says that she has no secrets, keeps from her mother and sister the true state of her relationship with Willoughby. On the other hand, the novel is studded with comic figures – Sir John Middleton, Mrs Jennings, Anne Steele – who wouldn't know a secret if they tripped over it in the dark.

But as this ingenious match-making coup suggests, concealment is as germane to *Sense and Sensibility* as secrets themselves. Here one might say that Willoughby conceals himself from Marianne, and that the novelist conceals his concealment from the reader. But it would be more accurate and helpful to notice that there is no continuous presence or intimation of this event in the narrative. It would be a rare reader who suspected that the insistence on Marianne's restless searching was a clue to something being concealed, and who carried that suspicion on through 200 pages. It is the narrator's secret, a bit of plotting, hidden until it be disclosed. Such secrets in the novel, like the back story of the two Elizas that Brandon reveals to

Elinor, can be much less interesting than the processes of concealment. For concealments, though they may well be the consequences of acts or events, belong to the inner life and are thus aspects of character portrayal. Elinor's keeping to herself the knowledge of Lucy's engagement, for example, which I have referred to as a secret, is better described as a concealment because it is presented as an enduring aspect of her personal life, and known to the reader over many chapters as such. Concealment, the psychological consequence or weight of secrets, *Sense and Sensibility* intimates, is everywhere, it is the very stuff of the moral life, not because secrets have to be kept, or not alone, but because feelings have to be kept private, and because social life exacts a tax not only on behaviour but also within the self. In the highly competitive and mercenary social world the novel depicts such concealment is endemic. Yet *Sense and Sensibility*, which hides so many secrets from the reader, in which concealments are so often practised by the characters, and where kinds of concealment thread through each other, is a novel that exhibits an extraordinary openness, even a brutal frankness, at the same time.

The word 'concealment' or its derivatives is certainly used often. A notable instance is in Colonel Brandon's speech after he has learned, as he thinks, that Marianne is actually engaged to Willoughby:

> 'Is every thing finally settled? Is it impossible to — ? But I have no right, and I could have no chance of succeeding. Excuse me, Miss Dashwood. I believe I have been wrong in saying so much, but I hardly know what to do, and on your prudence I have the strongest dependence. Tell me that it is all absolutely resolved on, that any attempt, that in short concealment, if concealment be possible, is all that remains.' (II: 5, 197)

Elinor understands this, oddly, as 'a direct avowal' of Brandon's love for her sister. But is this the only possible reading of his speech? The concealment Brandon speaks of might not only mean the hiding of his feelings for Marianne; it might also refer to his concealing his knowledge of Willoughby's history as seducer of Eliza Williams. Perhaps he is saying that the only way he can express his love for Marianne is by concealing information that might hurt her. In speaking in this oblique manner, in asking Miss Dashwood to intuit what he actually means, he is already practising a milder form of concealment. This speech, much like the rest of Brandon's speeches, is different in style from those of other characters and anticipates effects in Austen's later work that use incomplete syntax ('Is it impossible to — '; 'that any attempt, that') and reiterations to suggest a character's inner turmoil. Brandon is a man of rigid honour, and, as the reader learns later, has met

Willoughby in a duel. Perhaps his repetition of the word 'concealment' is employed by the writer to reflect moral reluctance, distaste, not only at having to keep Willoughby's perfidy a secret, nor only at having to hide his own passion for Marianne, but also at the notion of concealment in itself. It is as if the resort to concealment puts him in the same league, reduces him to the same level, as Willoughby, and he finds this desperately unpalatable. If this is so, it would align him with Marianne and his enemy, both of whom claim to despise concealment.

Only four pages earlier, Marianne has rebuked her sister: 'We have neither of us any thing to tell; you, because you communicate, and I, because I conceal nothing' (II: 5, 193). Strictly speaking, this is true: Marianne has certainly not concealed her feelings for Willoughby, and perhaps her neglecting to tell her mother and sister that, despite appearances, they are not engaged is a reflection of her adolescent naiveté, or something that she has not allowed herself to know that they might assume.[1] Elinor is 'distressed by this charge of reserve in herself'. But in this interview with Brandon, Elinor responds again with reserve, her own form of concealment. His words, the narrator comments, 'affected her very much. She was not immediately able to say anything, and even when her spirits were recovered, she debated for a short time, on the answer it would be most proper to give.' The first phrase here is an instance of a technique that is to be important in Austen's later narratives: intimating a silence in which the reader is invited to imagine the character's emotion. But 'debated' conveys the information that Elinor recovers intellectual command of herself, as she asks which is more important, to tell the truth – that she doesn't know for a fact what he assumes is correct – or to let Brandon down as lightly as she can. 'After some consideration', a phrase in a paragraph that in order to present Elinor as responsible and thoughtful inserts an implausible interval in the exchange, she decides to tell a white lie: 'she thought it most prudent and kind, after some consideration, to say more than she really knew or believed' – in other words, not to disclose her ignorance of the real state of affairs. This is to kill off Brandon's hopes of Marianne, by affirming what she does in fact not know, that the engagement has taken place. One is asked to admire the integrity of her inner process, but there is something dubious, as it turns out, about its result.

Elinor's character is the site of the novel's most interesting, ethically challenging and, in its way, disturbing investigation of concealment. Outwardly diplomatic, polite, accommodating, unlike her sister, she keeps her intense feelings to herself, partly because she knows that in the world they live in to say what you think or feel involves risk. The social milieu depicted in *Sense and Sensibility* is harsher, more cruel, than in any of Jane Austen's other published work, and not only because alone of the novels much of it is set in Regency London.[2] The Dashwood sisters have been cheated by an old man's folly of their expected inheritance and forced to leave the home the family has lived in for generations. Their (half-) sister-in-law, Fanny Dashwood, who succeeds to their place, ruthlessly mercenary and snobbish, is a foretaste of the new acquaintances they are to meet at Barton and again in the capital: the cold, insipid but equally snobbish Lady Middleton, the cold and selfish Mr Palmer, the vulgar but remorselessly ambitious Lucy Steele. These are the persons, among others equally uncongenial, who form their new circle of acquaintance, but whose values and styles are antithetical to the Dashwood sisters' own. Their company entails diplomacy, even flattery, to maintain the vapid equilibrium of genteel sociability.

In the exchanges between Elinor Dashwood and Lucy Steele the dramas of concealment are most compellingly, if problematically, activated. These dialogues, as Paula Byrne writes, possess 'a realistic quality that transcends the burlesque absurdities of similar comically-styled exchanges' in earlier eighteenth-century novels and plays.[3] Elinor is merciless to Lucy after the Dashwood sisters have passed a few afternoons with the Miss Steeles:

> Lucy was naturally clever; her remarks were often just and amusing; and as a companion for half an hour Elinor frequently found her agreeable; but her powers had received no aid from education, she was ignorant and illiterate, and her deficiency of all mental improvement, her want of information in the most common particulars, could not be concealed from Miss Dashwood, in spite of her constant endeavour to appear to advantage. Elinor saw, and pitied her for, the neglect of abilities which education might have rendered so respectable; but she saw, with less tenderness of feeling, the thorough want of delicacy, of rectitude, and integrity of mind, which her attentions, her assiduities, her flatteries at the Park betrayed; and she could have no lasting satisfaction in the company of a person who joined insincerity with ignorance; whose want of instruction prevented their meeting in conversation on terms of equality, and whose conduct towards others, made every shew of attention and deference towards herself perfectly valueless. (1: 22, 146)

This is a fine piece of writing, which effectively represents Elinor's unusual strength and clarity of mind. But it is difficult to credit the pity attributed to Miss Dashwood when in the same sentence it is followed by such a series of crushing condemnations, presented in all the authority of the resounding triadic phrasing most famously associated with Johnson.

Turned to characterological purposes here, the style seems extreme. 'Her attentions, her assiduities, her flatteries at the Park': such unnecessary insistence risks suggesting that Marianne is not the only figure in *Sense and Sensibility* to be affiliated with repetitious sentences and sweeping judgements. As far as one can tell, Elinor's assessments here are in complete accord with the narrative's. This relationship between the narrator and Elinor is in fact problematic throughout the novel.

Lucy cannot conceal her vulgarity and ambition from Elinor, but Elinor, who has taught herself to hide her emotions, may be more successful in concealing her dislike and contempt from Lucy. There are two private exchanges between them: the climactic chapter of the first volume of the novel, in which Lucy reveals her engagement with Edward; the second meeting is two chapters later, contrived and instigated by Elinor. These are followed by a series of more public encounters in London which finds Lucy 'returning ... to the charge' (II: 10, 248). As this phrase suggests, these are battles, more akin to duels than any other dialogues in this novel, or in any other by Jane Austen. Like the sisters in 'The Watsons', the fragment that was probably written in the years between the early and final versions of *Sense and Sensibility*, Elinor and Lucy are competing for a not overwhelmingly attractive husband with the energy and duplicity men employ in business and the professions.[4] In this novel, the confrontation between Brandon and Willoughby is only indirectly alluded to, half-concealed from the reader (II: 9, 239–40). Nothing in the relations shown between men matches the savage finesse and dramatic power with which Austen depicts women duelling for position and partners, not by the sword, but with words and deeds.[5]

The first conversation, like the more frequently discussed duologue between John and Fanny Dashwood early in the novel, consists of one party relentlessly manipulating the other. The focus is as much on the two women's facial expressions as on their speech. When Lucy first introduces the name of Ferrars, Elinor is caught off guard, since she has not been aware of any relation at all between Lucy and Edward: she '*did* think the question a very odd one, and her countenance expressed it' (I: 22, 147). 'Eyeing Elinor attentively as she spoke', 'fixing her eyes upon Elinor', Lucy then proceeds to mention that her connection with the family is with the 'elder brother', and Elinor turns to her 'in silent amazement'. With a pretence of hesitation, Lucy intimates that she might become 'very intimately connected' with Edward's mother; 'She looked down as she said this, amiably bashful, with only one side glance at her companion to observe its effect on her' (I: 22, 148). Elinor's viewpoint at this moment merges with the narrator's: or is this the interpretation of a third-party observer – an interpretation that, especially in the phrase 'aimiably bashful', pulls the rug from under Lucy's credibility? As Lucy moves closer to her object, Elinor's anxiety not to reveal her own feelings mounts. Her 'complexion varied', but secure, as she believes, in Edward's love for her, she is just able to stand her ground. Lucy proceeds to reveal the secret engagement – though she leaves it to Elinor to speak that word itself – and intimates she is confiding in her because she has 'the greatest dependance in the world' on Elinor's keeping her secret safe. Summoning all her self-control, Elinor then begins more deliberately to conceal her emotions ('solicitude' in this passage must mean anxiety):

> Elinor for a few moments remained silent. Her astonishment at what she heard was at first too great for words; but at length forcing herself to speak, and to speak cautiously, she said with a calmness of manner, which tolerably well concealed her surprise and solicitude — 'May I ask if your engagement is of long standing?' (I: 22, 149)

The way to parry Lucy's attacks is to put on a disguise, to hide her feelings if possible. But this becomes more and more difficult as Lucy strikes blow after blow.

The dialogue between John and Fanny Dashwood, a similar assertion of female power as she progressively whittles down the terms of the son's promise to his father, is sometimes compared with the way Lear's daughters strip him of his retinue, though Lear's daughters cruelly and tragically confront their father face to face.[6] The first encounter between Elinor and Lucy suggests another Shakespearean analogy: the exchange in *Othello* (Act III, scene 3) in which Iago attacks Othello's confidence in Desdemona's faithfulness. Lucy, like Iago, is given to the poisonous drip-feed. Both interrogations open with sly suggestion ('Did Michael Cassio, when you wooed my lady/ Know of your love?'; Lucy's introduction of Mrs Ferrars: 'The time *may* come ... when we may be very intimately connected') and proceed, little by little, to undermine their victim's confidence – Othello's belief in Desdemona, and Elinor's belief in Edward. Both are forced, step by step, to experience painful emotions that nonplus them and allow their opponent to deliver their next attack upon a weakened victim. And, like Iago, Lucy offers 'ocular proof' (though hers, as far as it goes, is genuine). She has come prepared to the encounter with materials hidden in her clothing, first 'taking a small miniature from her pocket', and putting this traditional lovers' token into Elinor's own hand.

In complete contrast with Othello, however, Elinor remains, at least outwardly, calm. Her dignity enables Lucy to extract from her the vital promise of secrecy. Then Lucy, boldly looking 'directly at her companion', torments or teases Elinor by saying that she has often thought of breaking off the engagement, which, as she might know, would be what Elinor must inwardly be longing for. (These interpretations inhere in their dramatic interaction, left to be intuited.) As this dialogue reaches its climax, the reader is not shielded from the overpowering distress that afflicts Elinor. Then, confident that she has Elinor where she wants her, 'taking a letter from her pocket and carelessly shewing the direction' (the address, which is in Edward's handwriting) Lucy flaunts it before her (1: 22, 154).

Elinor nearly collapses. But Lucy has another, more devastating wound to deliver. Once again, with apparent casualness, she mentions that she gave Edward 'a lock of my hair set in a ring when he was at Longstaple last . . . Perhaps you might notice the ring when you saw him?' (1: 22, 155). Is it going too far to suggest an analogy with Iago's apparently idle remark that he has seen Cassio with Othello's precious handkerchief and 'wipe his beard with' it? The association of hair with animality, and thus with sex, but also, peculiarly, with transcendence of the bodily, and thus of romance, makes it a potent talisman.[7] The assault on Elinor is the more terrible because, unknown to Lucy, she has, on seeing Edward's ring, 'instantaneously' assumed that the hair enclosed in it must be her own (1: 18, 114). The handkerchief and the beard, the ring on the hand and the lock of hair, are unnerving because they are visceral in their imaginative effect and confounding in their evidential power. Elinor is horrified to discover that for all her cautious management of her emotional life, she has fallen prey to her desires, seen what she wants to see. But when Lucy has apparently carried all before her, Elinor still retains her outward poise: she responds that she has indeed seen the ring on Edward's finger 'with a composure of voice, under which was concealed an emotion and distress beyond any thing she had ever felt before' (1: 22, 155). Though 'her heart sunk within her, and she could hardly stand', her struggle against her feelings is successful; her 'self-command', her capacity to conceal her distress, is insisted upon, and commended to the reader's respect.

So far, so good. But things become more problematic when Elinor initiates the second dialogue. She wants to find out whether her rival has any real affection for Edward. She is also bent on persuading Lucy that, despite her 'involuntary agitation' in their last encounter, 'she was in no otherwise interested' in the engagement 'than as a friend' (which of course is untrue). Even more strikingly, though she is certainly 'mourning in secret' (II: 1, 161) over the loss of Edward, 'she could not deny herself the comfort of endeavouring to convince Lucy that her heart was unwounded'. In seeking this second interview, Elinor is pursuing her own aims, rather than seeking in any way to genuinely assist her 'friend'. The reader has been conditioned to dislike and mistrust Lucy, and to take Elinor's side, but it is difficult to commend her tactics here: it is as if she has been brought down to her rival's level. As Byrne writes, 'there is a disquieting sense that the moral order of the novel is threatening to collapse: the danger is that Elinor's aptitude for dissimulation and disingenuousness is alarmingly akin to Lucy's'.[8] Lucy is more calculating, but lets her face reveal too much; Elinor's physical control helps her parry her enemy, but she is also bent, if not on deception, on manipulation.

Lucy is pleased that she reopens their discourse, since, as she says, she had imagined that she had offended Elinor previously:

> 'Offended me! How could you suppose so? Believe me,' and Elinor spoke it with the truest sincerity, 'nothing could be farther from my intention, than to give you such an idea. Could you have a motive for the trust, that was not honourable and flattering to me?' (II: 2, 167)

Elinor's second sentence puts forward a deceitful assumption: Lucy's motive has been to make sure that Elinor knows of her prior claim on Edward. Lucy knows that it is not true either: and Elinor knows that Lucy knows. She is here utilising a diplomatic strategy or polite convention that traps her interlocutor in a false position. Lucy must naturally accept this flattering account of her own motives, with the result that Elinor can consolidate her own position: that of the trusted, and trustworthy, friend. In this role, or disguise, Elinor can continue to attribute the best of motives to them both, and under that cover find out more about Lucy's feelings, which then plausibly enough allows her to enquire into the couple's financial prospects. Yet again there are disturbing notes in this exchange. The interception of her immediate reply with the comment 'Elinor spoke it with the truest sincerity' (which may well be true) might lead the reader to imagine that she speaks the second sentence with the same sincerity (or, as is conceivable, Austen does not quite register that Elinor's second sentence is deceitful). The little word 'it', which might colour Elinor's remark with moral heroism, might also read to a suspicious reader as a signal that Elinor is indeed acting a part, an actress speaking with 'truest sincerity' not being quite the same as honesty of feeling. On the face of it, though, she can be sincere because 'offence' is not what she has received from Lucy: she has been made devastatingly miserable, and, as she might guess, Lucy knows it.

The alliance of the narrator with Elinor is troublesome in these exchanges, but perhaps nowhere more so than in the commentary that accompanies the contrasting behaviours of the two sisters. When they are first in the company of the Dashwoods and the Miss Steeles, for instance, the narrator has remarked that it was 'impossible' for Marianne 'to say what she did not feel, however trivial the occasion; and upon Elinor therefore the whole task of telling lies when politeness required it, always fell' (1: 21, 141). Again, the phrasing is unnecessarily insistent, though there is a carefully delivered shock in the word 'lies', and the delaying of the verb to the end of the sentence makes rhythmically overt the weight of the 'task' that Elinor carries out. 'Lies' is very much what Frank Churchill in *Emma* describes as 'civil falsehood', but the bluntness of the word makes all the difference.[9] 'Lies' conveys a reluctance, even repugnance at the necessary tasks of social duplicity that is radically at odds with the behaviour that Elinor practises. The outrageously free-speaking comment is – excitingly – at a tangent with the discretion simultaneously being commended.

The tensions in the narrator are more successfully dealt with in the dialogues with Lucy, partly because of the trace of comedy that colours the ladies' exchange. Taking on the role and tone of her 'friend', Elinor can appear to sympathise with Lucy's predicament, while at the same time pointing out the material impediments to the engagement and finding out, for her own information, or satisfaction, just how implacable Mrs Ferrars' opposition is. In her turn cued, or trapped, by Elinor's self-presentation as her confidante, Lucy is displayed keeping up her own self-presentation as the devoted fiancée prepared to wait for years. Elinor pretends to accept the truth of Lucy's assertion of Edward's 'truth and constancy' and goes on, with the same apparent sympathy of the model counsellor, the supportive therapist, to remark that 'If the strength of your reciprocal attachment had failed, as between many people and under many circumstances it naturally would during a four years' engagement, your situation would have been pitiable indeed' (11: 2, 168). She is hinting, in fact, that neither Lucy's nor Edward's attachment is worth much now. 'Lucy here looked up', evidently smelling a rat. But Elinor 'was careful in guarding her countenance from every expression that could give her words a suspicious tendency'. Elinor's skills in concealment are being commended, but between the two women is a kind of narrative electricity because what is being communicated between their speeches is left to the reader to discern.

Marianne's 'noise' at the pianoforte has sheltered their dialogue from the hearing of others in the room. A pause in the music allows Lucy's sister, Anne, and Mrs Jennings to overhear. Between them they give away both that Elinor has a 'beau' and that Lucy has a beau, and that both beaux might well be the same beau. After this, no wonder the pair are nonplussed. 'Elinor blushed in spite of herself. Lucy bit her lip. A mutual silence took place for some time' (II: 2, 170). Lucy picks up her role the more quickly since she is still intent on getting some material help from her opponent. Before long, Lucy again dangles the prospect of voluntarily breaking off the engagement with Edward before her and pretends to ask her advice. Elinor produces 'a smile, which concealed very agitated feelings' (II: 2, 171). Lucy proceeds, speaking 'with great solemnity', more insincere than Elinor's sincerity, if less convincing, to tell her that if Elinor, as counsellor, advised her to put an end to the engagement, she would. Elinor parries this with her own lying flattery, saying 'the power of dividing two people so tenderly attached is too much for an indifferent person' (II: 2, 172). At this point the balloon of their elevated sentiments is about to collapse, and Elinor quickly decides to put an end to the conversation, 'lest they might provoke each other to an unsuitable increase of ease and unreserve'. 'Unsuitable' precisely catches the fact that class is here mobilised as decorum. Soon Elinor resolves not to encourage Lucy to any more intercourse, since it is 'dangerous to herself' (II: 2, 173). This might mean that she feels she risks being contaminated by Lucy's methods and duplicity, or that she risks letting her mask slip and reveal more of her feelings for Edward than is safe. It is impossible, in other words, to know how far the narrator, or author, is critical of Elinor's recourse to deception and manipulation in this scene. What is certain is that neither narrator nor character gives Lucy any quarter.

Lacking skill or training in self-command, in the concealment of her feelings, or in the techniques of genteel self-presentation, Lucy Steele is remorselessly exposed through her facial expressions and gestures. But since these encounters are almost exclusively dramatic, it is possible to attribute a tiny filament of authenticity to Lucy, to believe that some at least of what she avows might be true. When she speaks of her long-drawn-out misery, of her fear that Anne might reveal her secret, she is not lying, nor is her determination, perhaps even desperation, to hold Edward to his engagement quite unforgivable. It gives her a foothold in society, in a world where women without money and without male support are besieged. She is intelligent enough to know that she must claw her way upwards by her own efforts, and she has a sister who, like Elinor's, is a liability. Through Lucy Steele Jane Austen might be commenting on the desperate situation of marginal women. Elinor then might figure as a staunch defender of her own class privilege. Perhaps the novel is not so much about the necessity of diplomacy in personal interactions as an exposure, most acute in these scenes, of the 'horizontal aggression', as sociology terms it, to which those who cannot compete with the people above them in caste or status so often resort. Perhaps too there is unresolved bitterness behind what ultimately seems Austen's endorsement of Elinor's determined tactics.

In the next chapter Elinor and Marianne are invited by Mrs Jennings to stay with her in her London home in Portman Square, a prosperous address, but not the most fashionable. It is the winter 'season' and the Middletons arrive a week or so later, having hired a Conduit Street house, in the luxury of Mayfair. The Palmers are already in town, and a month or so later the two Miss Steeles arrive at their cousins' in Holborn, a decidedly less smart address. The milieu of the novel shifts to Regency London, where Austen's presentation of the social world becomes decidedly more hostile and still more problematic.

It is at Gray's, a shop in Sackville Street off Piccadilly, that Elinor encounters the fop she later realises is Edward's brother, Robert (II: II, 251–2). This gentleman, who stares at Elinor and thereby imprints on her 'the remembrance of a person and face, of strong, natural, sterling insignificance', and who holds up the waiting ladies while he examines 'all the different horrors of the different toothpick-cases presented to his inspection', is treated over almost three paragraphs with a vituperation, a 'brutality', that, as D. A. Miller memorably shows, 'overcomes character and narrator's voice alike'.[10] More obviously, the anger expressed by or on behalf of the waiting Elinor is a response to this selfish display of wealth wasted on self-indulgence and triviality. It is not too far away (since brutality is in question) from the well-known cartoon by Gillray in which a plump bon-vivant, uncannily like the Prince of Wales, is shown sprawling at the table and picking his teeth with a fork.[11] (Gray's was known to be patronised by the Regent.) This figure's fuss over the ridiculous item of a jewelled tooth-pick case epitomises the combination of wealth with personal insignificance that makes high-end society so intolerable to women like Elinor who must husband their gentility with the same discretion as they negotiate the sale of their mother's jewels.

In *Mansfield Park* the culture of London 'society' during the Regency is only indirectly shown, but through Mary Crawford's fuss over her ultra-modish accessory, the harp, together with her brother Henry's transporting of his high-bred hunters across half the country for his riding pleasure, the novel does glance at the extravagance and display practised as a natural right by people of the fashionable world.[12] When Mary Crawford writes to Fanny Price from Hill Street, another notable Mayfair address, she slips into the cynical and malicious tones of metropolitan society. In the London sequence of *Sense and Sensibility* this society is shown to be conducted with just as little kindness, even with a close to Proustian ruthlessness. Characters act themselves out in an exacerbated style: Mr Palmer's brusqueness is heightened into a lie when he denies having heard that the Dashwood sisters were in town, Lady Middleton's concern for social forms degenerates into amoral opportunism when she decides, despite Willoughby's treatment of her friends, to leave her card at his home and that of his wealthy bride. Networking is all-important. After the fop has left, bestowing on the sisters only a stare, Elinor's half-brother John comes into Gray's shop, and as they walk northwards through London to Conduit Street, John's stupidity, snobbishness and avarice are displayed over five pages of near-soliloquy. His boasting of Mrs Ferrars' putting 'bank notes into Fanny's hands to the amount of two thousand pounds' to help with their London expenses (II: 11, 254–9) to a sister who is living in what must count as middle-class poverty is almost the equivalent of Lucy Steele's taunts with her letter and ring in its hurtful visual particularity, if not precisely in its intention. John is just insensitive and stupid. The introduction of the mercenary, rude, rich Mrs Ferrars and her younger son, the vacuous dandy, completes the novel's cast of contempt-ible London characters, all except Mrs Jennings and Brandon bent on social advancement and the display of wealth, and favoured by nature with what Elinor and the narrator have called 'sterling insignificance'. This is the world, too, in which Willoughby, desperately short of money, has contracted his engagement with the heiress Miss Grey, who has £50,000 (a very great sum) to her name.

But if so many of the characters are coarsened by London, the novel's presentation of them takes on an answering stridency. In this milieu of competitive jockeying for social prestige, Lucy's speech is now presented in a barrage of stressed and italicised words that displays her intention grossly at odds with her speech:

> 'I should have been quite disappointed if I had not found you here *still*,' said she repeatedly, with a strong emphasis on the word. 'But I always thought I *should*. I was almost sure you would not leave London yet awhile; though you *told* me, you know, at Barton, that you should not stay above a *month* . . . I am amazingly glad you did not keep to *your word*.' (II: 10, 247)

There is now not the smallest doubt that Lucy is viciously jealous, nor that all Elinor's self-control has failed to persuade Lucy of her indiffer-ence to the engagement. Elinor's response is now similarly consigned into italics. She 'perfectly understood her, and was forced to use all her self-command to make it appear she did *not*'.

Though not in the habit of giving anything, as the narrator remarks, the Dashwoods give a dinner party, and Lucy, nervous at the prospect of meeting Mrs Ferrars, cries 'Pity me, dear Miss Dashwood!'; Elinor 'assured her, and with great sincerity, that she did pity her', to Lucy's amazement, who has hoped, as the narrator, unscrupulously switching the point of view, says, 'to be an object of irrepressible envy to Elinor' (II: 12, 264). Elinor pities Lucy because she knows that Mrs Ferrars is intent on Edward's marrying Miss Morton, Lord Morton's daughter, not the daughter of a schoolmaster. Her 'sincerity' is a result of this knowledge, not of any kindness to Lucy. It is as if sincerity itself has become duplicitous. There is a secret triumph in it that the narrator invites the reader to share. There follows a replay of their earlier confrontation when for two pages Lucy boasts of Mrs Ferrars' kind reception of her, and Elinor refuses to give her any encouragement (II: 13, 272–4).

Bound as she is by her promise to Lucy, Elinor must practise for chapter after chapter another, more enduringly painful order of concealment with her sister and mother. She must keep her knowledge of the engagement to herself, while at the same time she tries to overcome her feelings for Edward. More than once she suggests that her attachment to him is weakening in speeches that Marianne is shown immediately to detect as false. In fact, as her later confession to her sister when Edward and Lucy's engagement is known reveals, she has 'been most deeply interested' all the time she has struggled 'to appear indifferent' (III: 1, 299). This conflict of Elinor's inner life is presented only minimally, held back until it can be described with great eloquence, dramatic effect and Marianne's moral enlightenment in this chapter. Her other inner conflicts are often left to be deduced from her refusal to engage with the many people she despises. In a technique that is handled more subtly in *Persuasion*, minor characters – John Dashwood, Robert Ferrars, Mrs Jennings, Anne Steele – are allocated long and, depending on the figure, foolish or mercenary speeches, while Elinor's responses are minimal, though not in the least enigmatic. 'Elinor would not vouchsafe any answer', or 'she could only smile' in the face of her brother's self-exposure. 'She kept her concern and her censure to herself'; 'Elinor was silent'; 'To this, Elinor had no answer to make, and did not attempt any'; and more memorably, 'Elinor agreed to it all, for she did not think he deserved the compliment of rational opposition' (II: 14, 276). Her resentful emotions are often presented to the reader then only in the sound of their silence.

If on the one hand Elinor conceals her contempt, the narrative virtually revels in its capacity for wit, disdain and censure. While the heroine is offered as quelling or containing her hostile emotions, the prose around her is unremittingly scarifying and judgemental. Here is an example of the narrator letting rip, on Elinor's first meeting with Mrs Ferrars: 'a lucky contraction of the brow had rescued her countenance from the disgrace of insipidity, by giving it the strong characters of pride and ill nature. She was not a woman of many words: for, unlike people in general, she proportioned them to the number of her ideas' (II: 12, 265). This wit cannot be directly attributed to Elinor, because that would generate an unpleasant sense of her anger and frustration, or cut across the intention to present her as a figure of admirable self-restraint. The novelist at other times, as in the encounter at Gray's, cannot keep Elinor's judgements and her own distinct from one another. Another example is when the dinner at the Dashwoods is described:

> The servants were numerous, and every thing bespoke the Mistress's inclination for shew, and the Master's ability to support it. In spite of the improvements and additions which were making to the Norland estate, and in spite of its owner having once been within some thousand pounds of being obliged to sell out at a loss, nothing gave any symptom of that indigence which he had tried to infer from it; — no poverty of any kind, except of conversation, appeared, — but there, the deficiency was considerable. John Dashwood had not much to say for himself that was worth hearing, and his wife had still less. But there was no peculiar disgrace in this, for it was very much the case with the chief of their visitors, who almost all laboured under one or other of these disqualifications for being agreeable — Want of sense, either natural or improved — want of elegance — want of spirits — or want of temper. (II: 12, 265–6)

Elinor's despising the company has just been made explicit, so it is natural to take these destructive and contemptuous phrases as a summary of her experience. But there is little indication that the paragraph can be tied back to her, and its omniscient air certainly suggests the narrator. Whose 'want of spirits – or want of temper' is meant? 'The chief of their visitors' seems to exclude the Dashwood sisters. But it sounds very much as if 'want of temper' might include Elinor. In effect Elinor's want of temper is usually displaced into the narrative, where irony repeatedly descends into sarcasm, as when Robert Ferrars is said to 'candidly and generously' attribute what he calls his brother's *gaucherie* to his private education, or Lucy's 'good will' is spoken of, or Marianne gives a 'happy specimen' of her behaviour to Mrs Jennings (II: 4, 182) or a clumsy hint of hers is called 'this admirable discretion' (II: 13, 277).

The narrative conveys a strong sense of confederacy with Elinor, and perhaps in effect it represents what she is suppressing, but in dramatic terms Elinor is quarantined from the more scarifying and dismissive comments. This displacement of hostility into a narrative where it is openly expressed is a cruder technique than the embedded antagonism contained in the earlier dramatic rehearsal of Lucy Steele's repertoire of sly manipulations. There is little to be inferred about the characters in London, nothing in them but what they transparently, in their manners or talk, display. Judgements are absolute, without nuance or complicating reserve. But one result of this parade of the fashionable world's moral vacuity is certainly to underline the fact that Elinor and Marianne both have to deal with it. Though their ways of facing it are so different, they are at one with each other and with the narrator in virtually hating the London in which they find themselves. As Marcia McClintock Folsom has persuasively argued, the narrator's sarcasms about the characters and the ways of the world the Dashwood sisters have to confront works to secure the sympathy of readers for their dilemmas within it.[13] The whole novel is built around the sisters' dispossession – their loss of the house and the comforts that ought to have been theirs – and if it is this grievance that powers the narrator's open disdain and anger towards the display of wealth and wealth's privileges in the capital, it is this also which consolidates her sympathy for both her heroines.

It is in this London that Willoughby sends a letter that, without apology or regret, breaks off all contact with Marianne. In a scene that has been memorably discussed, she is found by Elinor stretched on her bed, with this letter in her hand, 'almost choked with grief'. She gives this and other letters into her sister's hand, 'and then, covering her face with her handkerchief, almost screamed with agony' (II: 7, 208). In a novel attentive to extreme emotions and filled with damning judgements, the repeated use of 'almost' might draw the reader's attention. Unlike Fanny Dashwood, who, learning that Lucy and Edward are engaged, falls into 'violent hysterics immediately with such screams as reached [her husband's] ears' (III: 1, 293), Marianne here does not allow herself to scream: with a gesture that intensifies its pathos, she is able at this moment to control the display of her feelings. The sisters are united in their grief and desolation, but Elinor reacts with merciless censure, appalled that a man claiming to be a gentleman could pen such an 'impudently cruel' letter, one which reveals him to be 'deep in hardened villainy', and for whom she can only feel 'abhorrence'. She meditates long on 'the contents of the letter, and the depravity of that mind which could dictate it' (II: 7, 210).

Marianne, though, will not relinquish her faith in Willoughby. She suspects that a third party has had a hand in the letter, for if Willoughby has changed, she declares, 'nothing but the blackest art employed against me can have done it'. When Elinor asks reasonably who could have instigated such slander, Marianne, in the usual wild terms that characterise her, declares 'I could rather believe every creature of my acquaintance leagued together to ruin me in his opinion, than believe his nature capable of such cruelty. This woman of whom he writes — whoever she be — or any one, in short . . . may have been so barbarous to bely me' (II: 7, 215). Elinor, who doubts all this, humours her, but Marianne continues hysterically: 'And yet this woman — who knows what her art may have been — how long it may have been premeditated, and how deeply contrived by her!' Her suspicions express her deep-seated distrust of the 'acquaintance', the many unpleasant and selfish people into whose company the sisters have been thrown. But the revelation that there was no formal engagement, which shocks Elinor, and the sheer unlikelihood of Marianne's suspicions being correct, mean that Elinor's view must carry a first-time reader (and perhaps even a re-reader) with it. Marianne's faith in Willoughby, in the face of such damning evidence, once again seems to underscore her foolishly romantic idealism.

Or so it seems. This letter, fully displayed in the novel's text, dated 'Bond Street, January', with the signature 'John Willoughby' in capital letters, is itself a form of concealment, its artful presentation inviting the reader to see it categorically as his. That this is too simple a conclusion is what Willoughby suggests almost at the climax of the dialogue between himself and Elinor that takes place during the night at Cleveland while Marianne is sleeping (III: 8). Pressed by Elinor, who has good reasons for hating him, to explain what seems the most material and damning evidence against him, Willoughby throws new light on it – to explain it in a way that confirms Marianne's apparently crazy suspicion. Sophia Grey, he declares, has more or less stood over him while he copied out a letter dictated by her jealousy and determination to wound the woman she suspected that Willoughby might love. If the reader takes his word for it, this letter replays in a different mode the duplicity and concealment of Lucy Steele, in which case it would be just as much, if not more, an example of the cruelty of a woman determined to protect her turf, as well as of the ruthlessness of metropolitan society. Looking back at the earlier scene such a reader, or rather re-reader, can only gasp at the daring of a writer who will allow her character to come so near the truth, and even hint at it in Elinor's word 'dictate' ('the depravity of that mind which could dictate it'), who can convincingly persuade one that Marianne is mistaken, and then vindicate her.

The narrator's word 'extraordinary' is often echoed by critics who describe this scene in which Willoughby exculpates himself. It is set off by the preceding chapter (III: 7) which relates the case-history of Marianne's illness. Here is an example of Austen's most accomplished eighteenth-century prose, in which concision is fostered by balance, antithesis and tripartite structures, and in which words like 'however' and 'therefore' play an important role. These sentences render the grave and anxious circumstances of the sick-room with dignity, and seem to respect Elinor's assiduous calming of herself; their stately reserve is only broken into by the dashes that signify emotional release when Elinor begins to detect signs of hope (III: 7, 355). Willoughby's arrival at night, after twelve hours of furious travel, is then managed as a dramatic entry, and the break between her seeing him at the end of one chapter and their exchanges in the next invites the reader to share Elinor's initial shock. The ensuing extended dialogue is notable for the pitch of dramatic intensity it attains, and perhaps more for its psychological realism.

In her *Jane Austen and the Theatre*, Penny Gay rightly calls this scene a 'coup de théâtre', and goes on to emphasise that Willoughby's movements and speeches constitute a 'performance of self-justification'.[14] There certainly are theatrical or histrionic elements in his speeches, but whether this should be attributed to the character's insincerity or to the author's recourse to heightened modes of presentation is unclear. I would claim that what makes the scene remarkable – and disturbing – is Willoughby's candour, an openness that sends shock waves through the novel's insistent and concerted representations, and even advocacy, of concealment. 'Oh! if you knew how much I love every thing that is decided and open!' Emma Woodhouse declares at the end of a chapter (*E* III: 16, 502). *Sense and Sensibility* is a novel coloured throughout by issues of self-restraint and reserve, but this scene is governed by Willoughby's purpose 'to open my whole heart to you' (III: 8, 361). That it is a gentleman's freedom to take leave, ride across country and then hold a woman captive as he speaks so fiercely and at such length of himself may not reverse or upset the novel's presentation of duplicity as inevitable constituents of life in society, but it suggests that the cautious rationality of Elinor is a mode of coping with her gender's disadvantages. If Willoughby's 'disposition' is 'naturally open and honest' (III: 8, 375), as Elinor allows herself to admit when she reflects on his history, a reader might allow that the vehemence of his language is not so much self-dramatising as expressive of that open character, and the more intense under the pressure of urgent emotional need. Having travelled so far, so fast, so desperately, his blood is up; the violence of his speech is hence plausible, and he is determined to excuse himself as far as possible in Elinor's eyes. But his exculpation is also, in the most graphic terms, his self-accusation.

Structurally, this conversation with Elinor illuminates earlier events whose significance has been carefully disguised from the reader (Marianne's desperate searching in Bond Street being a minor example): Brandon's sudden exit from the picnic, Willoughby's embarrassed leave-taking from Barton, the cruel letter itself. The novelist has blackened Willoughby's character thoroughly through this letter, not to speak of Colonel Brandon's revelation to Elinor of the younger man's past sexual adventures and his apparently unforgivable desertion of Eliza, the young woman Willoughby had seduced (or perhaps, as Austen soon allows Willoughby to imply, been seduced by). Elinor has every reason to hate this man whose treatment of her sister has been the primary cause of her desperate misery and ultimately her near-death. And so, prompted by the narrative's subterfuges, has the reader.

So complete is the *peripeteia*, the reversal of feeling and judgement that Austen now demands, that many readers and critics rebel against it and continue to view Willoughby's apparent confessions with scepticism, suspicion and even contempt. Claudia L. Johnson, to take one example, comments on the carelessness of his excuse that Eliza might easily have found out his address,[15] but it might be noted that Elinor, who is ready to pounce on everything he says, makes no comment and therefore seems to recognise this as a plausible explanation. Readings that see Willoughby contriving in this scene to hoodwink Elinor through his dramatising self-presentation, or attempting to seduce her into swallowing his side of the story, have to come to terms with two aspects of his speeches: the language that Austen gives him, and (inseparable from this) the psychological cogency of the motives and feelings he describes.

Willoughby is given speeches that, whether they alter one's opinion of him or not, trawl some deep waters. He lacerates himself for his weakness:

> when fully determined on paying my addresses to [Marianne], I allowed myself most improperly to put off, from day to day, the moment of doing it, from an unwillingness to enter into an engagement while my circumstances were so greatly embarrassed. I will not reason here — nor will I stop for *you* to expiate on the absurdity and worse than absurdity, of scrupling to engage my faith where my honour was already bound. The event has proved that I was a cunning fool, providing

with great circumspection for a possible opportunity of making myself contemptible and wretched for ever. (III: 8, 364)

The hostile glance at Elinor anchors his words in that moment of their confrontation and tempers what might otherwise certainly seem falsely intense in his speech. 'We know it's absurd,' he is saying, 'but don't we also know that this is how human beings behave, letting their weaknesses override what they know they should do?' The moral certainty of hindsight, the rationality that governs so much of Elinor's meditations, collapses before the treachery of human motivation, here captured in the words Austen gives to the character's description of his hidden, illicit, motives: 'cunning' and 'circumspection'. Later in the conversation, when from her silence he is able to judge that Elinor is moving towards sympathy, Willoughby declares, 'Miss Dashwood, you cannot have an idea of the comfort it gives me to look back on my own misery. I owe such a grudge to myself for the stupid, rascally folly of my own heart, that all my past sufferings under it are only triumph and exultation to me now' (III: 8, 368). In this compressed and even tortuous statement he seems to be telling Elinor that when he looks back, his 'misery' certifies the presence in him at least residually of conscience and integrity, of a part-self that, having been betrayed, can justly exact its revenge in punishment. It is an extraordinary idea, that one might find 'comfort' in self-hatred.

George Eliot and Lewes, whose repeated reading of Jane Austen was mentioned in the Introduction, might well have been impressed by this depiction of a man allowing himself to be governed against his own better impulses, and by the psychological plausibility that Austen can give to his own account of the strategies that allowed him to hide his 'remorse' from himself:[16]

> Time and London, business and dissipation, had in some measure quieted it, and I had been growing a fine hardened villain, fancying myself indifferent to her, and chusing to fancy that she too must have become indifferent to me; talking to myself of our past attachment as a mere idle, trifling, business, shrugging up my shoulders in proof of its being so, and silencing every reproach, overcoming every scruple, by secretly saying now and then, 'I shall be heartily glad to hear she is well married.' (III: 8, 369)

Willoughby is endowed here with an inner voice and, moreover, with the capacity to reflect upon his inner voice: though this is a dramatic speech, he is given the psychological depth that Austen later reserved for her heroines. He is allowed a good deal of insight into his own self-deceptions, struggling, even in this conversation, to get control over his impulses and, as he says, 'to know myself better' – another appearance in the novels of an important moral concept. But Austen's portrayal does not let the character off the hook, especially when he tells her of his misery in London:

> If you *can* pity me, Miss Dashwood, pity my situation as it was *then*. With my head and heart full of your sister, I was forced to play the happy lover to another woman! — Those three or four weeks were worse than all. Well, at last, as I need not tell you, you were forced on me; and what a sweet figure I cut! — what an evening of agony it was! — Marianne, beautiful as an angel on one side, calling me Willoughby in such a tone! — Oh! God! — holding out her hand to me, asking for an explanation with those bewitching eyes fixed in such speaking solicitude on my face! — and Sophia, jealous as the devil on the other hand, looking all that was — Well, it does not signify; it is over now. (III: 8, 370)

Willoughby has previously caught himself up for using hackneyed language that Marianne would not have tolerated. This lurid picture of himself as a victim won't wash, for Sophia has every reason to be jealous, and nothing but his own decisions 'force' him to 'play the happy lover' to her. His plea allows Austen to enlist him in the catalogue of figures in *Sense and Sensibility* who must conceal their emotions, but whatever sympathy a reader might muster, there seems something abject and coarse about him that speaks of a character essentially unreconstructed, who despite his vehement self-castigations is still full of himself. Even more disturbing is his extraordinary confession that, having seen Marianne's 'sweet face as white as death' at the moment when he rejects her advances, 'it was a kind of comfort to me to imagine that I knew exactly how she would appear to those, who saw her last in this world. She was before me, constantly before me, as I travelled, in the same look and hue' (III: 8, 370). Willoughby has previously declared that he finds 'comfort' in looking back on his own misery. Perhaps what he calls comfort here is merely the thought that he knew Marianne, knew her better than anyone else. But since comfort is the last word one would expect him to use, this is a disconcerting claim or confession, to say the least.[17] His speech is followed by 'a short pause of mutual thoughtfulness', and no wonder. Austen has presented a reckless man, vehement and uncompromising in his self-examination and self-exposure, and here her own imagination takes her into strange territory. Elinor's own established feelings about him are progressively vanquished as Willoughby talks. Despite her anger at his invasion, despite the scorn and contempt that Willoughby notices on Elinor's face as he confesses, despite her insistent attempts to hold on to the moral high ground and to restrain and correct his speech, she finds herself convinced by his explanation. She reprimands him, 'while her voice, in spite of herself, betrayed her compassionate emotion' (III: 8, 373). In this conversation, then, she is no longer wholly able to maintain the vocal self-command she achieved in her confrontations with Lucy, or with her brother.

'His character is before you,' Brandon has declared, 'expensive, dissipated, and worse than both': but Jane Austen reveals that Willoughby is a more complex, ambiguous and even tortured figure than Brandon, who is his enemy, can possibly allow. Perhaps Elinor's compassion should be felt by the reader, and – again perhaps – that would unsettle the novel's system of moral values, in which caution, circumspection, the white lies of diplomatic behaviour, have been seen as necessary modes of social practice, even if they are the reluctantly endured containments of the private self. The dramatic skill and acuity of this scene, like the confrontations between Elinor and Lucy Steele that I have analysed, is more compelling than the novel's central depiction of the Dashwood sisters. '*Sense and Sensibility* is not, as it is often assumed to be, a dramatized conduct book patly favoring female prudence over female impetuosity', Claudia L. Johnson wrote in her important and influential study of 1988.[18] But unfortunately this is not entirely true. The novel repeatedly insists on direct comparisons between the sisters, always to Marianne's detriment. As an example, take Marianne's ignoring of Mrs Jennings on their journey to London, and Elinor's compensating attentions (II: 4, 182). As events unfold, the adolescent Marianne certainly becomes a more interesting character, but this does not materially affect *Sense and Sensibility*'s reiterated approval of Elinor's self-control, rationality and concealment, and its relentless sarcasms at the expense of Marianne's romantic excesses, thoughtlessness and defiance of common sense. When Marianne declares on her recovery that 'My illness, I well knew, had been entirely brought on by myself' (III: 10, 391), this might read as another example of her habitually exaggerated speech, but it is more likely that the novelist expects the reader to understand the action in this light. 'Had I died, — ' she continues, 'it would have been self-destruction.' Marianne's illness is the result of her own foolishness, her inability or refusal (the novel scarcely discerns any difference between them) to control her 'excessive' feelings as Elinor so admirably, as we are taught, does.

In the contrast between the sisters, concealment is overtly presented as a subject of contention, a contested mode of conduct that threatens to divide them. But this manifest and quasi-didactic programme of *Sense and Sensibility* is interwoven with more problematic forms or orders of concealment, modes that overlap and entangle with each other. There are concealments on the author's part, parts of the plot which are kept secret until their revelation can pay off; there are the various concealments or deceits which all the main characters – Elinor, Brandon, Marianne and Willoughby – maintain often at their personal cost. These sometimes coincide with the narrative's own secrets. Most dramatically and pervasively, the older sister is shown habitually hiding her emotional responses and intellectual disdain, carefully controlling her facial expression and voice – to deceive Lucy Steele, or to avoid social collisions with her brother, his brother and others. Elinor Dashwood might in fact be considered as the avatar of that 'regulated hatred' D. W. Harding saw as the defining characteristic of Jane Austen's fictional practice, were it not for the fact that her hatred is both regulated and, by dint of the narrator's contiguity, released.[19] For the angry, sarcastic and judgemental narrative voice of *Sense and Sensibility* is hard to separate from the character's own: it is somehow both external to Elinor and internal to her – the expression of what genteel social life compels her to conceal. The heroine models the techniques of accommodation that the novelist judges to be wise, given the competitive and acquisitive world that the book depicts. But the author herself is inhibited by no such constraints and uses the novel to defy them. This internal contradiction is among the reasons *Sense and Sensibility*, though a brilliant debut, is also a problematic one.

When Elinor is dealing with Lucy she produces 'a smile, which concealed very agitated feelings', as we have seen. After its first chapters, there are few other than such false smiles in *Sense and Sensibility*. Austen's second published novel, *Pride and Prejudice*, though, is filled with smiles, and, if sometimes difficult to read, they do not conceal pain. None of the tensions of *Sense and Sensibility* pervade this book where both of the central characters are largely 'without disguise'. The next chapter opens with a smile that leads into its preoccupation with memory, its tricks, vicissitudes and, ultimately, its vital importance.

CHAPTER 3

Elizabeth's memory and Mr Darcy's smile

At Pemberley, Elizabeth Bennet encounters a picture of Mr Darcy:

> In the gallery there were many family portraits, but they could have little
> to fix the attention of a stranger. Elizabeth walked on in quest of the only
> face whose features would be known to her. At last it arrested her — and
> she beheld a striking resemblance of Mr. Darcy, with such a smile over the
> face, as she remembered to have sometimes seen, when he looked at her.
> She stood several minutes before the picture in earnest contemplation, and
> returned to it again before they quitted the gallery. Mrs. Reynolds informed
> them, that it had been taken in his father's life time. (III: 1, 277)

What smiles of Mr Darcy does Elizabeth remember? One of Austen's most
perspicacious critics captures a reader's difficulty at this point. 'In Pemberley before Darcy's portrait Elizabeth trusts a likeness even over her own
experience, or rather she invests this likeness with reordered memory',
Janet Todd writes. The smile on Darcy's face doesn't correspond to
anything that, as far as the reader knows, Elizabeth has previously known
about him, and she has to rethink her experience to recognise it. Elizabeth
projects onto the portrait, Todd suggests, what she herself feels at this
moment, recalling smiles that are 'rather at odds' with what the reader has
previously understood about Darcy.[1] Indeed, her 'remembering' of Darcy's
smile is surprising because, though the novel has once or twice shown
Elizabeth noticing a smile on his face, the reader has up to this point been
left to assume that this merely confirms her long-established opinion that
he is an ill-tempered man, and that these smiles are condescending, or
worse. Yet here the implication clearly is that Darcy's smile is warm and
attractive.

This moment is an interesting instance of *Pride and Prejudice*'s preoccupation with the tricks and vicissitudes, as well as the crucial importance, of
remembering and forgetting. It is only one of many in this novel in which
characters reach back into the past, or forget, or, sometimes, wilfully ignore

it. More tellingly, in tandem with its presentation of its characters' recall of
the past, the novel manipulates or manages the reader's own memory, or
what might be called their 'reading memory'. Presented with the recall of
the past by its characters, the reader is asked to recall that past too, but this
is not a simple process. Its characters often misremember, and the narrative
induces its reader to misremember too. The novel tells a story, developing
over time; but at the same time the text is a stable, static and enduring
record. So a reader has two forms of memory, one engaged, accumulated,
modified and sometimes fallible during the reading of the story, the other
retrospective and detached, with access to the 'true' past that the text in its
permanency records. In Austen's next novel, Fanny Price gives a thoughtful speech about memory: 'If any one faculty of our nature may be called
more wonderful than the rest, I do think it is memory', she declares. 'The
memory is sometimes so retentive, so serviceable, so obedient — at others,
so bewildered and so weak — and at others again, so tyrannic, so beyond
controul!' (II: 4, 243). All these differing aspects of memory, and more,
were not merely illustrated but activated in *Pride and Prejudice*.

Most educated people today are aware that their memories are very
fallible. You vividly recall a scene in a novel, but when some years later you
read the book again, that scene isn't there. You remember a childhood
incident when you were hurt, but your brother says it happened to him –
and has the scar to prove it. It's common, as many experimental studies
have shown, for people to think that they witnessed events that they only
heard about, or saw on television. Moreover, a memory, it is understood, is
conditional upon the circumstances in which it is formed – or malformed.
But it has not always been so. In the psychiatric and forensic professions, it
was long assumed that memories, and certainly those 'recovered' with the
aid of an interviewer or counsellor, were reliable.

Thinking about memory, and about remembering, has itself a long
history. In the seventeenth century Robert Hooke thought that memory
is 'as much an Organ as the Eye, Ear or the Nose', and that this organ is
situated 'somewhere near the Place where Nerves from the other Senses
concur and meet'.[2] This notion of the memory as a specific place in the
brain has been current for centuries. But perhaps in reaction to Hooke's
dogmatism, John Locke made some penetrating remarks on the subject of
'retention' in his *Essay Concerning Human Understanding* (1689), in which
he defined 'idea' as 'the immediate object of thought, perception or
understanding'. 'Our *Ideas*', he wrote, 'are said to be in our Memories,
when indeed, they are actually no where, but only there is an ability in the
Mind, when it will, to revive them again; and as it were paint them anew

on it self, though some with more, some with less, difficulty; some more lively, and others more obscurely'.[3] Locke's sentence seeks to avoid the traditional, and until recently common, assumption that memory is 'a single mental faculty varying only in strength and accessibility',[4] a store-house from which, unaltered and undamaged, the past can be retrieved, if with varying clarity. The metaphor in 'paint them anew' seems to imply both that remembering requires some form of energy and that the new painting differs from the original 'idea' and creates, so to speak, a new layer of meaning.

In this chapter, I draw on recent psychological and psychiatric under-standings of memory to demonstrate how accurate, and how prescient, Jane Austen's understanding of memory formation in *Pride and Prejudice* actually is. In the twenty-first century, it has 'become commonplace', as the historian Alison Winter writes, 'among academic psychologists: that memories have a constructive or reconstructive character. We do not merely forget information over time, we "reconstruct" the content of our memories by adding to and otherwise altering them.'[5] The contemporary conception of memory, as Winter writes, is indebted to the work of the Cambridge psychologist Frederic Bartlett, who argued, as early as the 1930s, that 'the mind transformed incoming sensations during perception', and that perception plays an important role in the way memories are both made and recalled.[6] It is now usually agreed among psychologists not only that memories are unstable and fugitive, but that the circumstances in which a remembered event or speech takes place, and the conditions under which the memory recurs, both play a determinative role in that memory's vividness, accuracy and reliability. Memories are like fashions, it seems: when they are revived, it is always with a difference.

'Cognitive psychologists', as Daniel L. Schacter writes, for instance, have understood 'for years that transience' – or the forgetting of material – 'is influenced by what happens as people register or encode incoming information: more elaboration during encoding generally produces less transient memories'.[7] This is clearly demonstrated in *Pride and Prejudice*. At the Netherfield assembly rooms, Darcy's remark 'She is tolerable; but not handsome enough to tempt me' is 'elaborated' for the reader, to use Schacter's term, by Elizabeth's 'telling the story with great spirit among her friends', and then by Mrs Bennet's relating to her husband 'with great bitterness and some exaggeration, the shocking rudeness of Mr Darcy'. A chapter or two later, when Elizabeth's friend Charlotte comes to visit, she teases Elizabeth, and Darcy's words are revived again: 'Poor Eliza! — to be only just *tolerable!*' (I: 5, 20). The effect of these reminders of the

original insult is to embed it in Elizabeth's mind, as becomes evident later
when in the proposal scene she declares to Darcy that 'From the very
beginning, from the first moment I may almost say', his manners
'impressed' her with his 'selfish disdain of the feelings of others'. And
because the elaboration also embeds it in the reader's memory, he or she
will have little difficulty in taking Elizabeth's side in their altercation.
(It becomes an almost theoretical matter, then, whether Darcy knew that
Elizabeth could overhear his speech.) But narrative procedures that on the
one hand ensure retention by readers can also be used, on the other, to
induce them not to remember information with which they have been
presented.

This is a small example of *Pride and Prejudice*'s exhibition and utilisa-
tion of the ways of memory. But the encounter with Darcy's portrait is
also, more tantalizingly, with his smile. And this encounter occurs in a
novel that is remarkable, even in Jane Austen's work, for being filled with
recurrent merriment, amusement, laughter – and smiles. Some of these
smiles are hidden, as under Mr Bennet's 'most resolute composure
of countenance' as his eyes communicate to Elizabeth his delight at
Mr Collins' fatuities, or left to be understood, like Elizabeth's amusement
at Jane's artless protestations – 'How can you be smiling so, Lizzy?' Sometimes smiles need to be disguised lest they offend, as when the Gardiners
keep their amusement at Mrs Reynolds' praise of her master to themselves,
or Lizzy turns away to hide a smile at an example of Darcy's pomposity.
Though Bingley keeps his countenance during one of Mrs Bennet's more
ridiculous speeches, Miss Bingley, less politely 'direct[s] her eye towards
Darcy with a very expressive smile'. Most commonly smiles are described
by adjectives or contextualised, given a setting or occasion that enables
the reader to imagine what kind of smile they were: Jane's smile 'of such
sweet complacency, a glow of such happy expression' after spending
the evening with Bingley; 'the insolent smiles' of his sisters; Collins' 'smiling
solemnity' when Elizabeth says she has enjoyed her stay at Hunsford;
Lady Catherine's 'gracious' or obviously condescending smile when her
guests dutifully praise her hospitality; Mrs Bennet's 'very complaisant
smiles' when Collins announces his matrimonial plans. This garland
of smiles, both hidden and open, is strung through the novel, playing its
role in its playful, even festive, comedy.

It is Elizabeth, of course, who smiles the most, and who is diverted at
behaviour (like Sir William Lucas bowing in the wind at Lady Anne's
coach (II: 5, 180)) often shared only with the reader. Lizzy's readiness to
smile intimates not only good spirits but a sceptical intelligence that is at a

tangent from the social world she observes. Together with her wit, her delight at 'whims and inconsistencies', her pleasure in the absurdities of her acquaintances, her ability to make fun even out of otherwise painful occasions like Darcy's 'tolerable', her smiles invite the reader into a private selfhood both amiable (a very important quality in the novel's scale of values) and disposed to satire. A reader is seduced, despite carefully judged narrational indices to the contrary, into believing that her smiles are a reliable index of her perception and intelligence.

Elizabeth is characterised not only, of course, by her smiles, but, especially in the novel's first volume, by her laughter. She laughs when she leaves Darcy and the Bingley sisters to form, as she says, a picturesque 'group' – which might refer to trees or rocks, but could also refer to cows (I: 10, 58). She can hardly stop herself laughing even when Collins says he might be run away with his feelings in a speech notable for its pomposity (I: 19, 118). And as she famously declares in front of Darcy and his friends at Netherfield, 'I dearly love a laugh,' (I: 11, 62). She even laughs 'heartedly' in Darcy's presence on one occasion, at his shrewd assessment of her enjoyment in professing opinions she doesn't in fact hold (II: 8, 195). A laugh, unlike a smile, is by nature open, expressive, and often joyous and healthy. (Not always, though: Elizabeth's exuberance is parodied in Lydia's mindless laughter.) As a rule, then, Elizabeth curtails her laughter in Darcy's company and permits herself only, often hidden, smiles.

More surprisingly, the text, read back from Elizabeth's remembering of Darcy's smile before his portrait, reveals that Darcy also often smiles: no fewer than eight times in the novel's first volume. Six of these smiling moments, in fact, are when he is alone with Elizabeth herself. But it is an especially attentive reader or re-reader (one who, I suggest, is deliberately reading against the pull of complicity with Elizabeth) who notices them. The first occasion is at the end of the conversation in Chapter 9 which is dominated by Mrs Bennet. Embarrassed by her mother's boasting of Jane's marriage prospects, Elizabeth hastens to turn the conversation and dismiss her mother's remark about a 'gentleman' writing pretty verses to her eldest daughter at the age of 15. 'And so ended his affection', says Elizabeth. 'I wonder who first discovered the efficacy of poetry in driving away love!'

> 'I have been used to consider poetry as the *food* of love,' said Darcy.
> 'Of a fine, stout, healthy love it may. Every thing nourishes what is strong already. But if it be only a slight, thin sort of inclination, I am convinced that one good sonnet will starve it entirely away.'
> Darcy only smiled; and the general pause which ensued made Elizabeth tremble lest her mother should be exposing herself again. (I: 9, 49)

It is possible to read the final sentence here as 'Only Darcy smiled – alone among the group it was Darcy who smiled.' This is the more plausible because the semi-colon that follows the words 'only Darcy smiled' might be taken to mark his reaction off from the rest. Or do the words mean, in effect, that 'Darcy might have laughed, but he smiled and that was all'? Most readers will assume that this is correct. Sympathising with the excruciating embarrassment that her mother's intrusive and maladroit remarks create for her daughter, one actively wants Elizabeth's wit to succeed. A laugh would clear the air, but none is forthcoming. But Darcy's smile here is more enigmatic than this. It might demonstrate once more his aloofness, his stiff and inflexible social demeanour; on the other hand, it and the silence following might (just) signal awkwardness, shyness. Perhaps he might feel, to borrow Elinor's thought in *Sense and Sensibility*, that she 'did not deserve the compliment of rational opposition', or – on the other hand – he might be lost in admiring her fine eyes. His smile is capable of different interpretations partly because there is nothing in the text that either reveals what his thoughts were or describes what his smile was like. Either way, most readers may find it difficult to reward Mr Darcy here, just for smiling.

The words 'smile' or 'smiling', by themselves, are almost opaque. Like the verb 'cried', applied so often to speech in this novel, 'smiling' conveys a bare minimum of information. 'Cried' indicates little more than a voice's increase in volume, leaving the reader to imagine the actual tone or inflection of an exclamation or exhortation. A 'smile', simply denoted as a smile, might imply a whole range of internal emotions, as is plain from the occasions on which smiles are in fact surrounded by indicative information in the novel. When Denny mentions that his friend Wickham has wished 'to avoid a certain gentleman', it is with 'a very significant smile', and Elizabeth certainly knows what that conveys. But in actuality a smile by itself can be almost unreadable. As an expert in facial expression has confirmed, the smile is 'the most common emotion qualifier', as well as 'the most common emotion mask', since 'the smile best conceals the appearance in the lower face of anger, disgust, sadness, or fear'[8] (as in Elinor Dashwood's 'smile, which concealed very agitated feelings'). Little, then, may be deduced from a smile simply as a smile, and certainly very little from the word smile (or its cognates) by itself. Darcy's smile works (or creates narrative engagement) because one may, here and later, at different readings imagine several different smiles: superior, disdainful, indulgent, contemptuous, delighted, warm.

During the evening at Netherfield in the next chapter, Darcy is teased not by Elizabeth but by Bingley, in a scene in which Elizabeth is in effect listening in on banter between old friends.[9] Bingley:

> 'I declare I do not know a more aweful object than Darcy, on particular occasions, and in particular places; at his own house especially, and of a Sunday evening when he has nothing to do.'
>
> Mr Darcy smiled; but Elizabeth thought she could perceive he was rather offended; and therefore checked her laugh. (1: 10, 55)

Should the narrator's description be read with the emphasis on '*thought*' (so that 'thought she could perceive' makes her perception dubious)? Perhaps; but, on the other hand, the phrase functions as an invitation to intimacy with the character's inner life and thus furthers the project of uniting the reader's attention with Elizabeth's. One might speculate that she is just prejudiced – in other words, projecting her own assumptions about Darcy onto the conversation. She is certainly not fully aware of what degree of teasing these two friends can enjoy between each other. Ought not this at least to qualify the assumption that Elizabeth makes here, and expresses in the next dialogue, in Chapter 11, that Darcy is 'not to be laughed at!' (1: 11. 62), or that he would be unable to take a joke? He certainly smiles, and it might well be a smile of dryly appreciative amusement at Bingley's teasing him, but the shift to Elizabeth's point of view erases that interpretation in the reader's mind. Mary Poovey has argued that *Pride and Prejudice* 'embeds its allusions to real situations in a complex system that simultaneously invokes these situations and manages their effects' which she terms 'Jane Austen's non-referential aesthetic'.[10] Borrowing Poovey's phrase, but turning it not towards real or historical material but towards the text's fictive dexterity, one might claim that here, as previously, Jane Austen simultaneously invokes an event and manages its effects.

In the next chapter occurs one of the most important exchanges in *Pride and Prejudice*. It will be worthwhile tracing its subsequent history in the narrative. Darcy, piqued perhaps by Elizabeth's satiric remark, 'Mr Darcy has no defect. He owns it himself without disguise', speaks at some length about his own character, or rather, one should say – since 'character' in this novel means one's public reputation or standing – about his nature. It is difficult to catch Darcy's tone as he explains, perhaps to himself as much as to his listener, what he thinks he is really like, and concludes with 'My temper might perhaps be called resentful. My good opinion once lost is lost for ever.' Alluding perhaps to Hamlet's own allusion to the 'defect' of nature in himself,[11] he goes on to say that 'There is I believe, in every disposition a tendency to some particular evil, a natural defect', and Elizabeth springs into action again:

> 'And *your* defect is a propensity to hate every body.'
> 'And yours,' he replied with a smile, 'is wilfully to misunderstand them.'
> (1: 11, 63)

Once again, the meaning of Darcy's smile is left to the reader to decide. The dialogue is broken into by the jealous Miss Bingley, crying 'Do let us have a little music.' That comic interruption – 'Louisa, you will not mind my waking Mr Hurst' – changes the mood and dismisses the conversation. Nothing is said about Elizabeth's reaction to this smile, though the last words of the chapter, which hint at Darcy's attraction to Elizabeth, may give a clue. 'Commonly,' as Ekman writes, 'smiling may be a submissive response to ward off or call a halt to another's attack.'[12] Perhaps that is a way of interpreting Darcy's smile here. There are other possibilities – that Darcy is unshaken by Elizabeth's attack, that he is coolly confident of his own position, and rather indulgently amused at her. There will be readers who feel they know very well what kind of a smile Darcy gives here. Is it a warm, friendly, open smile that Elizabeth remembers when she looks at his family portrait?

Elizabeth recalls this exchange when, all ears, four chapters later, she listens to Mr Wickham's catalogue of his injuries at Darcy's hands. Their dialogue takes place during a game of cards (thus when they are sitting close together), and this inserts brief pauses that tend to heighten its impact. It is clear that Elizabeth is in a state of high suggestibility during the conversation. Wickham's 'gentle but very intelligible gallantry', added to 'all the best part' of manly 'beauty' that has already attracted the Bennet sisters' notice, makes her very disposed to attend kindly to his tale of misfortune. When he insinuates that Mr Darcy is the root cause of his distress, she takes suggestion as a cat laps milk, not only because she already dislikes Darcy, but also because Mr Wickham has such nice manners, is so handsome and, no doubt, has such a lovely smile. When, posing as the wounded but forgiving hero, Wickham declares that he would never expose Darcy, for instance, 'Elizabeth honoured him for such feelings, and thought him handsomer than ever as he expressed them' (1: 16, 89). This hints broadly enough that she is taken by Wickham's physical charms. When psychologists study the circumstances in which memories are retrieved, they sometimes use the term 'demand characteristics' to identify the process whereby a subject, given the right conditions, will tend to produce the memory which their interlocutor has expected, and conveyed, either consciously or unconsciously, what he or she is asking for.[13] As Wickham steps up his accusations and plays the card of Darcy's inveterate 'ill-temper', Elizabeth produces from her memory the desired confirmation of his story:

> 'I had not thought Mr Darcy as bad as this—though I have never liked him, I had never thought so very ill of him—I had supposed him to be despising his fellow-creatures in general, but did not suspect him of descending to such malicious revenge, such injustice, such inhumanity as this!'
>
> After a few minutes' reflection, however, she continued, 'I *do* remember his boasting one day, at Netherfield, of the implacability of his resentments, of his having an unforgiving temper. His disposition must be dreadful.'
> (1:16, 90)

Like the scene in front of the portrait, this is a pivotal moment in *Pride and Prejudice*'s treatment of memory. It is also an exceptional moment in the history of the English novel, since it shows a character recovering a memory that is a misremembering and demonstrates the circumstances in which misremembering takes place.

In his chapter on 'Retention', John Locke had written that memories 'very often are rouzed and tumbled out of their dark Cells into open Day-Light by some turbulent and tempestuous Passion; our Affection bringing Ideas to our Memory, which had otherwise lain quiet and unregarded'.[14] It may be 'Affection' in the sense here of deeply engrained feeling that distorts Elizabeth's memory of Darcy's speech. It is a bad memory because it omits his immediately correcting her interpretation of the carefully articulated and surprisingly candid account he gives of his own failings. Darcy has noticed that there is a stubborn – wilful – resistance to his attempt at serious engagement with her, and perhaps it is resistance in the specific psychoanalytic sense of involuntary protection of a vulnerable part of the self. Elizabeth is unable to meet or recall Darcy's openness with her own, because, one might diagnose, she is still nursing her wounded pride.

Perhaps Elizabeth's 'few minutes' reflection' is better understood as 'a few moments' reflection', but in any case a reader is encouraged to believe that she is not simply eager to please Wickham by corroborating his story, but thoughtfully retrieving a speech from an incident that has genuinely made an impact on her. Since the speech she refers to occurs only a few chapters earlier, readers will recognise that she is remembering an actual occasion, one that they have witnessed taking place in the drawing-room at Netherfield at the end of Chapter 11, and thus they will tend to validate her memory. She does not, it seems, simply give in to Wickham's 'demand': she searches her memory for an event that occurred 'one day' and this makes it seem as if the occasion was some time ago. In the novel's time scheme it is probably less than a week, but because Jane Austen has diverted attention to Mr Collins' letter, his arrival and the family's reactions to him in the intervening four chapters, she has made a long interval appear to pass. All this contributes to make the reader accept at this point that Elizabeth's recollection is both sincere and reliable.

This exchange with Wickham is itself revisited (remembered) no fewer than three times in *Pride and Prejudice*. It plays an important role in Elizabeth's accusations in the proposal scene. 'Your character was unfolded in the recital which I received many months ago from Mr Wickham', Elizabeth declares, and proceeds to repeat the substance of Wickham's story of ill-usage (II: II, 214). But after she has received Darcy's letter, she finds herself having to reconcile his account of Wickham's history with what Wickham in this conversation has said to her. Jane Austen emphasises the impact that this has had on Elizabeth: 'She perfectly remembered every thing that had passed in conversation between Wickham and herself, in their first evening at Mr Philips's. Many of his expressions were still fresh in her memory.' But they take on a different colouring in the light of Darcy's account: 'She was *now* struck with the impropriety of such communications to a stranger, and wondered it had escaped her before' (II: 13, 229). The first part of this reflection suggests the answer to the second. As Austen demonstrated in *Northanger Abbey*, the formation of a memory depends on the focus of attention at the time of its making. What causes an event or speech to be retained in the memory is not merely its later elaboration, but more decisively the emotional arousal that accompanied the experience in the first place. 'Memory involves emotion as well as cognition', as Stephen Rose writes. 'Learning and remembering – memory – is a property not of individual synapses or nerve cells or brains, but of the entire organism, the person.'[15] The novel suggests that Elizabeth retains Wickham's speeches 'fresh in her memory' (I: 13, 227) because when she attended to them she was in a state of heightened receptiveness or sexual arousal. She hasn't recognised his manners as 'impropriety' for the same reason.

Much later, following Wickham and Lydia's elopement and patched-up marriage, Elizabeth is thrown into Wickham's company once more, and this first exchange is again recalled as they walk together in the garden at Longbourn. Wickham still seems keen to have her believe his side of the story, and brings up the issue of the living that he declares Mr Darcy senior bequeathed to him and that Darcy failed to honour. Elizabeth replies firmly that she has understood on good authority that it was left to him conditionally only, but this rebuttal only momentarily puts him off his stride. 'You have. Yes, there was something in *that*; I told you so from the first, you may remember' (III: 10, 363). If you turn back to their dialogue in Volume I, Chapter 16, you find that this might just be, to put it charitably, a 'confabulation', a creative memory, or half-memory, that shapes material from the past to meet the demands of the present moment.[16] Wickham does actually use the word 'conditional' there, but wraps it in a sentence that has a very different import. He says that Mr Darcy intended to give the living to him, but that his heir 'chose to doubt it – or to treat it as a merely conditional recommendation, and to assert that I had forfeited all claim to it by extravagance, imprudence, in short any thing or nothing' (I: 16, 89). Which is not at all the same. Declining to contest Wickham's assertion with her own exact memory of the conversation, Elizabeth then says she has heard too that he had declared he would never take orders. 'You did! and it was not wholly without foundation. You may remember what I told you on that point, when we first talked of it.' There is little evidence for this claim in the actual, textual, record of their conversation, nor presumably does Elizabeth herself recall it, since she now breaks off the conversation 'with a good-humoured smile'.

Thus while *Pride and Prejudice* treats the memories of its characters, the narrative manages the memory of its reader, sometimes encouraging and sometimes almost thwarting the retention of events. Simultaneously, the novel's text abides as an unimpeachable authority for these events or conversations. When a character recalls a speech, a reader able to resist the identifications encouraged by the novelist (or a re-reader) can turn back the pages and verify or confute what is dramatically recalled by a character. This indeed is one of the pleasures of this text. The novel – the real object that one holds in one's hands and whose pages one turns – is the material incarnation of the notion of memory that was current for so long: it is a true, stable, stored record of events always able to be accessed in its pristine form. However, this privileged epistemic status of the text is compromised by the fact that, like relics unearthed by archaeologists undamaged after many years, what is accessed still requires its own interpretation.

Turning back, then, from Elizabeth's memory of Darcy's speech – 'I *do* remember his boasting one day, at Netherfield, of the implacability of his resentments, of his having an unforgiving temper' – to the scene itself, four chapters earlier, one reads this:

'My temper I dare not vouch for. — It is I believe too little yielding —
certainly too little for the convenience of the world. I cannot forget the
follies and vices of others so soon as I ought, nor their offences against
myself. My feelings are not puffed about with every attempt to move them.
My temper would perhaps be called resentful — My good opinion once lost
is lost for ever.

    '*That* is a failing indeed!' — cried Elizabeth. 'Implacable resentment *is* a
shade in a character. But you have chosen your fault well. I really cannot
laugh at it. You are safe from me.' (I: II, 63)

'Implacable resentment' is Elizabeth's own phrase, not Darcy's. Whether,
as she later recalls, he is 'boasting' of his temper is at least disputable. What
she remembers, in fact, is her own immediate energetic and witty response
to his speech, which already carries with it, in 'you have chosen your fault
well', an assumption that he is boasting. If this were real life, one would say
that this is a classic example of the common phenomenon that Schacter
calls a 'misattributed memory', or, more precisely, a 'memory conjunction
error'.[17] This refers to a misremembering provoked by the phonetic
similarity or overlap between one word or phrase and another, with the
wrong one being entered into memory. The false memory is facilitated
because Darcy does use the word 'resentful' and because Elizabeth immediately translates his speech into her own terms. Already amused at what
she conceives as Darcy's arrogance, she is delighted to pounce on him
when – as she thinks – he gives himself away. To put this in Frederic
Bartlett's pregnant formulation, her mind is transforming incoming sensations through perception, so that (as we might imagine) she actually hears
Darcy say what she remembers.[18] And if the emotion attaching to a
remembered occasion is more powerful and perhaps more quickly renewed
than the actual memory itself, then it is possible to suggest that the
victorious emotion felt by Elizabeth at this moment is what lodges this
'memory' into her mind. Or, to put it more formally, one might claim that
Jane Austen's understanding of the dialogic transaction she portrays here
pre-empts contemporary two-person psychology.

    How one interprets Darcy's speech about his own temper is, as the
critical record suggests, a tricky matter. It can read like a confession as
much as a boast. His willingness to expose himself suggests an attraction to
and respect for Elizabeth that she, perhaps defiantly, repudiates. She certainly has forgotten, or prefers to forget, Darcy's immediate challenge to her
interpretation; whether she retains his accompanying smile cannot be
known. I have suggested that the conversation's sudden interruption leaves
it enigmatic: it might conversely be argued that aborting the conversation at

this point allows Jane Austen to plant the smile (and what it may imply) in the reader's memory. Thus returning to the text, while it exposes Elizabeth's misremembering, still leaves much to be puzzled over and interpreted.

As we have seen, the dialogue between Wickham and Elizabeth in which this misremembering occurs is itself remembered, and misremembered, later in the novel. Remarkably too, the original dialogue is again recalled during Elizabeth and Darcy's conversation at the Netherfield ball. When Elizabeth escapes from the dance Jane meets her 'with a smile of such sweet complacency' that Elizabeth responds 'with a countenance no less smiling than her sister's' (1: 18, 107). Though Darcy has twice smiled at Elizabeth during this dance, there is no such reciprocality on these occasions or even the barest indication that Elizabeth has noticed these indications of his good will (if that is what they are). What follows is the most serious, least flirtatious, dialogue between them so far. 'I remember hearing you once say, Mr Darcy, that you hardly ever forgave, that your resentment once created was unappeasable', Elizabeth begins. 'You are very cautious, I suppose as to its *being created*.' Here Darcy does not dispute her memory, only replying firmly 'I am'. The reason for this reply, and for his not disputing her memory, is that he is fully aware that she is referring specifically to his treatment of Wickham. About that matter Darcy has no regrets or compunction, and about Wickham he has determined not to speak. The reader cannot know this yet, and so Elizabeth's distorted memory is allowed to become more fully established still, contributing further to the plausibility of her dislike or even hatred of him. At the same time the notions of being 'blinded by prejudice' and judging 'properly at first' hint that it is not '*your* character', as she says, but her own that is being illustrated. The visual conceit initiated in 'illustration', picked up in his 'I could wish Miss Bennet, that you were not to sketch my character at the present moment' and reciprocated in her 'If I do not take your likeness now, I may never have another opportunity', simultaneously suggests an intellectual affinity between them, even spontaneous pleasure in their contest of wit, and thus plants another kind of memory in the reader.

The most enigmatic of Darcy's smiles occurs during their meeting at Rosings, several chapters and some months later. Elizabeth is seated at the piano; Darcy, 'moving with his usual deliberation', stations himself opposite her so that he can view 'the fair performer's countenance'. (The arch gallantry of the phrasing hints at the sexual motivation of his strategy.) Elizabeth herself fends him off with an 'arch smile' and then laughs heartily at his 'picture' of her own tendency to say things she doesn't believe in. She threatens to retaliate and shock his relations – Colonel Fitzwilliam and

Lady Catherine – with what she has to divulge. The 'dreadful' something she discloses is not, as one might reasonably fear, the story of his treatment of Wickham, but merely that 'He danced only four dances!' at the Netherfield ball, and thus lets him off lightly. Her teasing then continues as she at one moment toys with Darcy and the next turns away from him and enlists Colonel Fitzwilliam on her side. Why does Darcy think, as he has said, that he is ill-qualified to recommend himself to strangers? Fitzwilliam is ready enough to oblige: 'I can answer your question ... without applying to him. It is because he will not give himself the trouble.' Darcy protests, essentially saying that he's shy.

> 'My fingers,' said Elizabeth, 'do not move over this instrument in the masterly manner which I see so many women's do. They have not the same force or rapidity, and do not produce the same expression. But then I have always supposed it to be my own fault — because I would not take the trouble of practising. It is not because I do not believe *my* fingers as capable as any other woman's of superior execution.'
>
> Darcy smiled and said, 'You are perfectly right. You have employed your time much better. No one admitted to the privilege of hearing you, can think any thing wanting. We neither of us perform to strangers.' (II: 8, 197)

Darcy's response to Elizabeth's little lesson in good manners is one of the most enigmatic moments in their exchanges.[19] It poses the keenest interpretive challenge of all their dialogues. The problem is that, on the face of it, Darcy doesn't seem to understand what Elizabeth is saying through her analogy. Perhaps his smile means that he takes her point, despite not acknowledging this in his speech? Why does he assume that she is like him in 'not performing to strangers'? (Doesn't he know that she 'performs' all the time, as in this dialogue?)[20] The only sense this reader can make of it is that he's blinded by love and delighting to find an affinity between them. As Reuben Brower argued in a classic article, *Pride and Prejudice* presents the epistemological problem of knowing other people mainly through the misunderstandings between Elizabeth and Darcy; to which one might add that the epistemological challenge addressed to the reader most signally, here as elsewhere, is to interpret the uninterpreted matter of Darcy's smiles.[21] The conversation gets interrupted by Lady Catherine, 'who called out to know what they were talking of'. 'Elizabeth immediately began playing again.' Make of that what you will, dear reader.

Psychological understanding, then, is inseparable from narratological innovation in *Pride and Prejudice*. The text itself constantly deflects the reader's attention from features that the text itself constantly, even systematically, represents. So Jane Austen provides the material that underwrites the portrait scene at the same time as she manages its effects. Darcy's smiles have been there all the time. It is a complex narrative system – to borrow Poovey's phrasing again – but it is also psychologically complex in its effects. It not only represents the character's memory processes with prescient complexity, but also works with or manipulates readers' own attentiveness and memory with equal artfulness.

A retrospective reading would certainly suggest that Elizabeth misinterprets two later smiles. Talking of Charlotte's removal to 'an easy distance' away from her family, Darcy hints that, to her, 'any thing beyond the immediate neighbourhood of Longbourn ... would appear far'. 'As he spoke there was a sort of smile, which Elizabeth fancied she understood; he must be supposing her to be thinking of Jane and Netherfield' (II: 9, 201). His smile here may entice the reader momentarily into Darcy's private thoughts and suggest a quite different interpretation, one that a retrospective reading virtually compels. Like this interview, the proposal scene that follows soon afterwards is rendered exclusively from Elizabeth's point of view, and the reader's interpretation of Darcy's emotions relies repeatedly on Elizabeth's own construal of his facial expressions. When she first declines his proposal, for example, 'His complexion became pale with anger, and the disturbance of his mind was visible in every feature.' Minutes later Elizabeth sees that he is unmoved by any remorse for his separation of Bingley from Jane: 'He even looked at her with a smile of affected incredulity.' This 'affected', as it turns out, can only be Elizabeth's projection.

There are other moments in the violent confrontation that is the proposal scene when Darcy's emotions are expressed in physical gestures – in his walking 'with quick steps about the room', for instance. One of these follows Elizabeth's controlled but biting statement (and the more biting for its control) that

> 'You are mistaken, Mr. Darcy, if you suppose that the mode of your declaration affected me in any other way, than as it spared me the concern which I might have felt in refusing you, had you behaved in a more gentleman-like manner.'
> She saw him start at this, but he said nothing, and she continued,
> 'You could not have made me the offer of your hand in any possible way that would have tempted me to accept it.'
> Again his astonishment was obvious; and he looked at her with an expression of mingled astonishment and mortification. (II: 11, 215)

The 'start' was a feature of acting in the eighteenth-century theatre, often involving the actor's hands thrown up in horror or dismay, and very popular with audiences. When, in *Mansfield Park*, Sir Thomas suddenly finds himself onstage, the amateur actor Mr Yates, caught in the middle of declaiming a speech, gives 'perhaps the very best start he had ever given in the whole course of his rehearsals' (*MP* II: I, 213), much to the amusement of Tom Bertram, an interloper on the scene. Darcy's start is a more subdued affair, and if Jane Austen borrows from theatrical convention here, it is to naturalise it. Darcy's start is certainly, though, a brief physical convulsion that suggests the impact of an emotional assault.[22] No one, a reader might imagine, has ever said anything remotely like that to him before.

But this again would be a re- or retrospective reading. Like his smiles, Darcy's start is hardly noticed by Elizabeth, and easily passed over. There is no elaboration, no further notice of this moment, a blip in the midst of Elizabeth's angry dismissal; she immediately proceeds with her categorical statement of rejection, which results in Darcy's much more predictable look of 'incredulity and mortification', and the scene is soon over. For more than twenty chapters, and almost half of the novel, Darcy's start is forgotten, even if the memory of Darcy recurs to Elizabeth's thoughts and imagination repeatedly. When its meaning is recovered it is in a scene that continues but transforms *Pride and Prejudice*'s exploration of memory and remembering.

When Elizabeth re-reads Darcy's letter in Chapter 13 of the second volume, she subjects herself to a disciplined, systematic and even formal exercise of memory. She searches first for evidence in favour of Wickham that will refute Darcy's account of him; but what she recalls is merely her own infatuation. She tries to recall 'some instance of goodness', 'but no such recollection befriended her. She could see him instantly before her, in every charm of air and address', but she cannot bring to mind anything substantive to his credit. Step by step – 'she remembered . . . she remembered also . . . she could not help remembering' – Elizabeth not only recalls circumstances, but now puts them into a narrative context that discloses their significance, as in this example from a very different novel:

> These hours of backward clearness come to all men and women, once at least, when they read the past in the light of the present, with the reasons of things, like unobserved finger-posts, protruding where they never saw them before. The journey behind them is mapped and figured, with its false steps, its wrong observations, all its infatuated, deluded geography.[23]

Elizabeth's recall of her past mistakes has none of the sombre elegiac quality that Henry James bestows on his anguished Olive Chancellor's, who in *The Bostonians* is bitterly recalling her mistaken faith in Verena

Tarrant. Instead, Elizabeth Bennet's submission to the unsparing recall of the past energises her, because it employs her intelligence and exercises her independence of mind. The deliberate summoning of past occasions is now understood as essential to the formation of a selfhood unencumbered by thoughtless assumptions. Elizabeth realises now not only that she has been at the mercy of her own emotional promptings, but also that she has simply adopted the commonplace attitudes of the neighbourhood.

The significance of this process is formally declared in the paragraph of apparent speech that climaxes in Elizabeth's famous and resounding declaration, 'Till this moment I never knew myself' (11: 13, 230). The phrase, from an inscription on the temple of Apollo at Dephi, has been used down the centuries, and its cultural freight is intense: Austen is placing Elizabeth at this moment in the highest of ethical traditions, and emphasising it not only through Elizabeth's words, but also by putting her self-castigation into inverted commas. Elizabeth 'cries' her words of self-condemnation to herself, perhaps to the air, and the histrionics of this is allowed to convince the reader both that a momentous point has been reached, and of youthful spiritedness and optimism rescuing self-validation out of shame.

Elizabeth's confrontation of her own mistakes is matched and even exceeded in its daring by the dialogues between herself and Darcy that follow her acceptance of his second proposal. Here too, but still more powerfully, Austen presents the recovery of the past as an essential, necessary constituent of an adult ethical selfhood. After the long hiatus in which Darcy's feelings and motives are obscured, his second proposal is accepted, and two chapters follow in which remembering is depicted as a joint activity, and even as a therapeutic process. In Chapters 16 and 18 of the final volume, intercepted by the scene in which Elizabeth tells her father of her love for Darcy, these two people of very different temperaments work together to confront their mistakes and misunderstandings. This retrieval of the past energises them: it cements and celebrates their union at the same time as it exhumes and recognises the painful past.

Darcy's reaction to Elizabeth's acceptance of his second offer of marriage is treated with Austen's characteristic mischievous reticence about such scenes, but modulates quickly and even tenderly with the sentence 'Had Elizabeth been able to encounter his eye, she might have seen how well the expression of heartfelt delight, diffused over his face, became him' (111: 16, 407), a moment, one dares to imagine and suggest, when Darcy might just be smiling. In the explanations that follow, they quickly turn to the occasion that had seemed to put an end to their relationship for ever, 'that evening' of the first proposal, when they exchanged apparently unforgivable insults with each other. Elizabeth suggests that they can put it behind them; Darcy replies that he finds that impossible in a speech which uncovers what the novel has kept hidden for so long:

> 'I cannot be so easily reconciled to myself. The recollection of what I then said, of my conduct, my manners, my expressions during the whole of it, is now, and has been many months, inexpressibly painful to me. Your reproof, so well applied, I shall never forget: 'had you behaved in a more gentlemanlike manner.' Those were your words. You know not, you can scarcely conceive, how they have tortured me; — though it was some time, I confess, before I was reasonable enough to allow their justice.' (III: 16, 408)

Elizabeth has had a bad memory, but Darcy has a bad memory in a quite different sense. He remembers Elizabeth's words exactly: and the language he uses suggests that the pain they instantaneously inflicted, displayed at that moment in his start, was lodged indelibly in his body as well as in his mind. It is as if the pain of the memory keeps re-invading him with the fresh impact of an experience in the present. Darcy's could in fact be called a traumatic memory, not the memory of horrible events to which clinical psychologists apply this term, but the memory of more everyday and universal self-inflicted wounds, those that for instance Joseph Conrad describes in his Author's Note to *The Shadow-Line*, where he writes, appealing to 'universal experience', of the intense 'shame, and almost the anguish' 'with which one remembers some unfortunate occurrences, down to mere mistakes in speech that have been perpetrated by one in the past'.[24]

The psychoanalyst Ignês Sodré usefully defines trauma as 'the ego being overwhelmed by an experience it cannot deal with. Traumatic experience may return unmodified to the conscious mind as if it is never transformed into a proper memory, psychologically remaining perpetually in the present.'[25] The initial wound to Darcy's deepest sense of himself evidently inflicts recurrent psychological pain accompanied by a vivid recall of the moment. The recollection of his own words (together with, as one might expect, Elizabeth's reproof) has been 'inexpressibly painful' to him over many months. It was only when he began to accept the justice of her criticism that he could begin to place his experience in context and begin the work of self-reparation. Elizabeth replies soothingly to his speech, saying, in effect, 'I didn't really mean it like that', but, unreconciled, he goes on to allude to something that has not been shown to the reader of the earlier scene. 'The turn of your countenance I shall never forget, as you said that I could not have addressed you in any possible way, that would induce you to accept me.' Darcy here rephrases Elizabeth's original remark, in contrast to the specificity of his previously exact citation of the phrase that delivered the crucial wound. Nevertheless, the reiteration of 'I shall never forget' by a man who chooses his own words carefully is enough to convey that the memory of their confrontation has become enduringly painful.

The novel shows how Darcy's reparation takes place in the presence of Elizabeth, now the loved and loving partner, who listens patiently to his self-blaming. Elizabeth now seeks to banish these memories from Darcy's mind, or at least to alleviate his pain. She admits that she too has long been 'heartily ashamed' of her speech to him. But her shames are not at all the same thing as his. Even the 'misery of shame' (III: 11, 373) that Elizabeth has experienced at her mother's deliberate rudeness to Darcy on the recent occasion of their meeting is not so keen as Darcy's suffering, because hers is embarrassment, not regret. Darcy has suffered the anguish of regret at speech and behaviour that seemed to destroy all hope of his marrying the woman he loved, but, it is clear, he suffers even more strongly the anguish of betraying himself. Like Conrad, in whom the code of honour was as strong, Darcy has had to live with the knowledge that he has betrayed himself, his 'character', his deepest and most cherished conception of himself.

After the news that Wickham and Lydia are to be married reaches Longbourn, Jane, characteristically wanting everyone to get on and be happy, remarks that 'We must endeavour to forget all that has passed on either side' and that time would surely 'make their past imprudence forgotten'. Elizabeth will have none of this: 'Their conduct has been such,' she retorts, 'as neither you, nor I, nor any body, can ever forget. It is useless to talk of it' (III: 7, 337). Yet when Wickham and Lydia arrive at Longbourn, to Lizzy and Jane's amazement they 'seemed each of them to have the happiest memories in the world. Nothing of the past was recollected with pain' (III: 9, 349). If in nothing but their impudence, Mr and Mrs Wickham are a perfect match. Their narcissism is exactly contrasted with the need that Darcy feels to probe and unwind the causes that led to his mistake.

Elizabeth and Darcy must remember their shared past. They must recall the wounds they inflicted on each other, for even if these cannot be erased, bad memories brought into the open may lose some of their power to hurt. They focus now on Darcy's letter, which Darcy says he dreads her reading again: 'I can remember some expressions which might justly make you hate me.' 'Think no more of the letter', Elizabeth advises, 'every unpleasant circumstance attending it, ought to be forgotten. You must learn some of my philosophy. Think only of the past as its remembrance gives you pleasure' (III: 16, 409). Darcy knows that this is Elizabeth saying what she doesn't quite believe for the fun of it, and kindly tells her that her own 'retrospections must be ... totally devoid of reproach'. For him, though, 'Painful recollections will intrude' into his mind, he declares, 'which cannot, which ought not to be repelled', and he presses on to a retrospect of the childhood and upbringing that, he says, encouraged him to look down upon the rest of the world. There is something modern, even post-psychoanalytic, in his searching back into his childhood for the roots of his unconscious assumptions of privilege. Austen was too modest when she famously called her novel 'too light and bright and sparkling' if only because this focus on Darcy's trauma, and on the psychological work needed to alleviate it, carries its understanding of human nature to a new depth. If he has changed, if painful memory might be somehow metabolised into a change of character, it is due to her, he says, as he turns to his 'dearest, loveliest Elizabeth' – the first time he has called her by her first name in the novel. But as she later reflects, he has not yet learned to be laughed at.

This exchange takes place as they walk together, unconscious of time passing. In *Persuasion* Anne and Wentworth, who, like Elizabeth and Darcy, have shared the troubled history of a refused proposal, similarly walk idly together and, as the narrator puts it, 'return again into the past' (*P* II: 11, 261). The account of their reconciliation is generalised, distant, suffused with the glow of mellow happiness. The reader is kept at a distance as they sort out their recent misunderstandings. Only at the end of the chapter, and apparently after some days, does Anne speak directly of the past.[26] In *Pride and Prejudice* Jane Austen displays Elizabeth and Darcy not returning into, but immediately, actively and tenaciously retrieving the past over two chapters, and to very different effect. As they make the past present, the reader too makes a retrospect of the events of the novel, and now reads the finger-posts, understands the signs, that they scarcely observed before.

In the next chapter, Darcy smiles at Elizabeth after he has spoken to her father, a reassuring smile, or so a reader might imagine. In the ensuing interview Mr Bennet for the first time drops his mask of irony and speaks to Elizabeth, if indirectly, about the disappointment of his own marriage: 'My child, let me not have the grief of seeing *you* unable to respect your partner in life' (III: 17, 418).[27] But after Elizabeth convinces her father that she does truly love Darcy, and he gives his permission, the gravity that this has momentarily introduced into *Pride and Prejudice* dissipates, and,

Elizabeth's 'spirits soon rising to playfulness again', she renews the memory workout with Darcy, wanting to know when and why he fell in love with her, as acknowledged lovers so often do. She supplies her own answer: Darcy was attracted to her because he was sick of sycophantic females, because her impertinent questions and barbed remarks 'roused and interested' him. She adds that 'Had you not been really amiable you would have hated me for it; but in spite of the pains you took to disguise yourself, your feelings were always noble and just' (III: 18, 421). She now fully understands what she saw in front of his portrait, that beneath his starchy and aloof manner hid a generous and kindly man, the man who was revealed, and partly concealed, in his smiles.

Pride and Prejudice then, besides much else, deals with remembering, or rather with memory formation, storage and retrieval. Extraordinarily adept and prescient, it dramatises the constructive and reconstructive character of memory. Jane Austen seems to understand how memories work, and how both their making and recall is dependent on context and contingency. Moreover, her narrative understands and manages the reader's own memory. At the same time as material is introduced that qualifies or contradicts the 'truth' as seen by Elizabeth, the narrative blocks its translation into memory, and thus makes the reader's own reading memory an analogy or imitation of the memory phenomena it is dramatising. When the action brings about the concerted recovery of even painful memories, the resolution the reader finds is all the more satisfying because it acknowledges the real (narrative) 'truth' that has been there, latent, all the time.

Memories, acknowledged or unacknowledged, play an even more significant part in the life of Fanny Price, the so-often abused heroine of *Mansfield Park*, the novel that is the subject of the next two chapters. Self-knowledge, arrived at with such brio by Elizabeth Bennet, becomes a central and problematic concern in this novel, and the first of these chapters opens by considering Austen's investigation of the moral life of a woman, Mrs Norris, whose inner life is apparently conducted as self-disguise. The following chapter shows how Fanny's early history and adoption shape her psychology and her destiny, and offers a plea for an understanding of Austen's purpose in this novel that bypasses the dislike often regarded as the final word about her heroine. The truth about Fanny Price, it suggests, has often been hidden from readers and critics.

CHAPTER 4

The religion of Aunt Norris

In the middle of those chapters in *Mansfield Park* that relate Fanny Price's misery in the family home at Portsmouth, there occurs an interesting and odd moment. Her slatternly mother, with Betsy the spoilt youngest child on her lap, remarks idly that Betsy's godmother, her Aunt Norris, hasn't sent the child any gift, but that must be because she lives too far off to think of her. The narrator comments:

> Fanny had indeed nothing to convey from aunt Norris, but a message to say she hoped her god-daughter was a good girl, and learnt her book. There had been at one moment a slight murmur in the drawing-room at Mansfield Park, about sending her a Prayer-book; but no second sound had been heard of such a purpose. Mrs Norris, however, had gone home and taken down two old Prayer-books of her husband, with that idea, but upon examination, the ardour of generosity went off. One was found to have too small a print for a child's eyes, and the other too cumbersome for her to carry about. (III: 7, 447)

The narrator swerves away from Portsmouth for a moment, as if unable to resist adding one more twist to the comic variations on Mrs Norris' inveterate meanness. Though some of *Mansfield Park*'s earliest readers told the author how much they were 'delighted' by Mrs Norris, or, like Mrs Austen, 'enjoyed' her, modern readers more often find her too nasty to be amusing, and certainly there is more to this incident than comedy. For one thing, the reasons Mrs Norris gives herself for not sending the gift are so transparently inadequate. They might lead a re-reader to suspect that something more than parsimony is behind her reluctance here. These books will cost her nothing to send, so what is it that makes it impossible for her to act generously? What form of inner resistance hinders her from sending this present of an odd old volume?

For the moment one might note the telling nature of the gift (or non-gift). It was to be a prayer-book, a traditional and eminently suitable present for a god-mother to send to her god-daughter Betsy if, as in all probability is the case, the god-daughter has been christened Elizabeth after her, the widow of a clergyman of the Church of England. Reverend Norris' old prayer-books, though, would not simply be books of prayers, as a modern and secular reader might assume. They would be copies of the *Book of Common Prayer*, which is another name for the liturgy, or the official order of service in the Church of England. This contains, for example, the service for baptism, in which the god-parents make promises on the child's behalf to act as good Christians and to supervise the child's spiritual life. In a novel in which the hero, Edmund Bertram, is first preparing for ordination and then is ordained a minister of the Church, can Mrs Norris' omission be without significance? Fanny Price is in fact the auditor of a conversation between her newly ordained cousin and her would-be lover, Henry Crawford, about 'Our liturgy' only a few chapters before (III: 3, 393).

At the opening of *Mansfield Park* Mrs Norris proposes that the Bertrams do what they can to help her sister, Frances Price, who has married unwisely and now has nine children, by taking one of them to live with them. 'The trouble and expense of it to them, would be nothing compared with the benevolence of the action', she declares (I: 1, 6). Both Sir Thomas Bertram and Mrs Price assume that she means one of the boys. But her idea is that they take the 'eldest daughter, a girl now nine years old', who just happens to bear her mother's Christian name. Sir Thomas Bertram has serious misgivings, but she outmanoeuvres him, and her scheme is adopted. It becomes clear that it will not be she, but the Bertrams, who will have the expense of maintaining the child. The 'benevolent' or pleasurably self-congratulatory feelings Mrs Norris experiences, the narrator suggests, are dubious at best, and she provides a brief sketch of Mrs Norris' history:

> Had there been a family to provide for, Mrs. Norris might never have saved her money; but having no care of that kind, there was nothing to impede her frugality, or lessen the comfort of making a yearly addition to an income which they had never lived up to. Under this infatuating principle, counteracted by no real affection for her sister, it was impossible for her to aim at more than the credit of projecting and arranging so expensive a charity; though perhaps she might so little know herself, as to walk home to the Parsonage ... in the happy belief of being the most liberal-minded sister and aunt in the world. (I: 1, 9)

Apart from the glimpse at her reasons for not sending the prayer-book, this is the only moment in the novel in which the reader is allowed a view into Mrs Norris' inner life – inner life, in the sense of the thoughts, the formulated notions, she puts to herself. But this too is only a glimpse, since the author suggests, with what degree of irony a reader is left to judge, that she can only 'perhaps', or tentatively, reveal what Mrs Norris thinks. Nevertheless, 'Perhaps she might so little know herself' suavely introduces the ancient injunction which in *Mansfield Park* is to play a very large part in its conceptual structure and imaginative intention.

How the reader understands Mrs Norris, then, seems to depend almost entirely on her actions and particularly on her speech. Protesting her good intentions in the matter of the adoption she declares to the Bertrams, 'Is not she a sister's child? and could I bear to see her want, while I had a bit of bread to give her? My dear Sir Thomas, with all my faults I have a warm heart: and, poor as I am, would rather deny myself the necessaries of life, than do an ungenerous thing' (I: 1, 8). This is clearly enough an example of her lack of self-knowledge: it suggests that Mrs Norris believes herself to be a good woman. Generous even to a fault, Mrs Norris here simultaneously slips in the message that she herself is a victim, threatened, however remotely, with poverty. When shortly afterwards Reverend Norris dies, and there is some question of Fanny moving into the Parsonage with her, she fights off the suggestion like this:

> 'Here am I a poor desolate widow, deprived of the best of husbands, my health gone in attending and nursing him, my spirits still worse, all my peace in this world destroyed, with barely enough to support me in the rank of a gentlewoman, and enable me to live so as not to disgrace the memory of the dear departed — what possible comfort could I have in taking such a charge upon me as Fanny!' (I: 3, 33)

Once again she is a victim, unjustly and arbitrarily 'deprived' of her husband, her happiness 'destroyed', and condemned by the resulting implausible penury to struggle to support herself. But the seven stock sanctimonious phrases asking for pity and proclaiming loss ride on a breaking rhythmic wave that proclaims instead her hysterical need for self-justification, her virulent determination not to do her duty by her niece. At the same time 'all my peace in this world destroyed' and 'the dear departed' are specimens of idiomatic resources that express a debased and attenuated sanctimony, as if the minister's wife has only been able to access Christian idioms in a distorted form. To return to that conversation in the first chapter: protesting her benevolence to the not-yet-adopted niece, Mrs Norris declares, 'I am sure I should be the last person in the world to withhold my mite upon such an occasion.' The expression originates in the parable of the poor widow who contributes her mites (farthings or cents) to the temple treasury chest, according to the Gospels. The distance between the phrase's origin and Mrs Norris' appropriation of it when she is not yet a widow causes it to ring like counterfeit coin. Later in the novel, she tells Fanny that 'wherever you are, you must be lowest and last', and the phrasing here has a similarly remote origin in the Bible, so remote that Mrs Norris here twists a parable about kindness and charity ('So the first shall be last, and the last first': Matthew 20:16) into a weapon of domination.

Towards the end of *Mansfield Park*, the narrator comments cynically on the indifference that distance has wrought between the Ward sisters. 'Three or four Prices might have been swept away, any or all, except Fanny and William, and Lady Bertram would have thought little about it; or perhaps might have caught from Mrs Norris's lips the cant of its being a very happy thing, and a great blessing to their poor dear sister Price to have *them* so well provided for' (III: 13, 496).[1] 'Cant' is a famously Johnsonian word, and here it is used to define Mrs Norris' false consolation and real indifference. Samuel Johnson objected strongly to language in which people proclaimed themselves possessed of sympathetic emotions which they did not in fact feel. One of his definitions of cant in the *Dictionary* of 1755 is 'A whining pretention to goodness, in formal and affected terms'. He cites a couplet from Dryden's drama *Aureng-Zebe*: 'Of promise prodigal, while pow'r you want/ And preaching in the self-denying cant', which would fit Mrs Norris like a glove.

In Johnson's usage, 'cant' is more than falsity of expression: it is usually falsity of expression that masks hardness of heart. In issue 77 of his periodical *The Rambler* he writes, for instance, of 'the prattle of affectation mimicking distresses unfelt'. 'Cant', then, is talk which is objectionable not only because it is commonplace, but also because it is self-deceiving. 'When a butcher tells you that *his heart bleeds for his country*, he has, in fact, no uneasy feeling', he angrily and unforgettably tells Boswell.[2] But cant is not simple hypocrisy, since people who employ it deceive themselves into thinking that they are virtuous or sympathetic. Their vocabulary effectively blocks self-knowledge, or eases them into belief in their own pretensions. Mrs Norris, lacking any insight into, any knowledge of, her own motives, is no hypocrite. Vocabulary then, it is implied, has a kind of real or material presence: language effects, not simply affects, how people feel, and what people are. In other words, our language brings our knowledge into being.

Kathryn Sutherland has noted that 'One of Jane Austen's greatest contributions to the novel as fiction and epic is her deployment, deepened from novel to novel, of a narrative method inflected by the personal subjectivity of a self-conversing heroine.'[3] In an essay on 'Jane Austen's heroic consciousness' James Wood has argued that 'Austen maintains a hierarchy of consciousness', and that moreover, as he adds, 'the people who matter think inwardly and everyone else speaks. Or rather: the heroines speak to themselves, and everyone else speaks to each other.'[4] One might add to these comments that many figures in Austen's novels are shown to speak to themselves in the very same terms as they speak to others. An example is the kindly Mrs Jennings, a very different figure from Aunt Norris, in *Sense and Sensibility*. After a long paragraph in inverted commas in which Mrs Jennings wonders what the reason can be for Brandon's leaving so abruptly for London, the narrator comments, 'So wondered, so talked Mrs Jennings', as if suggesting that her speech might just as well be her inner 'wonderings' (*S&S* 1: 4, 83). Like her, what Mrs Norris says to herself may be no different from what she protests are her motives when she declares them to her relations. But what she says to others needs to be said repeatedly, as if to demonstrate its truth to herself.

Here is one of the more extraordinary of these speeches. Mrs Norris is telling Sir Thomas Bertram of her efforts to promote the courtship of his daughter Maria with the wealthy Mr Rushworth. This has involved a family visit to his mansion over 10 miles of rough road. The energy and drive of the speech come partly from her need to deflect Sir Thomas from his justifiable criticism of her supervision of the household while he has been overseas, and this is only part of it:

> 'My dear Sir Thomas, if you had seen the state of the roads *that* day! I thought we should never have got through them, though we had the four horses of course; and poor old coachman would attend us, out of his great love and kindness, though he was hardly able to sit the box on account of the rheumatism which I had been doctoring him for, ever since Michaelmas. I cured him at last; but he was very bad all the winter — and this was such a day, I could not help going to him up in his room before we set off to advise him not to venture: he was putting on his wig — so I said, 'Coachman, you had much better not go, your Lady and I shall be very safe; you know how steady Stephen is, and Charles has been upon the leaders so often now, that I am sure there is no fear. But, however, I soon found it would not do; he was bent upon going, and as I hate to be worrying and officious, I said no more; but my heart quite ached for him at every jolt, and when we got into the rough lanes about Stoke, where what with frost and snow upon beds of stones, it was worse than any thing you can imagine, I was quite in an agony about him. And then the poor horses too! — To see them straining away! You know how I always feel for the horses. And when we got to the bottom of Sandcroft Hill, what do you

think I did? You will laugh at me — but I got out and walked up. I did indeed. It might not be saving them much, but it was something, and I could not bear to sit at my ease, and be dragged up at the expense of those noble animals. I caught a dreadful cold, but *that* I did not regard. My object was accomplished in the visit.' (II: 2, 221–2)

It is not difficult to guess what really happened when Mrs Norris visited the old coachman in the privacy of his own room. A few hints about the dangerousness of the drive if only the postilions were available would be enough to tell him that his services are required, never mind his rheumatism. Mrs Norris is good at bullying servants under the guise of caring for them, and as for 'curing' his rheumatism – a bit of self-praise slipped in as backup to her general case – that must certainly be a self-delusion (one could imagine that the coachman told her he was better to get rid of her attentions). But what to make of her boast of getting out of the coach and walking up the hill in the snow to spare 'those noble animals'? What motive lies behind this self-sacrifice – or should it be called self-abasement? She is certainly acquiring private emotional capital when she speaks of 'the poor horses', as of the 'poor coachman', and by walking up the hill she is associating her efforts with theirs – implying that she will make any sacrifice for the sake of the family. Mrs Norris is of course intent upon proving herself to be kind and generous even to a fault, but this seems to carry the idea to absurdity. Perhaps that is Jane Austen's point: she is reciting an action that proves *to herself* that she is what she claims to be. What she does and what she reports to Sir Thomas are both directed to the same end of proving how much she is willing to do to promote the family's alliance with the Rushworths. She believes what she proclaims, that she is a really good person, devoted (as surely Sir Thomas must see!) to helping the coachman, the horses, and prepared to suffer in his interest, as well as in Maria's. And she really believes it because 'she so little know[s] herself'.

'A concern with self-knowledge', as Peter Knox-Shaw writes, is not 'in any way distinctively Christian'.[5] The injunction to 'know thyself', he argues, was readily incorporated into the rationalist ethics promoted by the Enlightenment, and perhaps especially in the practical and more domestic forms it took in eighteenth-century England and Scotland. To know oneself was to scrutinise one's motives and feelings in the light of temperate reason; it was to adopt a sceptical attitude towards the self's natural promptings. In this sense, one might add, it was a development out of that wary view of imagination taken by the founding father of the English Enlightenment science of knowledge, Francis Bacon, who saw human nature, as well as submission to learned authorities, as 'Idols', or obstacles to the advancement of learning.[6] Eighteenth-century philosophers like David Hume and Adam Smith, addressing the ethical domain, just as certainly insisted, in Knox-Shaw's terms, on 'the vital role played by reason in the self's construction of a proper relation to the world'. But at the same time, the Enlightenment in England, while far from being specifically Christian, 'found a home within the Christian churches', as J. C. D. Clark writes.[7] Scepticism towards motives and the distrust of zealotry, whether political or religious, was common to both. In Jane Austen's time, the advance of the radical Evangelical wing in the Church of England threw the sceptical rationalism of the main body of the church into greater relief.

Like all Protestant communions, the doctrines and prayers of the Anglican church emphasise the individual's own conscience and piety, rather than deference to a priest or obedience to a church hierarchy. The 'protest' of Protestantism is against the imperative to obey the edicts of the Pope, as delegated by him to a priesthood invested with access to spiritual wisdom denied to ordinary believers. Repudiation of the need for a mediator between God and man, or what is sometimes called the doctrine of the priesthood of all believers, is crucial to these faiths. More largely, the core of Protestant Christianity may be described as a conviction of the authority of the individual witness. This in effect means that the location of moral value lies in the personal conscience. One of its expressions may be that focus on the individual, solitary, communing self that became such a feature of the novel in English and of *Mansfield Park* in particular.

Jane Austen's father was a clergyman of the Church of England and two of her brothers also became ministers: hers was undeniably a devout, if undemonstrative, Anglican family. There is some evidence that despite her youthful enthusiasm for the Catholic Stuart dynasty, obvious in her juvenile spoof *The History of England*, the older Jane Austen shared the orthodox hostility towards Catholicism. In one of her letters written in 1813, Jane Austen writes of the poet Alexander Pope: 'There has been one infallible Pope in the World.'[8] It is the off-hand quality of this remark that suggests how much she lived in a culture of Anglican mistrust of what was seen as Catholic authoritarianism and dogma. In a letter to Francis Austen, in the same year, which incidentally includes a postscript in which she mentions that she has *Mansfield Park* 'in hand', she writes of her great respect for Sweden, a country 'So zealous as it was for Protestanism!' (her spelling).[9]

The self-knowledge that both Enlightenment ethics and Anglican theology concurred in believing was the goal of the moral life led, especially in the church, to the promotion of self-review and the scrutiny of one's treatment of others. This can be seen clearly in the three prayers that have been attributed to Jane Austen. The editors of Austen's *Later Manuscripts*, Janet Todd and Linda Bree, describe them as 'conventional variations on a familiar Church of England formula'.[10] As they suggest, these prayers, though written for communal use, insist that the Christian inspect his or her personal conduct and, when necessary, pass judgement on the self. Brian Southam, another editor of the prayers, concurred in pointing to their stress on 'the importance of self-examination'.[11] Their language derives from the *Book of Common Prayer*, but it is modified and simplified. Henry Crawford remarks in *Mansfield Park* that 'Our liturgy ... has beauties ... but it has also redundancies and repetitions, which require good reading not to be felt', and no one disagrees with him. In these prayers, as Southam writes, 'the heavily cadenced and ritualistic form of English of the Liturgy' is rephrased into an English accessible to the ordinary believer, so that, accordingly, 'sometimes we seem to overhear an unritualised near-speaking voice'.

On the first of the two sheets on which the prayers are written is the legend: 'Prayers Composed by my ever dear Sister Jane'. One prayer, entitled 'Evening Prayer', is on the first sheet, with the two other untitled prayers on the slightly larger second sheet. None of them are in Jane Austen's own handwriting.[12] One might certainly doubt the attribution to Jane Austen of the second two prayers, but (since they are on separate sheets) it is possible that they were bundled with the first as part of the Victorian wish to attribute piety to Aunt Jane. The first prayer may more plausibly be attributed to Jane Austen.[13] As A. S. Byatt puts it, this prayer is typical of the morality of the novels since it asks for help 'to be always on the watch so that you never hurt anybody else, so that you always notice other people's feelings'.[14]

It includes the following passage:

> Teach us to understand the sinfulness of our own Hearts, and bring to our knowledge every fault of Temper and every evil Habit in which we may have indulged to the dis-comfort of our fellow-creatures, and the danger of our own Souls. — May we now, and on each return of night, consider how the past day has been spent by us, what have been our prevailing Thoughts, words and Actions during it, and how far we can acquit ourselves of Evil. Have we thought irreverently of Thee, have we dis-obeyed thy Command-ments, have we neglected any known Duty, or willingly given pain to any human Being?[15]

In the last sentence the prayer turns away from addressing God and towards the speaking self. ('We', as in the rest of the prayer, is a formal, communal 'we' that stands in for the individual Christian.) It becomes momentarily dramatic. This specifically Protestant prayer, insisting on the individual's responsibility for his or her own salvation, now makes that individuality heard as a voice, addressing itself and asking questions of itself.[16] Such prayers may well be the crucible out of which emerged Jane Austen's fictional representation of self-communing.

In Austen's novels this address of the self to the self has no specifically religious dimension. It is certainly mostly the heroines who ask questions of themselves, who examine their own feelings and motives, in inner, private speech presented in interrogative terms. 'Had Edward been intentionally deceiving her? Had he feigned a regard for her which he did not feel? Was his engagement to Lucy, an engagement of the heart? No; whatever it might once have been, she could not believe it such at present' (*S&S* II: 1, 159–60). This inner debate of Elinor Dashwood might seem not so much a matter of self-examination as a review of Edward's conduct, but Elinor certainly is asking herself whether she has allowed her feelings to cloud her judgement. Other heroines at moments of high emotion do the same, as when Anne Elliot seeks to reason herself into common sense over Wentworth: 'How were his sentiments to be read? Was this like wishing to avoid her? And the next moment she was hating herself for the folly which asked the question' (*P* I: 7, 65). Even Emma, not so much given to self-questioning, asks 'How could she have been so brutal, so cruel to Miss Bates! — How could she have exposed herself to such ill opinion in any one she valued!' (*E* III: 7, 409) and, ultimately, in a quasi-conversion, spends quite a lot of time reviewing her mistakes.

The inner life of these heroines is represented in the shape of syntactically correct sentences. There is thus a transcription of the public or communal mode of prayer into the realm of private thought and emotion, with the consequence that this inner life is assumed to take a coherent, orthodox expressive form. As in these moments of anguish and dismay, the heroines do not pray for guidance, but they ask themselves for guidance in a non-religious version of the Protestant requirement of self-examination. As a rule – there are exceptions – when Austen uses quotation marks around a character's thoughts it is to suggest that there is a quasi-public quality to them. In none of the instances just cited does the author put quotation marks around these self-addressed questions.

The Enlightenment stress on self-knowledge as a goal, and the Protestant requirement of self-examination, converge and pervade *Mansfield Park* more than any other of Jane Austen's novels. It is unusual among Austen's books in offering insights into the private thoughts of a range of figures. Mrs Norris is the only character known to the reader almost entirely through her words and deeds – if we except Lady Bertram, whose sleepy remarks certainly occupy fewer pages. In the other novels there are many figures, even important ones, whose inner life is unknown. In these the heroine's consciousness controls, even if it does not limit, the narrative focus, and as a rule, passing, though telling, access to only one other person's private feelings – Marianne Dashwood's, Darcy's, Mr Knightley's, Wentworth's – is allowed. But the range of characters whose thoughts, emotions and projects, or 'views', *Mansfield Park* presents, at least briefly, includes Tom Bertram as well as, more crucially, Sir Thomas and Edmund Bertram, and the two Crawford siblings. Jane Austen shows the engaged Maria Bertram, for example, thinking about the wisdom of flirting with Henry Crawford: 'Maria's notions on the subject were more confused and indistinct. She did not want to see or understand. "There could be no harm in her liking an agreeable man — every body knew her situation — Mr. Crawford must take care of himself"'(1: 5, 52). The quotation marks used around her 'notions' imply that what she thinks might just as well be what she might say: there is no distinction between them. At the same time the dashes between the fragments of thought-speech convey Maria's unwillingness to dwell on these notions or excuses, in a rapid semaphore that allows her to brush aside other considerations latent, the syntax suggests, in the gaps between them. She has an inner life, an unexamined one.

Mary Crawford has similar feelings about her attraction to an unsuitable man, but Austen's technique of presentation differs: 'There was a charm, perhaps, in his sincerity, his steadiness, his integrity, which Miss Crawford might be equal to feel, though not equal to discuss with herself. She did not think very much about it, however; he pleased her for the present; she liked to have him near her; it was enough' (1: 7, 77). 'Not equal to discuss with herself' suggests that, like Maria, she might be turning away from her moral duty of self-examination. But 'perhaps' here accords Mary a degree of narrational respect or deference, and the tentative verb form 'might' allows that the processes within her are too subtle to be answerable to a straightforward irony or condemnation. Mary's half-thoughts, with their touch of self-abandonment, have something in common with Maria's, but the absence of quotation marks allows these to reside in recesses that are not easily accessible. They may not be representable in outward, dramatic form, but can be conveyed in self-comforting, evasive cadences.

A third passage representing sexual or romantic attachment augments the conceptual underpinnings of these two instances. Henry Crawford's extolling of Fanny Price's merits is not accorded quotation marks, and since there is no distinction between his speech and his thoughts, the effect here is a convincing rendering of his personal style, even of his sincerity:

> To see her with her brother! What could more delightfully prove that the warmth of her heart was equal to its gentleness? — What could be more encouraging to a man who had her love in view? Then, her understanding was beyond every suspicion, quick and clear; and her manners were the mirror of her own modest and elegant mind. Nor was this all. Henry Crawford had too much sense not to feel the worth of good principles in a wife, though he was too little accustomed to serious reflection to know them by their proper name; but when he talked of her having such a steadiness and regularity of conduct, such a high notion of honour, and such an observance of decorum as might warrant any man in the fullest dependence on her faith and integrity, he expressed what was inspired by the knowledge of her being well principled and religious.
>   'I could so wholly and absolutely confide in her,' said he; 'and *that* is what I want.' (II: 12, 340–1)

Henry asks questions, but he does not ask questions of himself. The writing that gives a rendering of Henry's thought-speech is supplemented by a sentence that introduces reflections contrasting with his own failure to reflect. It makes a similar point to the one made above: a person's vocabulary does not merely articulate thoughts or feelings, it brings them into being. Henry expresses his faith in Fanny in terms of her 'conduct', 'honour', 'observance of decorum', all words that have a largely secular ring, for behind them is the experienced man of the world's inveterate cynicism about women. When he declares that above all he could 'confide in' her, the usage of Austen's time suggests that he does not mean he could share private thoughts with her, but that he would have confidence in her, and that means confidence in her faithfulness. Behind this, not too far away, is his assumption that '*that*' is a rare thing. The rendering of his reasonings suggests to the attentive reader that there is no having such confidence in Henry himself. As the narrator puts it, he is unused to 'serious reflection'. In other words he rarely bothers to examine his own impulses, feelings and thoughts. This sentence about 'serious reflection' implies that Jane Austen was touched by one of the great movements of her time.

In the years before 1814 the adjective 'serious' would have acquired a distinctly earnest ring, since 'serious' was the word that the Evangelicals in the Church of England often used to distinguish their converts from the 'nominal' clergy of the main body of the church. Many in the later eighteenth century were absentee clergy, living some distance from their parishes, like Henry Tilney in *Northanger Abbey*, or delegated the work of visiting the sick and poor to badly paid curates. Because of the laxity of the clergy, the Evangelicals argued, the poor remained all too often in a state of wickedness and barbarity. They set themselves to remedy this situation by calls to Anglican ministers to remember the critical nature of their calling. To be 'serious' in Evangelical terms was to have undergone a conversion, to have received an inner conviction of one's salvation through Christ. This was at heart an emotional, even mystical event which rescued those who were converted from the natural wickedness of mankind, and inspired them to rescue others from sin and vice. The prestige of the Evangelicals had been immensely increased by their success in getting the bill for the abolition of the slave trade passed by Parliament in 1807, and by the time *Mansfield Park* was being written, the evangelical mood had permeated society.

This new seriousness is evident in the attention the novel gives to Edmund's defence of his profession during the visit to Sotherton (1: 9, 107–9). He is clearly responding to the Evangelicals' call for increased commitment from Anglican ministers when in the face of Mary's scathing comments on London clergy, he outlines his conception of 'manners'. *Thoughts on the Importance of the Manners of the Great to General Society* was the title of an influential volume published in 1788 by Hannah More, the most successful publicist for the Evangelical cause, and Edmund sounds almost as if he had it at his fingertips: 'The *manners* I speak of, might rather be called *conduct*, perhaps, the result of good principles; the effect, in short, of those doctrines which it is their duty to teach and recommend; and it will, I believe, be every where found, that as the clergy are, or are not what they ought to be, so are the rest of the nation' (1: 9, 109).

Yet there is a clear distinction. That the clergy must take their ministry seriously is a position that no Evangelical would dispute; but modelling good conduct is a very different matter from bringing Christ's message to the heart. When Mary Crawford jokes in a letter to Fanny that Edmund may have found 'some old woman at Thornton Lacey to be converted', she is confusing his Anglican earnestness with Evangelical mission (III: 9, 457). Her flip metropolitan attitude shows that she does not understand that conversion, the attainment of an unimpeachable inner light, is quite alien to the theology that Edmund upholds, and to the conception the author holds of the moral life. Jane Austen may be appropriating the adjective 'serious' in her condemnation of Henry Crawford, but she is not signalling evangelicalism. She is conveying the suggestion that, here as elsewhere, her presentation of her various characters' inner life draws upon Protestant theology and practice. In this conception, moreover, there is no absolute assurance of truth, and no ethical questions can be completely resolved, no conviction of one's own righteousness, no knowledge of the self that can be objective or complete. The focus in *Mansfield Park* on the complexity of inner moral, or psychological, life thence calls forth some of Jane Austen's most dexterous, nuanced and original writing, activating a conception of inner reality that has as little in common with the fundamentalist version of Protestantism that was Evangelicalism as it has with Catholicism. While the emphasis on self-review in this text articulates the Protestant conviction that the individual is responsible for his or her moral life, and that this cannot be delegated to a superior authority, the sceptical treatment of her characters' thought processes equally suggests how fallible, how vulnerable to self-deception the thinking solitary self might be.

Jane Austen's rendering of Sir Thomas Bertram's inner life is more finely calibrated and extensive than the briefer glimpses into the workings of Maria's, Mary's and Henry's minds. Sir Thomas is a Christian gentleman who apparently takes his religion seriously; in the first paragraph of the novel he is presented as a man of 'principle as well as pride', and he gives, for example, a 'little harangue' to Henry Crawford about the duties of a clergyman (ii: 7, 288). The novel's handling of his thoughts and behaviour is in effect a demonstration of how worldly ambitions and 'pride' continually sap the 'principle' to which he believes himself to adhere. Both aspects of his character are seen clearly when he decides to speak to Maria about her proposed marriage to Rushworth. His reported speech is kind and firm: he offers to get her out of the difficulties and embarrassments of a broken engagement – an offer that, given upper-class culture of the time, is remarkably generous. But when Maria declares he is quite mistaken, and decidedly affirms that she wishes to marry Rushworth, he is 'satisfied, too glad to be satisfied perhaps to urge the matter quite so far as his judgment might have dictated to others' (ii: 3, 234). Here again, 'perhaps' and 'might' allow, or seem to allow, a degree of leniency towards the figure. But as Sir Thomas' loose 'reasonings' for being satisfied are laid out one by one in the text, the wishful thinking that they display culminates in nothing less than the author's contempt. 'Such and such-like were the reasonings of Sir Thomas — happy to escape the embarrassing evils of a rupture, the wonder, the reflections, the reproach that must attend it, happy to secure a marriage which would bring him such an addition of respectability and influence, and very happy to think any thing of his daughter's disposition that was most favourable for the purpose.' One reason for attributing these phrases directly to the author rather than the narrator is that they resemble the treatment of Charlotte Lucas' reflections on her decision to marry Collins in *Pride and Prejudice*, and reflect how commonplace is this capacity of people to deceive themselves into a morally indefensible decision. Sir Thomas remains, however, uneasy about it, for at Maria's wedding he is agitated as no one else apparently is (II: 3, 237).[17]

A reader may feel that Maria Bertram deceives her father, and that would be some mitigation. Fanny does not deceive her uncle about her feelings for Crawford, but her demeanour, as he observes it, makes plausible his growing interest in promoting a match between them. The presentation of Sir Thomas' encouragement of Henry Crawford's courtship of Fanny registers with great subtlety the intricate pathways such self-deceptions can take:

> though infinitely above scheming or contriving for any the most advantageous matrimonial establishment that could be among the apparent possibilities of any one most dear to him, and disdaining even as a littleness the being quick-sighted on such points, he could not avoid perceiving in a grand and careless way that Mr. Crawford was somewhat distinguishing his niece — nor perhaps refrain (though unconsciously) from giving a more willing assent to invitations on that account. (II: 7, 277)

The complexly wrought sentence that traces this moral labyrinth allows for the possibility that its first phrases belong to Sir Thomas' own conception of himself. Its awkward intricacy is his effort to hold worldliness at a distance. He puts what he is thinking outside that self-conception, which, in other words, is a fantasy or idealised self of unworldly principle. He does not allow himself to know what he is thinking. But, as more obviously with his failure to help Maria, the real or worldly self actually, or 'unconsciously', governs his actions. It is partly because he has, not quite known to himself, invested psychological capital in the possibility of Fanny's marriage to Crawford that he loses his temper so shamefully at her obdurate refusal of an offer he deems so acceptable.

Sir Thomas', Maria's, Mary's and Henry's refusal or incapacity to acknowledge or enquire into their feelings form the context for *Mansfield Park*'s ground-breaking presentation of the conscience of Fanny Price. It is in the East room, a private place which perhaps references the 'closets' to which earlier heroines like Richardson's Pamela retired to consult their thoughts, that Jane Austen sites Fanny's self-interrogations. When the East room is first described, Fanny has been under intense pressure from her cousins to take part in *Lovers' Vows*, and cruelly berated by Aunt Norris in public for her refusal. 'To this nest of comforts Fanny now walked down to try its influence on an agitated, doubting spirit — to see if by looking at Edmund's profile she could catch any of his counsel, or by giving air to her geraniums she might inhale a breeze of mental strength herself.' The narrator's gently humorous, even indulgent, note suggests that Fanny's ensuing deliberations be regarded with charitable kindness:

> she had more than fears of her own perseverance to remove; she had begun to feel undecided as to what she *ought to do*; and as she walked round the room her doubts were increasing. Was she *right* in refusing what was so warmly asked, so strongly wished for? What might be so essential to a scheme on which some of those to whom she owed the greatest complaisance, had set their hearts? Was it not ill nature — selfishness — and a fear of exposing herself? And would Edmund's judgment, would his persuasion of Sir Thomas's disapprobation of the whole, be enough to justify her in a determined denial in spite of all the rest? It would be so horrible to her to act, that she was inclined to suspect the truth and purity of her own scruples, and as she looked around her, the claims of her cousins to being obliged, were strengthened by the sight of present upon present that she had received from them. (1: 16, 179)

Fanny is an inexperienced 18-year-old, and her self-questioning here has a simple, even naive, quality. This is a young woman struggling to be honest with herself, as no one else in the novel struggles. In her predicament, she certainly does not pray for guidance, yet this series of questions replicates the form in which the Anglican or Protestant Christian is instructed to review their moral life in prayer. 'Have we neglected any known Duty, or willingly given pain to any human Being?'; 'Was she *right* in refusing what was so warmly asked, so strongly wished for?': to ask questions of oneself is also, as in Jane Austen's own prayer, to remind oneself of one's responsibilities to others, and though Fanny's conception of what she owes, or might owe, to other human beings has been distorted by her education in gratitude at the hands of Aunt Norris, and by the gifts that furnish her room, this in effect is what she does.

Compared with Maria, with Mary, with Sir Thomas even, Fanny's attempt to decide what she ought to do in this crisis is something like an exemplary instance of that conversation of the self with itself which distinguishes Austen's heroines from those around them. It is perhaps rather less a conversation with, than a catechism of, herself. (The definition in Johnson's *Dictionary* is 'To question; to interrogate; to examine; to try by interrogatories.') It is as if Fanny is assigning priestly authority to a part of herself that has the right to judge of her feelings. These are questions that she must somehow or other decide on her own. But the italics in which her interrogations are represented ('Was she *right*. . .?') convey an anxiety in excess of the situation, and the incessant pestering of the self that follows suggests that self-review is here exacerbated into a form of nervous anxiety. Fanny's conscience is so tender that it is like a wound. The most acutely self-probing thought, 'Was it not ill-nature — selfishness — and a fear of exposing herself?', is allowed only momentarily to emerge.

Her deliberations are cut short by Edmund's entrance. He tells her that he has decided to join the players and take the part of Anhalt. Fanny, who sees Mary's influence in his every speech, succumbs to her jealousy of Mary and, as Edmund leaves her, throws up the attempt to understand herself. 'The doubts and alarms as to her own conduct, which had previously distressed her . . . were become little consequence now. This deeper anxiety swallowed them up' (1: 16, 184). Fanny may have exemplified the practice of self-examination, but she is not an exemplary heroine. It is emotion – and not especially creditable emotion – that carries the day. Other important passages of self-examination in the East room follow, but each, like this, is cut short, left incomplete, so that the momentum towards self-knowing is shown never to achieve its goal.

If Fanny were to be read, as many critics have read her, as a 'Christian heroine', though, Mrs Norris, the novel's other marginalised and dependent female character, might certainly be understood as her opposite, as a figure of false, inauthentic or bogus Christianity. Self-defended by her repertoire of cant, she can be read as an indirect commentary on the currency in the first decade of the century of Evangelically inspired self-righteousness. First readers may be inclined to dismiss her as 'evil', or as a 'witch', but if a re-reader attends carefully it is possible to guess at more, to glimpse more of her psychology and motivations than is known to herself. Aunt Norris certainly is very nasty. Her harassment or bullying of her niece comes as close to physical cruelty as the opportunities or decorums of polite social life allow. The 'little white attic, next to the servants' that she proposes be Fanny's bedroom has no fireplace; the East room grudgingly allowed her use has a fireplace, but no fire is to be lit in it; Fanny is to suffer in the cold. Fanny must fetch and carry across the Park at Mrs Norris' bidding, even in the hot sun, and is expected to walk across the Park in the cold February dusk to an appointment at the Parsonage. Fanny is scolded out of the house to go riding, scolded from the window when she is looking at the night sky, scolded from one end of the drawing-room to the other to pick up her needlework. When Fanny reflects on her life at Mansfield, she is allowed to use the word 'tyranny', and there can be no mystery as to whose tyranny she is thinking of.

One obvious explanation is that, like George Eliot's disappointed and bitter Mrs Transome, she finds 'the opiate for her discontent' in exercising 'every little sign of power her lot [has] left her'.[18] She is certainly depicted as enjoying power over her inferiors: she relates with relish the housekeeper at Sotherton's dismissal of two maids for a trivial infringement of customary decorum; she tells the family with similar jubilation, coupled with a contemptuous imitation of his working-class speech, of her triumph in catching the carpenter's boy (10 years old, like Fanny when she arrives) carrying off a spare piece of timber.[19] Her restlessness (she must badger Sir Thomas when he has gathered his family around him on his return; she must meddle with and 'injure' the fire the butler has built) is also clearly readable as a symptom of her craving to be important. A genteel widow, like an elderly spinster, has little social clout in the world Jane Austen presents, but Mrs Norris has secured what she can in the way of prestige by attaching herself to her sister's rich and important family, made the easier because her sister is lazy enough to hand over the education and later her chaperoning of the daughters to her. She dotes on the eldest; and her creed, as she tells Lady Bertram, is that 'my sole desire is to be of use to your family'.

But it isn't enough. There is something else in Mrs Norris that needs to be appeased and gratified. What is it that leads to her procuring of Fanny and her relentless harassment of this all-too-acquiescent niece? Jane Austen sets up the particular domestic and family situation that is going to be explored in the subsequent narrative in her first sentences in this novel, as is her practice, even in her unpublished work.[20] 'With only seven thousand pounds,' Maria Ward 'had the good luck to captivate' Sir Thomas. As Kay Souter points out, the paragraph's subsequent play on the word 'oblige' (Miss Ward being 'obliged to be attached', Frances Ward marrying 'to disoblige her family') 'emphasises the extent to which the oldest and youngest sister are locked into sibling reactivity', since 'oblige' implies that they choose their partners in response to the middle sister's good luck.[21] Then, as Janet Todd writes, the sisters 'enter into a lifetime of sexual and social rivalry'.[22] The seeds have been sown for the eldest sister to feel resentment and jealousy towards both her younger sisters, jealousy of Maria that is displaced into identification with the Bertram family but which can be exercised, if not exactly expressed, towards the wayward sister, Frances, who has married, apparently, for love. So, unknown to herself, her keenness to adopt a child of Frances and then to contrive that Fanny internalises her own social inferiority allows her to play out her resentment. Under the cloak of charity and benevolence, again unknown to herself, because she has no other language than cant, she can both exercise power and assuage her frustrations. But her habitual idiom (to give another example, she says that she is 'slaving' at the costumes for the theatricals) does not only continually assert her benevolence and altruism, it also reveals that she needs continuous self-soothing and self-appeasing, and that is because in her deepest sense of herself she is a victim.

But what is the connection between Mrs Norris' bullying and her meanness, just as insistently recorded in the novel? It too is suggested early in that first chapter's brief archaeology of miserliness already quoted: 'Had there been a family to provide for, Mrs Norris might never have saved her money, but having no care of that kind, there was nothing to impede her frugality, or lessen the comfort of making a yearly addition to an income which they had never lived up to' (1: 1, 9). 'No care of that kind' means no children to watch over, care for and love; 'comfort', to become an import-ant word in the novel, is here a miserable replacement for the fulfilment she has missed, as much in her sexual life as in her family. Mrs Norris' 'love of money' is a psychological substitute for other forms of gratification. Meanness, then, is explained through the lack of children. But what causes her meanness to feed into and coexist with her bullying? One sister's children have been almost adopted as her own, and spoilt as substitutes, but what psychopathic energy accounts for her remorseless intimidation of her other niece?

Before the moment when she finds it impossible to send the prayer-book to her god-daughter, there is another comic variation on Mrs Norris' meanness. Fanny and William are going to travel 'post' in a carriage to Portsmouth paid for by Sir Thomas, and Mrs Norris, realising that she can cadge a lift with them, opines that she'd like to come too: 'she had not seen her poor dear sister Price for more than twenty years . . . she could not help thinking her poor dear sister Price would feel it very unkind of her not to come by such an opportunity'. The two are horrified, but they need not be: she soon recollects that 'though taken to Portsmouth for nothing, it would hardly be possible for her to avoid paying her own expenses back again' (III: 6, 430). 'So, her poor dear sister Price was left to all the disappointment of her missing such an opportunity': the incantatory cant formula that she uses (as earlier in the novel, too) performs its function of twisting selfish feelings into apparently creditable ones. The narrator's mocking insistence on this phrase surely signals its opposite: that Mrs Norris has little but hostile feelings towards her sister.

To return to that decision, or rather reluctance, of Mrs Norris' to send the gift to her sister's child and her own god-child. Yes, it is easily smiled at as another instance of her inveterate meanness. But there must be other reasons the initial impulse to send the gift is countermanded – other motives buried in Mrs Norris' psychological life that are hidden from herself. That is no reason a reader might not speculate about her inner processes. One might imagine, for instance, that if her thought-speech were accessible it could run like this: 'Why should I send a gift to my sister Fanny's child? She has nine children, I have none. She has a full and busy life. I am alone, friendless and unloved. I should be rewarded, not she and her child.' Mrs Norris would never admit to herself that she is friendless and unloved: hence another reiterated phrase she uses when there is some question of Fanny moving in with her, 'I must keep a spare room for a friend' (1: 3, 34). This is a spare room she doesn't need for a friend she doesn't have, just like the prayer books she doesn't need that she won't send to the god-daughter she never visits. The original empty signifier, this is another piece of cant, a fiction that disguises her friendlessness from herself but also serves to ward off the possibility that she might actually have to do a kindness. Such are the ways of the unconscious that there is only a short step from rancorous and envious notions about Frances to another, even more irrational idea: 'My sister has robbed me of the children I ought to have had.' (Just as Maria has robbed her of the husband that, as eldest, she might have had.)

This will strike some as going too far. Perhaps it is. But the impression that this figure leaves with its modern readers is of such a powerful unappeased ego, of such unresolved conflicts, that some exploration into psychopathology is warranted, not because one treats Mrs Norris as a 'real person', but because Jane Austen's text lays down evidence that almost inevitably leads to a psychiatric diagnosis. As Janet Malcolm has remarked, 'It is only behind the doors of analysts' consulting rooms or between the covers of great novels that these mysteries of family love and hatred receive their deeper elucidation.'[23] Towards the end of *Mansfield Park*, when Maria has disgraced the family by her adultery and the marriage she has fostered is in ruins, the narrator describes a different Mrs Norris:

> She was an altered creature, quieted, stupefied, indifferent to every thing that passed. The being left with her sister and nephew, and all the house under her care, had been an advantage entirely thrown away; she had been unable to direct or dictate, or even fancy herself useful. When really touched by affliction, her active powers had been all benumbed. (III: 16, 518)

That phrase 'an altered creature', with its suggestion of a deep and unfathomable change, suggests that the house of cards that Mrs Norris has built around herself has finally collapsed. Without an inkling of self-awareness, Mrs Norris has been condemned to act out in the world – in bizarrely pointless activities, in meddling, in bullying, in adding to her savings, in slavishly doting on Maria, the eldest sister, like herself – the conflicts within. She is represented in *Mansfield Park* almost entirely in her speech and through her actions, because where there is no inner life there is no mode of representing what might be there but through the outer life. The figure is thus the dialectical opposite of the novel's heroine. Fanny's consciousness and inner thoughts are progressively focused upon in *Mansfield Park*: in the first volume she is mainly an observer and listener; in the second more access and prominence are given to her private thoughts; and this momentum culminates in the chapters in the third volume when, isolated in Portsmouth, exclusive access to her experience is given. This incremental attention to the heroine's inner life and moral struggles means that structurally as well as ethically these two figures are contrasted.

It is a fundamental premise of Protestantism that the individual is charged with the investigation of his or her moral life. This premise, this accepted and internalised assumption, powers Jane Austen's satirical and contemptuous treatment of Aunt Norris. Mrs Norris has neither the wit (and she is certainly not very bright) nor the humility to ask questions of herself, and it is according to the degree with which her characters ask questions of themselves that Jane Austen accords them respect. But Austen's understanding of the inner life goes beyond the moral or ethical terms in which Fanny Price addresses herself in that scene in the East room. Latent in the family history of the Ward sisters are the forces that shape Aunt Norris and her relationship to her niece. Mrs Norris therefore is the creation of an author who has an intuitive grasp of unconscious or semi-conscious psychology. Fanny Price too is shaped by that history, and by the adoption that is Mrs Norris' unconscious revenge on her sisters. In the next chapter I explore the damage to Fanny's life that her adoption and displacement bring about, and examine further Jane Austen's ground-breaking rendering of psychological forces that are inaccessible to conscious thought.

CHAPTER 5

The story of Fanny Price

Fanny Price, the 10-year-old daughter of a marine on half-pay and one of a family of nine children living in the backstreets of the raucous naval city of Portsmouth, is adopted – more or less adopted – by the rich family of the Bertrams, who live at Mansfield Park, an extensive estate far away in the quiet English countryside of Northamptonshire. Today you can comfortably travel the distance in a few hours, but in the early nineteenth century it was an arduous two-day journey via London. After Fanny's adoption, communication between the two families almost ceases, and it is eight years before she returns to see her birth family. Fanny, who is small for her age, whose clothes are poor, whose education has been minimal, who lacks the airs and graces of her cousins, who is shy and nervous, is left to adjust to a new life in a family where everyone goes about their own business, and scarcely anyone has the slightest insight into her feelings. But like many adoptees and wards, she is expected to be grateful to those who have taken her in and to repay their benevolence. It is scarcely too much to say that she must adjust not only to a new family and a new house, but also to a distinctly different, even alien, culture. She is required to adopt the Bertrams' ways as her own and to forget, if she can, the years of her childhood. But assimilation, as she discovers, is not so easy.

Many novels about orphan children, some of them classics, were published in the eighteenth and early nineteenth centuries. *Mansfield Park* focuses not on an orphan, but on a ward or an adopted child, and is certainly the first to explore the impact, the psychological consequences, of a 10-year-old being wrenched from one environment to grow up in another. In the world today, especially in Western nations, where children are increasingly adopted from far-off places, the drama of Fanny's conveyance and transplantation has become newly arresting. In the twenty-first century, novels and memoirs about the traumas of adoption now abound.[1] Nor is this the only contemporary genre in which displacement from one environment to another is a key issue. Narratives of emigration and displacement, stories of adaptation or estrangement within a new country and culture, now also form a substantial and increasing volume of writing in English. Much can be lost in the translation not merely from one language to another, but from one world to another, and piercing nostalgia for the homeland, as well as the necessity to succeed in, or at least adapt to, the new conditions, often forms the traumatic core of these narratives. It has been plausibly claimed, indeed, that we are all migrants now and that the project of 'post-colonial' studies is in part built on recognition of that fact.[2] It might also be suggested that the travails of emigration and displacement are conditions of a modernity whose narrative history began in Jane Austen's time.[3] The currency of such stories now enables us to read *Mansfield Park* as their precursor.[4]

When Fanny is at length allowed to go back to Portsmouth, not because anyone thinks that she might want to reconnect with her biological family, but because Sir Thomas expects that the experience will give her a salutary shock, feelings that have been long repressed and displaced well up in her. 'The remembrance of all her earliest pleasures, and of what she had suffered in being torn from them, came over her with renewed strength, and it seemed as if to be at home again, would heal every pain that had since grown out of the separation' (iii: 6, 426).

The trauma of childhood displacement is often expressed in metaphors similar to those that Fanny is given to use to herself in this passage, as in, for example, Margaret Humphreys' *Oranges and Sunshine*, which contains interviews with and letters from former child migrants sent to Australia, Canada and other British Commonwealth countries in their thousands during the middle decades of the twentieth century.[5] Now as adults they look back, often with bitterness, on the damage this caused. 'I was one of the so-called Home Girls who, in the space of one morning, was torn away from my school, my home, and all my playmates at the age of eleven', writes a Canadian woman. 'Ann Prichard', an Australian woman sent from Britain as a 10-year-old to Queensland in the 1950s, writes with similar distress: 'Torn from already fragile roots, and transplanted into a semi-arid environment ... Now, astride two cultures, I have roots in none. Robbed of a past, I was now robbed of a future. No amount of counselling can restore my feeling of worth.'[6]

Those memories of suffering whose strength is now 'renewed' when Fanny anticipates returning home have not been dwelt on in earlier chapters of *Mansfield Park*, but rather left for the reader to intuit and understand. Fanny is not bitter or resentful of her 'removal', unlike the speakers in Humphreys' text, but she is, I shall argue, similarly damaged by it.

Among the many other concerns of this magnificent novel, Jane Austen explores and displays the indirect, subtle and partially hidden ways in which this particular, distinctive young woman's psychological wounding is expressed. She also allows the reader to understand that Fanny's psychological techniques (for want of a better term) are means towards a tentative self-healing.

Neither refugee nor an emigrant, Fanny does not suffer the terrible travails that so many survivors report, but the prevalence of narratives of adoption and exile creates a context of awareness; newly focused attention to 'every pain that had . . . grown out of the separation' will allow a re-reading of *Mansfield Park*. Formal adoption was not a legal possibility in 1800, and Fanny's reception into the Bertram household is on sufferance: there is always the theoretical possibility that she will be sent back home. Her Aunt Norris sees to it that she is not accepted as one of the Bertram family and that she knows it (her room is to be in the attic, with the servants). Crucially, since she is taken in by the Bertrams at an age when she has already formed ties to her home and her birth family, hers is a narrative of displacement. Fanny is a heroine damaged early by her upbringing, as well as by her quasi-adoption, who experiences intense conflict between gratitude to her adopted family and the deepest rebellion against them – a rebellion so deep that it can scarcely be acknowledged in her consciousness. To read *Mansfield Park* with this focus allows one to escape a critical tradition that, reading the novel largely as a moral or ethical argument, has so often failed to treat its central character with any patience, and expressed incomprehension through misdescription and disparagement.[7]

Fanny Price arrives at Mansfield, having been told on the way how grateful she should be by her aunt, meets her new family and then is more or less left to herself. Jane Austen had very probably read Robert Southey's *Life of Nelson*, first published in 1813, in which Fanny's experiences on arrival at Mansfield are anticipated.[8] Its opening pages describe Horatio's painful parting from his favourite brother, William, and then the 12-year-old boy's first hours on his ship:

> He paced the deck the whole remainder of the day, without being noticed by any one; and it was not till the second day that somebody, as he expressed it, 'took compassion on him.' The pain which is felt when we are first transplanted from our native soil, when the living branch is cut from the parent tree, — is one of the most poignant which we have to endure through life. There are after griefs which wound more deeply, which leave behind them scars never to be effaced, which bruise the spirit, and

sometimes break the heart: but never do we feel so keenly the want of love, the necessity of being loved, and the sense of utter desertion, as when we first leave the haven of home, and are, as it were, pushed off upon the stream of life.[9]

Left to wander the great house, as Nelson was left to wander his ship, Fanny 'finds something to fear in every person or place'. 'The grandeur of the house astonished, but could not console her', the narrator dryly remarks. 'The rooms were too large for her to move in with ease . . . and the little girl who was spoken of in the drawing room when she left it at night, as seeming so desirably sensible of her peculiar good fortune, ended every day's sorrows by sobbing herself to sleep.' The austere Johnsonian concentration, the underplayed pathos of Austen's prose as she summarises Fanny's first days at Mansfield are as telling as Southey's autobiographically charged metaphors. Her cousins mock her small stature, the governess remarks on her ignorance, the servants sneer at her clothes, and 'when to these sorrows was added the idea of the brothers and sisters among whom she had always been important as play-fellow, instructress, and nurse, the despondence that sunk her little heart was severe' (I: 1, 16). It is not being 'cut from the parent tree' that makes Fanny's separation from all she had been used to so painful, nor 'the want of love, the necessity of being loved', but the necessity of having someone to love and to care for: the loss of her brothers and sisters, and especially her own brother William, who himself is soon to leave home and, at the age of 12, like Horatio Nelson, join the navy.

Fanny's love for William, and his for her, maintained in the difficult circumstances of their vast and lengthy separation, is a most important thread in the novel. Theirs is the novel's only sound, uncomplicated family relationship. It keeps her early experiences alive for her, and for the reader. It anchors part of her in her past. The first moment of friendship she experiences at Mansfield is when her cousin Edmund, finding her sitting crying on the stairs, discovers that she misses William most of all – 'her constant companion and friend; her advocate with her mother (of whom he was the darling) in every distress'. Edmund helps her write to William, and since she has no one to love, though he is six years older, he soon becomes a kind of surrogate for her brother.[10] Some months after 'her removal', as it is bluntly called, William is invited to spend a last holiday with her before he goes to sea. The narrator's sketch of the next few years of Fanny's life is unsentimental; she grows up 'not unhappily' among her cousins, though the phrase leaves a lot unsaid (I: 2, 24). In Chapter 6, the story having jumped forward to when Fanny is 18, and the Crawfords have

arrived on the scene, Mary's witty remarks about the brevity of brothers'
letters lead her to an impulsive intervention: "'When they are at a distance
from all their family," said Fanny, colouring for William's sake, "they can
write long letters'" (1: 6, 70). It transpires, then, that Fanny and William
have kept writing to each other, despite the obvious difficulties, over the
many years he has been away. Fanny mentions this fact with tears in her
eyes; it allows Austen to allude to 'the foreign stations he had been on' and
thus briefly bring the naval struggle against Napoleon's forces into the
novel, and indicate Fanny's awareness, however indifferent other characters seem, of the imperial world beyond the sequestered estate.[11] Another
interruption, a few chapters later, shows again how much her brother is
present to her mind. 'Poor William!' she exclaims: "'He has met with great
kindness from the chaplain of the Antwerp!'" ... very much to the purpose
of her own feelings, if not of the conversation' (1: 11, 129). Edmund and
Mary are arguing about the reputation of the clergy; they ignore Fanny's
contribution. Another few chapters further on, and Fanny's contact with
William is evoked even more poignantly in the description of her East
room. These spaced and small reminders of her brother are telling: through
William she conducts a private emotional life partially estranged from the
family she now lives among. William too is cut off from his parental home,
but his gender, his character, his confidence in himself (first born, he has
been his mother's favourite), not to speak of the 'great kindness' he has
received from a father figure, is to highlight Fanny's very different circumstances and more difficult accommodations.

Fanny and William Price come from a poor home; their mother,
Frances Ward, brought a substantial dowry into her marriage with a
marine, but now that he is pensioned off, the income from that dowry is
more or less all they have to live on. At £7,000, it would return £350 a year
when invested, but this was barely enough to maintain such a large family,
especially with a husband who is fond of hard liquor. The Prices move
from rented house to rented house, though they keep servants and are
therefore at least marginally genteel. But it is a chronically disorganised
household, since Frances Price is an incompetent housekeeper, and the six
boys are certainly favoured over the girls. Her mother seems to let Fanny
go without a qualm: her surprise that a girl is chosen rather than a boy is
confirmed when, much later in the novel, the narrator writes that 'Her
daughters had never been much to her' (III: 8, 450). In her thank you letter
to the Bertrams Mrs Price describes her eldest daughter as 'somewhat
delicate and puny'. All the signs, in fact, are that Fanny has suffered from
a poor and inadequate diet. At 10, she is 'small of her age, with no glow of

complexion', clear indications of her early malnourishment. The damage done to a child who gets inadequate nutrition during childhood up to the age of 10 cannot be fully corrected by an adequate diet later, as Jane Austen must have known. Thus Fanny, besides being shy, remains physically frail during the first half of *Mansfield Park*. Sir Thomas and Mrs Norris are pleased to find that, though 'far from clever', Fanny has a 'tractable disposition' (1: 2, 20) and congratulate themselves on the adoption. Lady Bertram sees 'no harm in the poor little thing'.

Jane Austen's critics have often found it difficult to come to terms with Fanny's physical health. Lionel Trilling wrote that 'Fanny is in a debilitated condition through the greater part of the novel', Marilyn Butler suggested that she is 'feeble'; for Tony Tanner she was 'weak and sickly' ('sickly' is what Elizabeth Bennet was pleased to label Lady Anne de Bough) and, again, 'debilitated'. These critics surrounded their deprecatory comments with important reservations and commentary, Butler for instance immediately remarking that the 'real significance of [Fanny's] character is not its weakness but its strength'.[12] But as very often happens with medical or quasi-medical language, apparently neutral terms – like the word 'unhealthy' itself – can readily, and as if unconsciously, carry or imply moral disapproval. Fanny Price's assumed lack of health has been described not just as unfortunate, but as morally unsound. An egregious example of this is Nina Auerbach's remark, in a much-cited article, that 'there is something horrible about her, that compels ... toward the deformed, the dispossessed'.[13] The depreciation of Fanny's physical being is often linked to what is seen as a deplorable emotional disposition, as when the feminists Sandra Gilbert and Susan Gubar write of her 'invalid deathliness', or William H. Galperin, more sinisterly, of her 'nearly metastatic ambition'.[14]

It is pertinent to read Fanny Price's body and demeanour in the context the novel firmly provides. On arrival she is contrasted with the Bertrams, a 'remarkably fine family, the sons very well looking, the daughters decidedly handsome, and all of them well-grown and forward of their age', so that there was 'as striking a difference between the cousins in person as education had given to their address' (1: 2, 14). Their 'address', self-presentation and 'countenance', their good health, upright carriage and confidence are a result of the family's easy circumstances, just as initially Fanny's shyness and lack of self-confidence are most probably the consequence of her mother and father's neglect. Perhaps her demeanour is expressive of more than neglect and deprivation, and more can be read into it than shyness. In *Lost in Translation*, her memoir of displacement, Eva Hoffman, for example, describes how, as a young teenager transported from Crakow to Vancouver, she comported herself:

> When I'm with my peers, who come by ... self-confidence naturally, my gestures show that I'm here provisionally, by their grace, that I don't rightfully belong. My shoulders stoop, I nod frantically to indicate my agreement with others, I smile sweetly at people to show I mean well, and my chest recedes inward so that I don't take up too much space – mannerisms of a marginal, off-centred person who wants both to be taken in and to fend off the threatening others.[15]

Jane Austen allows Tom, her older cousin, to deride Fanny as 'creep-mouse', which suggests the downward gaze and self-effacing movements of a servant. Perhaps Fanny too has 'shoulders bent with the strain of resentment and ingratiation'. Hoffman's account of her behavioural style among her new Canadian peers speaks of something that is expressed through Fanny's own bodily presentation and social demeanour at Mansfield. Outwardly modest, retiring, she is wary of being caught out, careful not to call attention to herself, to ingratiate herself, if possible; but, lonely and adrift, she also needs to fasten onto someone. It is no wonder she clings to her cousin Edmund, kind, steady and somehow representative of a world she wants – as of course she wants – to belong to. Though perhaps at the same time, like the young Eva, she harbours resistance, if not resentment.

Trained by her birth family to think herself inferior, Fanny's education in self-abasement is continued through her adoptive family's indifference, or worse. Continually harassed by Aunt Norris, slighted, ignored and occasionally made fun of, she is not in fact what she seems to them – a passive and acquiescent surface. 'Ill-used' (her cousin Julia's word in a moment of compunction), Fanny needs to find ways to accommodate the recurrent insults to her selfhood. The narrative is devoted to the gradual disclosure of that selfhood's natural insurgency and of the ways, or techniques, Fanny uses to manage her own unacceptable, and even rebellious, emotions. One of these is over-compensation, displayed early in the novel in Chapter 4 when, as a 15-year-old, seeking to get Edmund on her side, she reiterates how much she loves Mansfield: 'I love this place and everyone in it', she declares when she is trying hard to avoid being sent to live with her Aunt Norris. The young Fanny's default coping strategy is to persuade herself that Mansfield really is her home.

After a significant lapse of time, the novel settles down to describe events in the summer and autumn of 1808.[16] Fanny is now 18, and the Crawfords, brother and sister, arrive at the neighbouring Parsonage.

Edmund, 24, is quickly attracted to the sophisticated Mary, who is lively, witty and daring. There follows the famous scene in which Fanny watches Edmund give Mary a riding lesson on a horse that he has arranged for Fanny herself to ride. Ousted from the house by Aunt Norris, ready for her own exercise, she catches sight of Edmund and Mary on their mounts across the park. 'After a few minutes, they stopt entirely, Edmund was close to her, he was speaking to her, he was evidently directing her management of the bridle, he had hold of her hand; she saw it, or the imagination supplied what the eye could not reach' (1: 7, 79). Jane Austen writes from within Fanny's feelings, and her agitation is felt as the mounting rhythm of the sentence mimics her increasing heartbeat, which culminates in something like a gasp, as rendered by the semi-colon (perhaps originally a dash) and the clinching, heart-stopping moment when her jealous desire finds its food: 'the imagination *supplied* what the eye could not reach.' Fanny has undergone the same training and the same physical contact with Edmund that she imagines him offering Mary. There is naturally no direct acknowledgement that what is being felt is sexual jealousy, but Mary is riding Fanny's mount, given to her by Edmund; she is a rival, taking Fanny's rightful place. She tries to calm herself by invoking her habitual and ingrained self-abasement – 'She must not wonder at all this' – but it doesn't work. Instead, her aroused emotion gets channelled into anger against Mary's brother, Henry, and elaborated in a brief indictment of Henry's neglect of his sister, which helps her to exonerate Edmund despite his complicity in this betrayal and preserve his idealised image. It is desperately forced, this strategy, though it helps a little, so she is now able to try to rescue something out of her nasty and turbulent emotions by claiming compassion for the poor mare. (To a re-reader, the fact that Mrs Norris claims to pity poor horses too belies this psychological manoeuvre.) In this passage Austen uncovers with great power and concision, and for the first time in the novel, psychological events of arousal and containment, of passionate feelings unacceptable by the self and therefore having to be disguised.

Then Fanny has to confront Mary's apology, or non-apology: 'Selfishness must always be forgiven, you know, because there is no hope of a cure' (1: 7, 80). This witticism blocks any opening for Fanny's unquiescent emotions.[17] The narrator merely writes that 'Fanny's answer was extremely civil'. Her agitation so recedes into the narrative that it becomes virtually invisible, only to be revived by implication, when, mounted on her horse at last, she glimpses Edmund and Mary 'walking down the hill together to the village'. Here, as increasingly in *Mansfield Park*, the reader is asked to carry the knowledge of Fanny's passionate inner life forward through small hints, for this is a text in which indicative silences are left to perform a good deal of emotional work.

Fanny has been lent the horse because Edmund believes the outdoor exercise will give her more strength. But Fanny is not 'sickly' or 'invalid' in the ordinary senses of these words. She is only unwell in one scene, which follows almost immediately in the same chapter. The insult to her self-esteem, the envy and jealousy that Fanny has experienced must now be endured for the next four days, as Edmund and Mary, unabashed (and he infatuated) take away her mount for rides together with Henry and her cousins. Fanny is left to the mercy of her aunts in the big house. It is a hot July, and while all the other young people enjoy themselves, Fanny is made to cut roses for one aunt and run errands back and forth across the park in the blazing sun for the other. In what seems the exaggerating idiom of her teenage years, she has earlier declared to Edmund 'I can never be important to any one' (1: 3, 29). But what could more clearly re-enforce the truth of that feeling than the treatment she is now enduring? Edmund and Julia arrive back so late in the evening that it must be at least dusk, and Fanny is not to be seen. She has retreated to a sofa in the darkness at the end of the 'very long' Park drawing-room. When Edmund asks for her, Aunt Norris scolds her for being lazy.[18] Obediently, she comes forward and takes up her needlework again. Edmund rather comically thinks he can remedy everything by bringing her a glass of wine. Yes, she may be indisposed, but the translation of emotional distress into physical symptoms, of depression and anxiety into exhaustion and headache is now so widely understood that to dismiss Fanny Price's physical being here or elsewhere as 'debilitated' is unconscionable.[19] The narrator makes it clear that 'the pain of her mind had been much beyond that in her head'. Emotional life and physical being are registered as indistinguishable in such a receptive subject as Fanny.

'Fanny is timid, silent, unassertive, shrinking, and excessively vulnerable.' Tanner's essay, though written forty years ago, is still current, the epitome of much other slighting commentary.[20] Despite her modesty and self-doubt, Fanny is demonstrably far from always silent or (another frequently used derogative) 'passive'. In the first extended conversation between them in the novel, the young Fanny is shown, despite her youth and insecurity, to resist Edmund's attempts to persuade her that she will be happy if she goes to live with Aunt Norris. 'I cannot see things as you do', she says, before reverting to her habitual deference – 'I ought to believe you to be right rather than myself' – though she does not in fact give in (1: 3, 30).[21] A more significant instance of self-assertion occurs after Henry

Crawford's seductive remarks to Maria Bertram in the grounds of Sotherton, and his invitation to her to get around the locked gate, with his assistance:

> Fanny, feeling all this to be wrong, could not help making an effort to prevent it. 'You will hurt yourself, Miss Bertram,' she cried, 'you will certainly hurt yourself against those spikes — you will tear your gown — you will be in danger of slipping into the ha-ha. You had better not go.' (1: 20, 116)

Fanny's awareness of Henry's suggestive innuendos, Maria's helplessness at his hands and their combined contempt for Rushworth, who has been sent off to fetch the key, produce an alarmed intervention that is all the braver for coming from a previously disregarded social inferior, whose overhearing of their flirtatious exchanges they have seemed to regard as insignificant as a servant's. Fanny clearly perceives, and says, that Maria is risking moral rather than physical harm. Moreover Fanny takes an active part in the disagreements in the next chapter over Edmund's ensuing ordination. When, for example, Edmund seems to concede a point to Mary – 'We cannot attempt to defend Dr. Grant' – Fanny steps in with several sentences of reasoned argument in which she does defend Dr. Grant's choice of profession (1: 11, 130). Mary's response, tart and witty, effectively curtails the argument, but Fanny here certainly speaks her mind. It is true that she sometimes seems little more than Edmund's echo. When he delivers a long and rather pompous speech about the role of the modern clergyman, and Fanny responds '"Certainly," with gentle earnestness,' it is hard not to share Mary Crawford's amusement as she remarks, 'There. . .you have quite convinced Miss Price already' (1: 9, 109).

Perhaps the explanation why so many readers believe Fanny is deplorably passive lies in a signal feature of the novel's narrative structure: that the interludes portraying Fanny's inner life, which as a very early critic of *Mansfield Park* perceived, is full of 'restlessness and jealousy', are sharply contrasted with the group scenes that depict her demure social demeanour.[22] Fanny needs to keep quiet in company, she needs to tread lightly: she wants to be accepted, to belong; if not to fit in, to be at least inconspicuous. And she is the more wary because she is so much more intelligent than the family who, in a kindly manner or otherwise, look down upon her. Her apparent passivity is a coping strategy. This aspect of her position is exemplified most clearly at the moment when she refrains from asking Sir Thomas more questions about the slave trade, lest she should show up the indifference or ignorance of his own daughters (II: 3, 231–2). But when the narrative does enter her consciousness, especially when she is alone in the East room, the reader is presented with a selfhood arduously struggling to attain calm and integrity against repeated assaults and incursions. The contrasting modes of her presentation work together, then, to dramatise the consequences of her displacement. By temperament and training self-effacing, she does rarely assert herself: but that – in contrast to her intense inner life – is the point.

Towards the end of the first volume of the novel the Bertram siblings and their visitors decide to put on a contemporary hit play to entertain themselves. Fanny reads a copy and is shocked. This is the first decade of the nineteenth century, she is a very young 18, she has led an isolated and sheltered life, and it is not too much to say that *Lovers' Vows*, though much performed, seems to her obscene. At its centre is an unmarried mother's reconciliation with her illegitimate son, and it features too the provocative approaches of a young lady to a clergyman who is her tutor. Mary, who is to play the coyly seductive Amelia, finds her way to Fanny's sanctuary, and Edmund, playing the clergyman, soon follows, with a similar request that Fanny will take him through some awkward, possibly embarrassing, exchanges. Edmund and Mary are thrilled to find they have the same idea, and get Fanny to act as prompter as they act out the scene. The presentation of this episode in the novel re-enacts the psycho-dynamics of the horse-riding incident. There, the object of Fanny's turbulent emotions was partially obscured; here it is almost totally hidden, through Austen's complete omission of any of the play's text. One is not told what the performers are saying to each other. The reader must thus infer the nature of Fanny's responses to what Mary has already indicated is a suggestive dialogue between the clergyman and the young woman who is his pupil, and which thus not only allows Mary to speak to Edmund in terms no English lady should ever permit herself, but also at a more obscure, and therefore disturbing, level dramatises Fanny's own longings for her mentor Edmund's love.[23]

> She was invested, indeed, with the office of judge and critic, and earnestly desired to exercise it and tell them all their faults; but from doing so every feeling within her shrank; she could not, would not, dared not attempt it; had she been otherwise qualified for criticism, her conscience must have restrained her from venturing at disapprobation. She believed herself to feel too much of it in the aggregate for honesty or safety in particulars. To prompt them must be enough for her; and it was sometimes *more* than enough; for she could not always pay attention to the book. In watching them she forgot herself; and agitated by the increasing spirit of Edmund's manner, had once closed the page and turned away exactly as he wanted

help. It was imputed to very reasonable weariness, and she was thanked and pitied; but she deserved their pity, more than she hoped they would ever surmise. (1: 18, 199–200)

With the words 'she could not, would not, dared not', the passage segues from the narrator into Fanny's feelings, an agitated mixture, as the rhythm suggests, of resistance and fear. The sentence 'She believed herself to feel too much of it in the aggregate for honesty or safety in particulars' is particularly deft since it shows Fanny attributing her nervousness or fear to the depth of her moral disapproval, while the introductory phrase 'She believed herself to feel', permitting a reading that underlines her scrupulousness, also sows a little doubt about whether she really understands or can accept her own motives. Her feelings break through at the italicised phrase '*more* than enough'. Though she proposes to herself that all she can properly do is remain detached, in fact she becomes, as when she looked across the park, mesmerised by another oblique display of sexual attraction. The negatives and understatements of the passage conceal what one might deduce is ultimately nothing less than passionate anguish. 'She deserved their pity more than she hoped they would ever surmise' leaves it again to the reader to fill the text's reticence with Fanny's emotion.

With the stipulation engineered by Mrs Norris that she never has a fire in there, and since it is no longer wanted as a schoolroom, Fanny has been allowed to make use of the East room as her personal domain.[24] In this novel so much concerned with place and displacement, this is her 'nest of comforts', as the narrator, for once indulging in metaphor, calls it. The room's furniture and contents are more carefully delineated than any other in Jane Austen's novels. It is both a creation of Fanny's hopes and dreams, and a real, material space, and so in effect simultaneously a representation of her psychology and, implicitly, an ironic commentary on its strategies. But this unexpected visit from Mary and then from Edmund is not the first time that this refuge has been invaded; nor is it the last.

In his chapter 'Nests' in *The Poetics of Space* focusing on the human longing for material protection, Gaston Bachelard comments that 'If we go deeper into daydreams of nests, we soon encounter a sort of paradox of sensibility. A nest – and this we *understand* right away – is a precarious thing, and yet it sets us *daydreaming of security*.'[25] We long for protection and shelter, withdrawal and concealment, but a nest is by its nature fragile, vulnerable. The East room in fact is the very emblem of Fanny's condition as a displaced person. It's a room of her own, but not quite.

Still furnished as the old schoolroom, and filled with discarded objects, like an attic, Fanny has succeeded, to some extent, in making it over into her own space. 'Her plants, her books — . . . her writing desk, and her works of charity and ingenuity, were all within her reach; — or . . . if nothing but musing would do, she could scarcely see an object in that room which had not an interesting remembrance connected with it. — Every thing was a friend, or bore her thoughts to a friend' (1: 16, 178). The repetitions evoke Fanny's need to convince herself. She is telling herself 'I am at home, I belong here', but it is a daydream of security. To maintain the illusion, the comfort of the dream, her mind must brush away memories:

> though there had been sometimes much of suffering to her — though her motives had been often misunderstood, her feelings disregarded, and her comprehension undervalued; though she had known the pains of tyranny, of ridicule, and neglect, yet almost every recurrence of either had led to something consolatory; her aunt Bertram had spoken for her, or Miss Lee had been encouraging, or what was yet more frequent or more dear — Edmund had been her champion and her friend; — he had supported her cause, or explained her meaning, he had told her not to cry, or had given her some proof of affection which made her tears delightful — and the whole was now so blended together, so harmonized by distance, that every former affliction had its charm. (1: 16, 178)

This is the closest the novel and Fanny's thoughts have come to an acknowledgement of her miseries at Mansfield. Though they are veiled in generalities, there is enough specificity to attribute 'tyranny' to Mrs Norris, and 'ridicule, and neglect' to her cousins Maria and Julia. The long sentence that follows Fanny's thought processes is carefully crafted to mimic her emotional skirting of pain. It puts the acknowledgement of suffering in a parenthesis, and so allows the final emphasis to fall on the consolatory thought that 'the whole was now so blended together, so harmonized by distance, that every former affliction had its charm'. Fanny quarantines her bad memories and then allows herself to believe that she does not remember them. Banished into distance, perhaps; but the reader cannot so easily forget that at this moment of the novel's action Fanny is seeking solace in the East room after a vicious attack by Mrs Norris that has occurred only the evening before. How would afflictions acquire charm, unless through a willed embrace of self-deception? William Deresiewitz tellingly quotes Wordsworth's *Lines Written Above Tintern Abbey*: 'for such loss, I would believe/ Abundant recompense'.[26] Fanny 'would believe', she wishes and hopes, yet under the mantle of longing that she throws over the East room's discarded furnishings and bric-a-brac can still be discerned the awkward, ugly shapes of painful reality.

But Fanny's self-comforting is not treated forensically. The attitude of the narrator is more kindly, or even tender, than this. Fanny's nest of comforts is understood as a place of self-healing, or rather perhaps of self-salving. The next sentence combines amusement with tenderness, itemising and elaborating the bits and pieces that furnish the room, and ending with another recall of William, the thread that connects Fanny to her earlier and happier life. Next to the set of family profiles (the adoptive family) 'thought unworthy of being anywhere else, over the mantlepiece, and by their side and pinned against the wall' is 'a small sketch of a ship sent four years ago from the Mediterranean by William, with H. M. S. Antwerp at the bottom, in letters as tall as the mainmast' (1: 16, 179). The young Fanny has wanted to put something real, something that speaks of older life, alongside, and implicitly challenging, the stilted, formal emblems of the Bertrams. Like their children's drawings that people stick up on their office walls, or the photographs of family members we carry in our wallets, or use as screen savers, William's boyish sketch is a reminder in places of alienated consciousness of the reality of love in the world. Its presence in the room is both pathetic and sustaining, an action no stronger than a flower.

Fanny Price then performs a good deal of emotional or psychological work to persuade herself that Mansfield is her home. There is another sideways glimpse of this labour in a scene where, uncharacteristically, she does talk a good deal. Some time later, she is sitting in the garden of the Parsonage with Mary and gives a longish speech, covering almost a page, about memory, easily read (or perhaps more often skipped) as an example of Fanny's bookishness. She begins by noticing the process of change in the garden, how over three years the 'rough hedgerow' has been transformed. 'Perhaps in another three years we may be forgetting — almost forgetting what it was before', she muses (11: 4, 243). She then speaks of 'the operations of time, and the changes of the human mind!' It is possible to suggest, with the psychoanalyst Ignês Sodré, that 'forgetting — almost forgetting' implies here the wish to forget or deny bad memories, as symbolised by the rough hedgerow (the dash and repetition, signifying here again, as so often in Austen's presentation of speech, a break in rationality and the momentary intrusion of unwanted emotion).[27] The thoughtful reflections already quoted in the chapter on *Pride and Prejudice* follow:

'If any one faculty of our nature may be called *more* wonderful than the rest, I do think it is memory. There seems something more speakingly incomprehensible in the powers, the failures, the inequalities of memory, than in any other of our intelligences. The memory is sometimes so retentive, so serviceable, so obedient — at others, so bewildered and so weak — and at others again, so tyrannic, so beyond controul!' (II: 4, 243)

Fanny wants to avoid anything approaching personal or intimate communication with Mary – anything that might lead to Mary confiding in her, or that might stir up her own feelings. She keeps the conversation and the pretence of friendship going by talking of general, even philosophic, matters. She is used to her personal feelings or life-history being of no interest to anyone, but from where else than her own experience does Fanny garner the knowledge that memories can be 'so tyrannic, so beyond controul'? Does Jane Austen imply that she is referring to memories like those of 'tyranny' that she combated in the East room, those that rise again in full force when she learns she is to go home? Seeing that Mary isn't interested, she changes the subject to the garden scene in front of them. Mary replies condescendingly that 'till I came to Mansfield, I had not imagined that a country parson ever aspired to a shrubbery or any thing of the kind'. 'Parson' is a derogatory way to refer to a clergyman at this period, and Fanny must be acutely conscious of the slight of her host implied in Mary's 'aspired'. Her speech might be considered offensive, but Fanny can take no offence. Concealing whatever feelings she might have, she renews the conversation on her terms, with an apostrophe to 'The evergreen! – how beautiful, how welcome, how wonderful the evergreen!' The abrupt switch to another subject half-comically reveals what Fanny actually feels about Mary's remark.[28] She continues to talk energetically, gushingly, defensively, but the feelings that simmer beneath this conversation do not emerge until a moment later, when Mary does allude indirectly to her own hopes for a future with Edmund. Now 'Fanny's heart beat quick', and she is unable to keep the dialogue going (II: 4, 245). The exchange implies not only Fanny's unease in Mary's company but also, at a deeper level, her own remembered experience and the impossibility of its being directly expressed.

Another telling incident, occurring a chapter later, on the occasion of Fanny's invitation to dine at the Parsonage, leaves Fanny's responses to be deduced. Because it is her first formal invitation, she decides she ought to wear her best dress – the only going-out gown she has. It is a winter evening, and dusk is gathering: '"Now I must look at you, Fanny," said Edmund, with the kind smile of an affectionate brother, "And tell you how

I like you; and as well as I can judge by this light, you look very nicely indeed. What have you got on?"' Fanny explains that she is wearing the dress her uncle gave her on her cousin Maria's marriage. She hopes Edmund doesn't think it too fine: 'A woman can never be too fine while she is all in white. No, I see no finery about you; nothing but what is perfectly proper. Your gown seems very pretty. I like those glossy spots. Has not Miss Crawford a gown something the same?' (II: 5, 259).

The comedy of male indifference to female attire ('woman is fine for her own satisfaction alone' dryly comments the narrator of *Northanger Abbey* (I: 10, 71)), along with Fanny's gratification, abruptly takes a turn into something else. Edmund has never looked at her in this way or commented on Fanny's dress before, so this is a special moment. She must be pleased and grateful; at last he is noticing her. But the pleasure she might receive vanishes (although the reader may find it amusing) when it becomes clear that Edmund is actually thinking about Mary. Fanny is used to being disregarded, but it is a moot point whether the repetition of such slights lessens their pain. The text here again is silent, moving briskly on to the next incident, an effect akin to those in *Pride and Prejudice* which throw the onus of interpretation of a dialogue onto the reader. But 'the kind smile of an affectionate brother' in this passage underlines, like so many touches in the novel, the chasm that lies between Fanny's desire and Edmund's own feeling.

For desire is what it has become. Fanny's conversation with Edmund about her possible removal to Mrs Norris' occurs in Chapter 3, when she is a young 15. At the end of that chapter, when Sir Thomas leaves for Antigua, Fanny is 15, about to become 16 (I: 3, 38). The action resumes in Chapter 4, when Fanny is 18. The years between – the years of Fanny's puberty, when she evolved from being a girl to becoming a young woman – are omitted.[29] In the primal scene, the initiatory moment of her love, when she was 10, Edmund bridged the two worlds, the family she had been wrested from and the family to whom she must adapt, by his unexpected kindness, and made a more symbolic bridge by sending William a guinea of his own under the seal of Fanny's letter. His brotherly mentoring, his spokesmanship have continued to offer the reassurance that this bridge provides. But at 18 the advent of Mary Crawford has aroused in Fanny feelings that are different. Love, mingled with need and dependency, has morphed into adult desire. These feelings, hardly known or admitted to, grow in the course of the novel's subsequent action into a passionate, tenacious longing for Edmund, to keep Edmund for herself. Her desire is first disclosed to the reader under the aegis of neglect or jealousy during the riding incident, for everything in her circumstances and training means that it must be disguised, even from herself. Fanny has wanted to belong, but now she belongs in a terribly exigent way. It has always been a condition of her adoption that she is 'not a Miss Bertram', that her 'rank, fortune, rights and expectations will always be different' (1: 1, 12). But Fanny's adult love for Edmund disturbs all of that settled regime.

In the drawing-room, immediately before the chapter about Fanny's retreat to the East room, she is besieged by the Bertrams when she says that acting is impossible for her. Edmund's intervention on her behalf only intensifies her Aunt Norris' vindictiveness. '"I am not going to urge her," — replied Mrs Norris sharply, "but I shall think her a very obstinate, ungrateful girl, if she does not do what her aunt and cousins wish her – very ungrateful indeed, considering who and what she is"' (1: 15, 172). Everyone there is appalled, because Mrs Norris exposes the truth that underlies the family's attitude towards Fanny, but one that should never be spoken so brutally. From the first hours of her adoption, Fanny herself has lived with the knowledge that her reception into Mansfield Park can only be repaid by gratitude, that, being poor and rejected by her mother, she is dependent on the Bertrams' kindness for everything that her new life affords.[30] She has received a comfortable home in the healthy countryside, a lady's education, and with these the promise of provision for her future. These are material gifts that she can never pay back; all that she can offer in recompense – as Mrs Norris here ruthlessly points out – is acquiescence, obedience, conformity. And because she has been tutored into submission by her parents (and because her adoption has shown that for them she is disposable), she has accepted this as a condition of her being. Gratitude has become second nature to her, displayed almost as a pathology when, Edmund having invited her to comment on Mary's criticism of her uncle, she leaps to censure the new arrival for ungratefulness. Clearly a projection of her own conditioning, this is one of the moments when Edmund ('Ungrateful is a strong word. I do not know that her uncle has any claim to her *gratitude*') corrects her (1: 7, 74). Earlier he has joined in the family consensus that Fanny's adoption has proved a success because she has such a 'grateful heart'. In the East room the sight of the presents that her cousins have bestowed on her is enough to throw Fanny: 'she grew bewildered as to the amount of the debt that all these remembrances produced' (1: 16, 179–80). These gifts and the other less tangible ones form a hidden, unwritten contract that has locked their recipient into an unavailing reciprocity.

Within the framework of obligation in which Fanny Price has grown up, Jane Austen now sets another, more sinister variation on gift relations. Things come to a head when Henry Crawford, master seducer, too old apparently to go out shooting every day, decides to take up another sport, this time to make 'a small hole in Fanny Price's heart' (11: 6, 267). Eventually, hoist with his own petard, he confesses to Mary that he has fallen in love with the girl he has laid siege to and will seek to marry her. She is poor, true, but she has excellent connections, he is rich enough, and the idea of the marriage pleases both him and his sister. At this point the narrator intervenes, perhaps to make plain what her earlier treatment has taken the risk of understating. Fanny is enabled to resist Henry's overtures, because, as Austen now plainly says, her heart is 'guarded in a way unsuspected' by either of the Crawfords. Her affection is already 'engaged elsewhere': she is secure from his attack because of her 'love of another', a love that is obviously itself romantic or sexual (11: 6, 270). Otherwise, this realist novelist of romances explicitly declares, a tender-hearted and impressionable young lady of 18 like Fanny would scarcely have escaped 'heart-whole from the courtship' of a man of the world like Crawford. Very soon afterwards, William, 'the so long absent and dearly loved brother,' sends a letter from Portsmouth which makes Fanny tremble with joy at the prospect of seeing him again at Mansfield (11: 6, 270).

William Price, brought up as 'the darling' of his mother, self-confident, integrated, ambitious, is in temperament the antithesis of his sister. He has found a new home in the navy and is eager to continue his career. Enthralling the assembled family with his stories, ready to ride out with Crawford, spirited and engaging, a Captain Wentworth in the making, he is received, despite his junior status in the navy, as unquestionably an acceptable guest. With William, Fanny enjoys that 'unchecked, equal, fearless intercourse' that for many years her adoption has denied her: they talk over their childhood, and in a passage of unusual warmth the author allows herself to celebrate their togetherness (11: 6, 273–4). William gives Fanny an amber cross, a gift that is the more precious because, for once, it has no strings attached. But William's reinsertion into the novel at this point only serves to deepen the dilemmas of his troubled adopted sister and to bring her conflicts to an acute climax.

From the outset of his campaign, Henry Crawford attacks Fanny through the manipulation of affective ties, and now specifically through her love of William. The loan of his valuable hunter to her brother is only the first of his attempts to make Fanny feel indebted to him. The lead-up to Fanny's coming-out ball, arranged by Sir Thomas, himself with ulterior as well as generous motives, gives him another opportunity. More importantly, persuading Mary to persuade Fanny to accept a necklace from him is a means by which, without his confronting her, Henry can virtually compel Fanny into accepting this symbolic token of his affection, and, as she half-perceives, to recognise his desire to possess her. This 'gift' is more like a trap. But it is through William Price's ambitions to rise in the navy that Crawford finds the most persuasive means to exert leverage over Fanny Price's feelings.

Price makes no secret of his frustration at being stuck in the rank of midshipman. When Crawford overhears Fanny saying that she is sure Sir Thomas 'will do every thing in his power to get you made' (II: 7, 290), he sees (as a reader must gather in retrospect) another opportunity to increase, as he thinks, her affection for him and demonstrate beyond a doubt the genuineness of his feelings for her. On his return from London, where he introduced William to his uncle, Crawford announces to Fanny that he has succeeded in getting her brother promoted. Perhaps his success in persuading his uncle, the admiral, might testify to his love for her (though Crawford is a man who likes to get his way), but the result is bullying, because it works by targeting what he has seen are Fanny's tenderest feelings. And despite her overflowing joy at William's being made a lieutenant, Fanny understands immediately that Henry has been 'conferring an obligation', that 'Your kindness to William makes me more obliged to you than words can express' (II: 13, 349) and that therefore she is once again under pressure to make a return. This is not enough to make her accept his proposal, though, which – coming hard on the heels of the news of William's promotion – causes her great distress.

The necklace Henry plants on Fanny with Mary's connivance is not the only gift she receives just before the ball. Returning with it, she finds Edmund in the East room at her writing-table. He presents her with a gold chain on which to hang William's cross, saying that it is 'a token of the love of one of your oldest friends'. Fanny is 'over-powered by a thousand feelings of pain and pleasure' (II: 9, 303): pleasure because of 'love', pain because of 'friend'. The previous scene has shown Mary swindling Fanny into believing that she herself has had the idea of giving her a necklace. Delighted to hear of her gifting, Edmund tells Fanny that she and Mary resemble each other in 'true generosity and natural delicacy', and leaves her saying that he 'would not have the shadow of a coolness arise . . . between the two dearest objects' that he has 'on earth' (II: 9, 306). In the East room once again Fanny is left to struggle there with her feelings:

He was gone as he spoke; and Fanny remained to tranquillise herself as she could. She was one of his two dearest — that must support her. But the other! — the first! She had never heard him speak so openly before, and though it told her no more than what she had long perceived, it was a stab; — for it told of his own convictions and views. They were decided. He would marry Miss Crawford. It was a stab, in spite of every long-standing expectation; and she was obliged to repeat again and again that she was one of his two dearest, before the words gave her any sensation. Could she believe Miss Crawford to deserve him, it would be — Oh! how different would it be — how far more tolerable! But he was deceived in her; he gave her merits which she had not; her faults were what they had ever been, but he saw them no longer. (II: 9, 307)

Here heightened emotion is conveyed through the transformation of punctuation devices bequeathed to Austen by the novelists of sensibility. The deployment of repetitions, dashes and exclamation marks serves the representation both of thoughts and of acute emotional pain. Fanny's attempts to keep on top of her feelings are continually interrupted, undermined, by the anguish that is conveyed through these devices, as they co-operate with and augment the rhythm of the paragraph. They make this rhythm jerky, disordered. The conventional 'It was a stab' of Fanny's anguish (like that which Willoughby in *Sense and Sensibility* calls that 'hackneyed metaphor . . . a dagger to my heart': III: 8, 368) is revivified or literalised when the phrase's involuntary repetition seems to turn it into an action, a wound driven deep, as if into Fanny's body. When Fanny tries to subdue her dejection 'by the influence of fervent prayers for [Edmund's] happiness', one might be reminded of the sentimental heroine Emma Courtney pouring out her soul in 'fervent aspirations' for the 'happiness' of another man whose love must be relinquished,[31] were it not that one's sympathy for Fanny is qualified by the jealous blaming of Miss Crawford she has just allowed herself and the exclusion of Mary from these prayers.

The rhythms of this passage, then, evoke the body, at the same time as its phrasing in words and sentences articulates thoughts. But words – the carriers of consciousness – can be made to penetrate the body and change 'sensation'. In the next paragraph Fanny again calls upon language to deliver her from the insurgency of her desires:

It was her intention, as she felt it to be her duty, to try to overcome all that was excessive, all that bordered on selfishness in her affection for Edmund. To call or to fancy it a loss, a disappointment, would be a presumption; for which she had not words strong enough to satisfy her own humility. To think of him as Miss Crawford might be justified in thinking, would in her be insanity. To her, he could be nothing under

any circumstances — nothing dearer than a friend. Why did such an idea
occur to her even enough to be reprobated and forbidden? It ought not to
have touched on the confines of her imagination. She would endeavour to
be rational. (II: 9, 307)

What is hidden in that unreferenced 'it' in the second sentence (the
unreferencing taking the reader into recesses of Fanny's desire)? It is that
Fanny's love for Edmund has given rise, in the secret chambers of her
thought, to the dream of marriage with him. 'To think of him, as Miss
Crawford might be justified in thinking' alludes now to her thinking of
Edmund as a potential partner. 'Why did such an idea occur to her even
enough to be reprobated and forbidden?' Once more unspecified, the
'idea' is not permitted to cross the barrier into representation or articula-
tion, repudiated at the very same moment as the taboo thought emerges.
Fanny dares not let the word 'marriage' enter her consciousness. 'Such an
idea', simultaneously presented and concealed, becomes again merely an
'it' in the next sentence: 'It ought not to have touched on the confines of
her imagination.' The repeated need to thrust the thought down is
represented in the repeated form of the sentences that define it.

'Confines' is an arresting and revealing word. Her imagination has
confines, boundaries like an estate, walls like a garden, but the term
confines, like the fence at Sotherton, implies, and in fact cannot mean
anything other than, that there is something outside the confine, itself
powerful or dangerous enough to be excluded. So that here is a picture of
the mind, like Henry Tilney's in *Northanger Abbey*, in which 'imagination'
is to be kept separate from another aspect, or 'idea', that the mind has
produced, that is something altogether more dangerous. There are
thoughts that merit being called crazy or 'insane': 'To think of him as
Miss Crawford might be justified in thinking, would in her be insanity.'
To be in love with Edmund is one thing; to dream of, to fantasise about,
marriage to him, is quite another. Marriage would violate the social
hierarchy that with one part of herself, the 'rational', adjusted, trained self,
she has accepted as inevitable. To allow herself to imagine the 'it' of
marriage to Edmund and all that that involves (the barriers of the mind
are permeable, and she cannot stop herself imagining it) is to transgress
and unsettle the whole social order which she inhabits and which inhabits
her. But this is nevertheless what she wants. To feel love is not enough; it
must be translated into marriage for Fanny's deepest needs to be assuaged.
Marriage to Edmund would mean, though this thought must be deeply
buried, that she fully belonged, was fully at home, in her adoptive place.
All this is conveyed in the rhythms and dexterities of Jane Austen's prose.

'How am I ever to look him in the face and say such things? Could you do it? But then he is your cousin, which makes all the difference' (1: 18, 197). Mary's assumption in the play-reading scene that Fanny could not conceivably have any romantic feelings towards her cousin will only have increased Fanny's pain, but it is not because Edmund is her cousin that Fanny seeks to put down the insurgency of her desire. The vehemence, approaching to horror, with which she castigates herself here has suggested to many readers that what she is warding off is the thought of incest, a sexual attraction to a cousin that is really taboo.[32] And it is indeed possible to conceive of Fanny's need for Edmund as a kind of warping, her confined circumstances having distorted the normal course of sexual attraction. But in Jane Austen's world (as in most of the world today) the prospect of marriage between cousins, *per se*, was nothing to fear; in fact the opposite was the case, since cousin marriage would ensure that wealth remained within the family and promised family support, and a reasonable expectation of shared interests and views.[33] What powers her self-reproaches in these paragraphs is rather that Edmund's identity as her cousin (a term she twice addresses him by in this scene, as is her habit, so as to keep her feelings at a distance) is inseparable from his being her uncle's son, or, in other words, his identity as a Bertram. The narrator, generalising for a moment in the midst of evoking Fanny's mental struggle, writes that 'she had not words strong enough to satisfy her own humility'. It is not because he is a blood relation that Fanny castigates herself for dreaming of marriage to Edmund, but because that cousin is the son of a baronet, she is the daughter of a marine on half-pay, and she owes his family 'her duty', a duty she has accepted as gratitude, obedience, submission and abiding by the rules. Like many displaced persons as well as adoptees, her non-entitlement has become a condition of her being.

It is because she has lived by the rules that Fanny has won her acceptance within the family, has secured her aunt Bertram's affection, and has earned her forbidding uncle's kindness and regard. But she is inwardly breaking the rules, and the self that has needed to belong to Mansfield is at war with this other craving to marry her cousin, which so transgresses, affronts the settled order. She has a right, everyone's instinctive right, to her own desires and to choose her own fulfilment. She is shown to know this, but in her thoughts she is violating the compact, the unspoken contract that her reception into the household depends upon. If she were to marry Edmund, that would be something like complete assimilation, but meanwhile she can only stay true to her feelings, her 'pre-engaged heart', and withstand the accusations that her baffled and furious uncle levels at her when she turns out to be so different from the pliable, acquiescent adoptive daughter he had thought her: 'You do not owe me the duty of a child. But, Fanny, if your heart can acquit you of *ingratitude* — ' (III: 1, 368).

This critical scene in which her uncle visits the East room with Crawford's proposal is narrated largely from Sir Thomas' point of view. The reader briefly shares his sanguine expectations and anticipation of pleasure, so that his bafflement, and even his fury, seem understandable. Fanny's own emotions are conveyed almost entirely through his observation of her physical appearance, with the result that, once again, the reader is left to imagine her distress. He tries to find out whether some previous attachment might be behind Fanny's otherwise inexplicable refusal. 'This is beyond me', he exclaims. 'This requires explanation. Young as you are, and having seen scarcely any one, it is hardly possible that your affections —— '

> He paused and eyed her fixedly. He saw her lips formed into a *no*, though the sound was inarticulate, but her face was like scarlet. That, however, in so modest a girl might be very compatible with innocence, and chusing at least to appear satisfied, he quickly added, 'No, no, I know *that* is quite out of the question — quite impossible.' (III: 1, 365)

Fanny's blush belies her lips; her throat contradicts her blush. She can neither betray herself by telling the truth, nor betray herself by lying. One critic has found the character 'constitutively duplicitous', but this charge presupposes a disposition to deceive that is belied by Fanny's horrible anguish here at having – almost – to lie. It seems rather that Jane Austen stays intransigently faithful to her imagined character in showing that, even as she defends her love, and stays true to herself, Fanny is ashamed. Her socialised identity is at war with her instincts. She continues to hide her feelings, but she is not misleading her uncle when a few minutes later she more calmly consents to his supposition that Edmund will marry Mary Crawford. She is afraid that if she told Sir Thomas about Crawford's misbehaviour with Maria, she would drag her cousin into the mire without furthering her own cause, but it is hard to imagine how anyone, let alone someone in her situation, would risk this. In the days following, she toughs it out: even though she cannot avoid feeling grateful to Crawford for his attentions, she can do nothing but resist them (III: 2, 378).

It is true that when Edmund returns, and takes his father's side, she leads him to believe that her resistance to Crawford is based on her objections to his principles. 'I am persuaded that he does not think as he ought, on serious subjects', she declares, and Jane Austen certainly risks her here sounding slightly like an Evangelical moralist. But if, as Richard Cronin remarks, 'Fanny is surely saved by her duplicity from Evangelical heroism',[34] the deceit, if it is that, is again exigent: Fanny speaks as much of the truth as she can – that she has disliked and distrusted Crawford since she observed his toying with Maria. Because Edmund is in love with Mary, and completely oblivious to Fanny's feelings for himself, this is the only defence available to her.

Edmund sees that Fanny 'must need the comfort of communication' and joins her on what he calls 'a comfortable walk'. And so it is – 'Fanny had not felt so comfortable for days and days' – until it becomes plain that he is bent on persuading her to accept Crawford. 'You have proved yourself upright and disinterested, prove yourself grateful and tender-hearted', he says insinuatingly, playing the paternalist card that everyone plays. She continues to defend herself and her actions, but when he calls her 'My dearest Fanny' while 'pressing her arm closer to him', and goes on to enthuse about Mary's kindness, the physical contact throws her off balance (III: 4, 401, 407). Summoning in herself an energy that must partly derive from her animosity towards Miss Crawford, Fanny gives a sustained and authoritative defence of her position. 'Let him have all the perfections in the world, I think it ought not to be set down as certain, that a man must be acceptable to every woman he may happen to like himself', she argues. But when in the same speech she goes on to refer to her own 'situation' – 'In my situation, it would have been the extreme of vanity to be forming expectations on Mr Crawford' – she does make a false move (III: 4, 408). It is not because of her inferior social position that she has failed to respond to his advances, but because she is in love with Edmund. The fact that this cannot possibly be said leads to her misrepresenting her motives. She soon realises her mistake: 'She feared she had been doing wrong, saying too much, overacting the caution which she had been fancying necessary' (III: 4, 409). In a very tight corner she defends herself with as much of the truth as she can, but she does slip into betrayal of herself here. Jane Austen is almost ruthless in her understanding and exposure of the psychological complexities of a figure whom many critics have condemned for the rigidity of her virtue.[35]

Sir Thomas decides to send her back to Portsmouth for a while, and Fanny is overcome. Home is to 'heal every pain that had since grown out of the separation' from her own family. She longs '[t]o be in the centre of such a circle, loved by so many, and more loved by all than she had ever been before, to feel affection without fear or restraint, to feel herself the equal of those who surrounded her' (III: 6, 426). At home, she will be 'safe from every look which could be fancied a reproach', even from Edmund's: 'At a distance unassailed by his looks or his kindness, and safe from the perpetual irritation of knowing his heart, and striving to avoid his confidence, she should be able to reason herself into a properer state' (III: 6, 427). 'Unassailed' attributes to Edmund's looks the violence of physical assault and, like the 'stab' that his words in the East room gave her, registers them as if they were wounds given to her body. Each one of these phrases discloses more piercingly than before in *Mansfield Park* an aspect of the terrible tax that her reception into the grand house has entailed, and that the narrative has often preferred to assume. Confirming that constraint has become second nature to her, the narrator writes shortly afterwards that she can only half-acknowledge her own feelings. Fanny writes to suggest she visit Portsmouth, and Mrs Price's kind reply leads her to imagine with equal longing that 'she should now find a warm and affectionate friend in the "Mamma" who had certainly shewn no remarkable fondness for her formerly'. Naturally, so to speak, Fanny blames herself for this, forgives her mother and imagines that, now she knows better how to be useful, 'there would be leisure and inclination for every comfort, and they should soon be what mother and daughter ought to be to each other' (III: 6, 428).

'Comfort', a complex word, recurs many times in *Mansfield Park* and is central to Fanny Price's psychology. Its older meaning suggested support, consolation, even redemption, so that Christ was often called, as in the King James Bible (John 16:7), the 'Comforter'. (This meaning is discernable in Edmund's desire to comfort Fanny.) At the other end of the spectrum, comfort denotes the freedom from anxiety that material prosperity provides. More generally, and more precisely in Fanny's case, the word presupposes a sub-text, or prior condition, of pain, anxiety or distress, upon which it supervenes. It is a compromise formation, one might say, between desire and actuality, the second-best runner-up to happiness. Within Fanny's psyche, comfort, as in the East room, signals the release from anxiety, from the constant harassments of her everyday existence; it is comfort, not happiness, nor fulfilment, that she habitually envisages as a psychological goal. Uncherished as a child, victimised as a teenager, taken from her own family to a new and indifferent environment, such a person, Jane Austen understands, can usually hope for a modest happiness at best, a bargain with reality. It is this understanding in fact that underpins and excuses the novel's own compromising conclusion.

Portsmouth does have the medicinal effect Sir Thomas expects, if not in the way he expected it. This disordered and tumultuous household leads in turn to Fanny's idealisation of the Bertram ménage:

> At Mansfield, no sounds of contention, no raised voice, no abrupt bursts, no tread of violence was ever heard; all proceeded in a regular course of cheerful orderliness; every body had their due importance; every body's feelings were consulted. If tenderness could be ever supposed wanting, good sense and good breeding supplied its place; and as to the little irritations, sometimes introduced by aunt Norris, they were short, they were trifling, they were as a drop of water to the ocean, compared with the ceaseless tumult of her present abode. (III: 8, 453–4)

Portsmouth has turned out to be the longed-for home where Fanny cannot feel at home, a place where she is once more of no account, ignored, rejected and misunderstood. She had tried to make the clutter of the East room at Mansfield signify that she was cared for, and here, but even more desperately (the desperation conveyed by the mounting and relentless phrasal repetition), she turns Mansfield into a fantasy world of comfort, even if it is only a comfort made out of negatives. The narrator reminds the reader that Fanny's 'frame and temper' are 'delicate and nervous': the cadencing, for example, in 'they were short, they were trifling, they were as a drop of water to the ocean' exactly reproduces her nervous hysteria, the helpless cliché that climaxes the thought sequence revealing just how wracked and besieged she is. Disillusioned, harassed and lonely, she reaches a point where her intelligence has succumbed to misery.

Imprisoned in Portsmouth, a city surrounded by barriers, Fanny is the more or less impotent recipient of news from London, condemned haplessly to guess or construe from her correspondents meanings that might have the most intimate consequences for her own life, and more vulnerable than ever to the seductions of Henry Crawford. But these arduous chapters in which she follows the progress of Edmund's courtship by psychological radar simultaneously wear away or dissolve her last fragile ties to the home of which she had dreamed and leave her with only one option. 'William was gone ... William was gone' (III: 8, 449, 450), and, with his promotion and career, their earlier uncompromised, loving closeness. Now she must make the second best, the best. 'When she had been coming to Portsmouth, she had loved to call it her home, had been fond of saying that she was going home; the word had been very dear to her; and so it still was, but it must be applied to Mansfield. *That* was now the home. Portsmouth was Portsmouth; Mansfield was home'

(III: 14, 499). Thus Fanny's displacement turns towards assimilation or acceptance, perhaps the natural consequence of an unnatural beginning.

For while her mother turns out to have 'no desire of her friendship, no inclination for her company', her place begins to be taken by Lady Bertram. As Sodré points out, Tom's illness arouses real maternal feeling for the first time in Lady Bertram, and this change is reflected in her letters to Fanny.[36] In their comically otiose style they too assume that Mansfield is Fanny's home, and even 'trust and hope, and sincerely wish you may never be absent from home so long again' (III: 14, 499). (To put it more harshly, Fanny is the daughter substitute whom she expects to stay on as her companion.) Lady Bertram loves her selfishly, maybe, but loves her nonetheless. Her letters are her niece's 'private regale': they feed the desperately lonely Fanny's hunger for acceptance. So that when Maria's adultery becomes known, and its dire consequences for the whole family become clear, she is recalled to Mansfield and Edmund comes to pick her up, Fanny travels happily despite his own deep depression. As the coach enters the Park, 'Her eye fell every where on lawns and plantations of the freshest green; and the trees, though not fully clothed, were in that delightful state, when farther beauty is known to be at hand, and when, while much is actually given to the sight, more yet remains for the imagination' (III: 15, 517). The narrator and the character are for a moment in perfect sync. This is the only sentence in the novel when the estate of Mansfield Park is celebrated, and Fanny, who is filled now with hope, identifies with it. The gladness that surrounds Fanny's return is wonderfully augmented by the chapter's final paragraph:

> By one of the suffering party within, they were expected with such impatience as she had never known before. Fanny had scarcely passed the solemn-looking servants, when Lady Bertram came from the drawing room to meet her; came with no indolent step; and, falling on her neck, said, 'Dear Fanny! now I shall be comfortable.' (III: 15, 517)

'Came ... came with no indolent step': the formal, even rather archaic, wording bestows upon Lady Bertram's action a gravity that, for example, 'came eagerly' could not have. It prepares for the transformative moment of 'falling on her neck'. The phrase evokes two Biblical moments of homecoming: Joseph's return to his father after many years and, more especially perhaps, the return of the prodigal son in Luke (15:20): 'But when he was yet a good way off, his father saw him, and had compassion, and ran, and fell on his neck, and kissed him.' Like the Biblical passage, Austen's sentence uses punctuation to dignify the moment – in the Bible, a succession of five commas, here two semi-colons and two commas. These pauses, micro-halts one might call them, act against the impulsive, passionate race to embrace they describe, and, together with the fact that Lady Bertram's 'comfortable' still retains a vestige of its august and spiritual meaning, carry the comedy of her inevitable selfishness to a moving, even exalted, conclusion. This is a moment when the novel's trajectory towards Fanny's assimilation is poised on the finest of balances.

In the novels and plays that Jane Austen knew, lost children at last reconciled to their parents, or discovering their true identity, are commonplace. Frances Burney's Evelina, for example, who has thought herself an orphan, at last meets the father who abandoned her, Sir John Belmont, and amid much mutual kneeling, tears and embraces they are reconciled to each other.[37] Revealed to be the child of a baronet, she has enough blue blood to qualify as the bride of the aristocratic Lord Orville. Clara Reeve's *The Old English Baron*, published the same year, and often understood to be the first 'female Gothic' novel, features a poor youth who is the ward in the family of a baronet: he turns out to be the heir. Emmeline in Charlotte Smith's first novel, who, as the subtitle has it, is 'the Orphan of the Castle', is believed to be illegitimate, but the plot reveals that her parents were in fact married, and what is more she is the owner of the castle in which she has grown up. Orphans and foundlings who are reconciled with their lost relatives and turn out to be nobly born crop up everywhere. The scene in *Lovers' Vows* that allows Crawford and Maria to embrace brings Agatha together with her long-lost illegitimate son; less controversially, John Home's *Douglas*, the well-known play that Tom mentions in *Mansfield Park* (1: 13, 149), concerns a boy brought up in poverty who becomes a famous warrior, and is in fact the long-lost son of the play's tragic heroine, Lady Randolph.

There were many precedents, then, for this story of a ward or adopted daughter to become finally, as many critics have imagined, 'the mistress' of Mansfield Park, for the novel to end with poor cousin Fanny returning in the triumph of fairy-tale happiness, and the celebration or redemption of the great estate. These were all stories, though, in which the child is proved to be the legal inheritor.[38] It was possible, too, that Fanny's idealisation of the place itself would become the author's, as the 'cult of the English country house', as Evelyn Waugh put it in the middle years of the twentieth century, certainly persuaded some readers that it does.[39] All of Jane Austen's novels critique romance, and in this one she critiques specifically what Freud called the 'Familienroman', the family romance.[40] The novel has returned Fanny to Mansfield and convincingly shown that her heroine's psychological journey has reached a haven or resting place. The estate has become for her the comfortable, stable, enclosing mother and father she has inwardly longed for, the place that assuages the wounds of her troubled displacement. But that does not mean that the past is forgotten. She is not revealed to be the estate's true heir, she does not become an authority figure, not a mistress and still less a redeemer, but a welcomed child.

The genre Austen is writing in means, however, that she must now marry Fanny to Edmund and meet the formal requirements of romance. And there is disharmony between her account of Fanny as a damaged figure for whom only partial happiness or comfort is only ever going to be likely, and this demand. So a kind of compromise is what the last chapter gives her reader. The narrator, now avowedly the author, can promise now only 'tolerable comfort' at its opening, though in effect it is a chapter that has caused many readers not comfort but dismay and uneasiness. Edmund falls in love with Fanny, and they are married, as the comedic/romantic genre demands, and everyone else's future is sketched, though with the greatest attention given to 'poor Sir Thomas'' self-reproaches. The court-ship of the hero and heroine is, however, barely imagined as plausible. 'I purposely abstain from dates on this occasion,' writes the author, 'that every one may be at liberty to fix their own, aware that the cure of unconquerable passions, and the transfer of unchanging attachments, must vary as to time in different people' (iii: 17, 544). The defensive, uneasy irony misfires: could anyone believe that Edmund and Mary's relationship conforms to the romantic clichés that are mocked with such glibness here?

Perhaps light may be thrown on the ethos of this chapter by the moment in *Pride and Prejudice* when Elizabeth imagines marriage with Darcy, when all chance of it seems to have vanished:

> His understanding and temper, though unlike her own, would have answered all her wishes. It was an union that must have been to the advantage of both; by her ease and liveliness, his mind might have been softened, his manners improved, and from his judgment, information, and knowledge of the world, she must have received benefit of greater import-ance. (iii: 8, 344)

Mansfield Park now has recourse to the same subjunctive, provisional verbs. 'My Fanny ... must have been happy, in spite of every thing. She must have been a happy creature ... She had sources of delight that must force their way' (iii: 17, 533). 'My Fanny' allows the author to express especial fondness (as for a child), but the phrase also admits that the figure is a fictional creation, the property of an author who can manipulate fate as she wishes, and this is what she does. Fanny Price is not the only character in this chapter whose future is now imagined in the same mode: Mrs Grant 'must have gone with some regret', if Henry had 'persevered, and uprightly, Fanny must have been his reward': Edmund's happiness 'must have been great enough to warrant any strength of language in which he could clothe it to her or to himself'. Phrases such as 'it may reasonably be supposed', or 'we may fairly consider' are scattered through the chapter. In *Pride and Prejudice*, Elizabeth's ideas are followed by this sentence: 'But no such happy marriage could teach the admiring multitude what connubial felicity really was', the clichés of which speedily dispatch her thoughts into the never-never land of fantasy. With its vagueness about time, so sharply contrasted with the day-to-day accuracy of the preceding chapters, *Mansfield Park* propels its characters into a future for which the author now takes no responsibility.

The novel certainly concludes with Edmund and Fanny moving after some time at Thornton Lacey to Mansfield, but its last sentence, while rounding off in the style expected, reminds the reader of the difficult past. Following the convenient death of Dr Grant,

> they removed to Mansfield, and the parsonage there, which under each of its two former owners, Fanny had never been able to approach but with some painful sensations of restraint or alarm, soon grew as dear to her heart, and as thoroughly perfect in her eyes, as every thing else, within the view and patronage of Mansfield Park, had long been. (III: 17, 547–8)

Fanny's enduring dread, first of Mrs Norris and then of Mary Crawford, is explicitly recalled in this final sentence. But novelists can be allowed clichés like 'thoroughly perfect' in their final words, as Jane Austen does again in *Emma* when she writes that the predictions of Emma and Knightley's friends 'were fully answered in the perfect happiness of the union'. Austen waves her magic wand at the end of her narrative and in this very last sentence brings Fanny Price to the Parsonage, under the 'patronage' of Mansfield Park, but this is not a story of ambition fulfilled, nor of the country house culture renewed, but, as her final flourish suggests, of healing imagined.

The treatment of Fanny Price as a displaced person here inevitably raises questions about the relation of her portrayal to accounts of the novel that read it, and treat her, quite differently. The character, I have suggested, is a forerunner of the many figures in later literature who are torn between different worlds, and I have implied that *Mansfield Park*'s achievement is in its eliciting of the hidden life, the inner conflicts and accommodations of this divided and ultimately much oppressed figure. There are many readings that treat the novel in effect as a sophisticated morality play in which Fanny and Edmund model virtue, and the Crawfords vitality, or read it as a quasi-political drama in which conservative values are either endorsed or subverted. More pertinent for my argument is the fact that another category of displaced person and another trajectory of displacement have preoccupied readers and critics of *Mansfield Park* for the past three decades. It was Edward Said in 1993 who first proposed that Fanny was a 'transported commodity'.[41] A child whose uprooting from Portsmouth to Mansfield analogises the transport of slaves from west Africa to the Bertram estates in the West Indies has proved an extraordinarily potent figure, and has certainly revivified the criticism of *Mansfield Park*. But Fanny Price is not in any reasonable sense a commodity. She is not purchased, nor taken to be employed, exploited or made use of, except by Mrs Norris, whose motives are, importantly, hidden from herself.

Fanny Price is not a slave. But nor is she a displaced person, refugee or asylum seeker. She is not a 12-year-old who has walked across the Balkans from contemporary Afghanistan to seek refuge in Paris; she has not been brought from overseas as the 'home girls' were to work as a housekeeper on a family farm in Canada; she is not an 'unaccompanied minor' now waiting to be 'processed' in an Australian off-shore detention centre. In writing of her displacement I do not wish to elide these crucial differences, but to suggest that our awareness of the traumas of displacement and adjustment might dispose us to consider the case of Fanny Price more attentively and sympathetically, and in particular to give due attention to the hidden impact of her removal as it affects her life at Mansfield. As the critical record suggests, it has been peculiarly difficult for readers in the past to read the story of Fanny Price with the sympathy given and requested by her author.

In this chapter I have suggested some of the techniques by which Austen makes manifest the subtle involutions of her lonely main character's conscience. But by contrast, the notionally crowded scenes of *Mansfield Park* – the dance and the ball – are treated cursorily. In *Emma*, the very different heroine inhabits a village in which close-knit gatherings are the rule, and there Austen finds a new mode by which to suggest their crowded sociability. In sites where the projects and destinies of different characters closely interweave with each other, Emma's overhearing is the taken-for-granted and therefore hidden mode in which a very different fictional world from *Mansfield Park* is manifested.

CHAPTER 6

Emma's overhearing

A young lady arrives at her uncle's English country estate and finds the house 'a picture made real':

> The large, low rooms, with brown ceilings and dusky corners, the deep embrasures and curious casements, the quiet light on dark, polished panels, the deep greenness outside, that seemed always peeping in, the sense of well-ordered privacy in the centre of a 'property' – a place where sounds were felicitously accidental, where the tread was muffled by the earth itself and in the thick mild air all friction dropped out of contact and all shrillness out of talk.[1]

Readers might imagine Mansfield Park like this, given Fanny's own nostalgic idealisation, but this passage could hardly be by Jane Austen. For Austen's imagination is not pictorial or picturesque; the narrative rarely steps back and invites the reader to see rooms, or the way light falls within them, or to dwell on the atmosphere created by the physical surroundings her characters inhabit. The 'dining-parlour' of Northanger Abbey, she writes, 'was a noble room, suitable in its dimensions to a much larger drawing-room than the one in common use, and fitted up in a style of luxury and expense which was almost lost on the unpractised eye of Catherine', and certainly lost, one might feel, on the curious modern reader (*NA* II: 6, 170). Catherine's indifference to anything new in the way of interior appointments might be the excuse for equally vague characterisations of the various chambers that General Tilney shows her through, but the same reliance on her reader's knowing what rooms would be like is evident in all of Austen's novels. At Pemberley, the Gardiners and Elizabeth are shown into 'a very pretty sitting-room, lately fitted up with greater elegance and lightness than the apartments below' (*P&P* III: 1, 276), which leads Elizabeth to reflect, as she walks towards a window, that Darcy, who has initiated this refurbishment, must be a kind brother. But no details are given, or perhaps needed: the true significance of this brotherly gesture is left to be inferred later. At the other end of the genteel social scale, Miss Bates and her mother 'occupy the drawing room floor' of a house belonging to 'people in business', further defined as 'a very moderate sized apartment, which was every thing to them' (*E* II: I, 166). That is all. Very little more information is added about the Bates' rooms in the course of the novel, although their confinement and the awkward stairs leading to them are certainly to become important factors, as it turns out, in the novel's action. Where rooms are concerned, Austen usually satisfies herself merely with indicative gestures. Everything is done in broad, simple strokes that principally focus on what one is tempted to call real-estate values. Windows, doors, tables, chairs and desks are only mentioned when the activities of characters require them. This paucity of visual information in the novels struck Lewes, who in his mid-nineteenth-century appreciation wrote that 'So entirely dramatic, and so little descriptive, is the genius of Miss Austen, that she seems to rely upon what her people say and do for the whole effect they are to produce on our imaginations.' And moreover that 'the absence of all sense of outward world – either scenery or personal appearance – is more remarkable in her than in any writer we remember'.[2]

But there are certainly exceptions to the minimalism of visual description, especially when a room's appointments can be used to provide important information about the character who inhabits it, as with Fanny's East room or Captain Harville's rented cottage. The 'less of splendor and more real elegance' that Pemberley's appointments have in contrast to Rosings is, perhaps, a guide to its owner's good character. Occasionally too Austen uses interior lighting to telling effect. Early on a January morning in London Marianne Dashwood kneels against one of the window seats 'for the sake of all the little light she could command from it', the half darkness in which she is writing desperately to Willoughby making especially poignant her flow of tears (*S&S* II: 7, 205). Sir Thomas Bertram, home after his long voyage, asks where Fanny is, and leads her 'nearer the light' to look at her, and the small illuminated circle within the surrounding darkness of the room creates a touching temporary intimacy between the two (though Austen does not specify whether the light is candles or an oil lamp) (*MP* II: I, 208).[3] Candles play an important part in the ball at the Crown Inn ('This is meeting quite in fairy-land' enthuses Miss Bates), as well as in the winter afternoon at Portsmouth when Fanny Price's uncouth father holds the only candle between himself and the newspaper – a moment she finds herself recalling when, in a famous passage, she compares sunlight in the country with its 'glare, a stifling, sickly glare' in the town (*MP* III: 7, 442; III: 15, 508). Austen reserves the information that the drawing-room at Hartfield faces west until Emma's elation after Knightley's proposal can be reflected in the 'beautiful effect' of the setting sun (III: 14, 473).

Despite her usual mere gestures at description, Jane Austen does in fact often give her reader a strong sense of the rooms, the spaces and the places through which her characters move, and this is especially true of the later novels. The rooms are not particularised, but their dimensions always play an important role, and are often a compelling material factor in the dramas that are enacted within them. A reader can often imagine where characters are standing or sitting, and follow their movements across rooms.[4] If the absence of visual description is not felt as a lack, however, this is largely because spaces are created by aural rather than by visual means. Jane Austen's is not a highly visual world, but it is, by way of compensation, an intensely and intricately aural one. This is not because Jane Austen often defines or describes the tones in which her characters speak, since this is far from the case: in this too she is a minimalist. Just as the reader must often impute their tones, or imaginatively 'hear' how a character speaks, the effects of spatiality in her novels are imperceptibly present, implicated, left to be garnered or absorbed through the reader's imaginative osmosis.

An important means by which spatiality is created, however, is through the recurrent tactic or motif of her protagonist's overhearing of others' talk. It is through overhearing, since it invokes simultaneous proximity and relative distance, that intimate spatiality is brought into play and the determining physical conditions of the genteel social life that is her subject are implied. In *Emma* and *Persuasion*, the topics of this and the next chapter, overhearing plays more than an incidental role, and indeed is critical to the specific dramas each of them unfolds.

Mr Darcy's unfortunate remark about Elizabeth Bennet's merely 'tolerable' appearance is not the only significant moment of overhearing in Jane Austen's novels. Far from it, in fact. Darcy himself later overhears Mrs Bennet boasting of the marriage prospects of her daughters, while only a few pages earlier his own conversation has been overheard by Mr Collins (*P&P* I: 18, 108). There is even a pre-echo of the *Pride and Prejudice* incident in *Northanger Abbey*, when at the Bath Assembly Rooms Catherine Morland decides that Captain Tilney, though more dashing than his brother, is not so pleasant, 'for, within her hearing, he not only protested against every thought of dancing himself, but even laughed openly at Henry for finding it possible' (*NA* II: 1, 133). Less self-possessed than Elizabeth, Catherine would not dream of taking offence. Later, a more

startling episode of overhearing is staged: trapped on a bench in the Pump
Room with Isabella and the Captain, Catherine is the shocked witness
of a suggestive duologue conducted in half-whispers between the pair
(1: 3, 149–50).

In *Sense and Sensibility*, Elinor Dashwood, overhearing the conversations of Marianne and Willoughby, concludes, wrongly, that they must be
engaged. A more complex instance of overhearing occurs later in the novel.
Brandon and Elinor are talking privately near a window; Mrs Jennings
imagines and hopes that Brandon is proposing:

> though she was too honourable to listen, and had even changed her seat, on
> purpose that she might *not* hear, to one close by the piano forté on which
> Marianne was playing, she could not keep herself from seeing that Elinor
> changed colour, attended with agitation, and was too intent on what he
> said, to pursue her employment. — Still farther in confirmation of her
> hopes, in the interval of Marianne's turning from one lesson to another,
> some words of the Colonel's inevitably reached her ear, in which he seemed
> to be apologizing for the badness of his house. This set the matter beyond
> a doubt. (III: 3, 318)

Mrs Jennings is misled by her hopes, and her misinterpretation of what she
hears is comic: the narrator discloses 'what had really passed' soon after.
The interception of her attention by Marianne's playing, some distance
away, fosters a sense of the interior space and makes the occurrence seem
natural. But the result, Mrs Jennings' total misconstruing of the overheard
conversation, is the stuff of farce.[5]

Overhearing is in fact a very common device of the theatre. Concealed
in closets, hidden behind trees or hedges, whipping behind arrases, characters in both comedies and tragedies are always listening in on other
people's solitary speeches or private exchanges. Sometimes, like Lady
Teazle, behind a screen in *The School for Scandal*, or Beatrice, 'couchèd
in the woodbine coverture' in *Much Ado*, what a character covertly hears
changes their lives, and it always furthers the plot.[6] The conditions of the
theatre mean that the focus in these scenes of eavesdropping is usually on
the dialogue that is overheard: characters who are in hiding, like Polonius
for instance, do not usually display their emotions to the audience. But
sometimes in Shakespeare's plays a more complex effect is achieved, as for
example when the audience enjoys Malvolio's speeches and at the same
time is privy to the glee of the conspirators concealed in the box-tree.

Jane Austen's deployment of overhearing certainly owes much to the
drama. One especially important effect, presaging those that Austen
achieves by other means, can be illustrated by the extraordinary scene in

Troilus and Cressida (Act V, scene 2) in which an amorous dialogue between Diomedes and Cressida is overheard by Troilus and Ulysses.[7] The two men stand aside on the stage, 'where the torch may not discover us', but, unknown to them, they too are overheard by the cynical Thersites, nearby yet also concealed. A tussle between Cressida and Diomedes, he making as if to leave her, she pleading with him, is accompanied by exchanges between the hidden onlookers, so that the quarrel between lovers at centre stage is broken into ('aside') by Troilus' tormented jealous outcries and by Ulysses' increasingly desperate attempts to stop him from breaking out of his hiding place. The struggle between one pair is counterpointed, to riveting effect, by the struggle between the other. The whole is also interrupted or accompanied by Thersites' gleefully sleazy comments. So through the employment of overhearing, this scene in *Troilus* affords the simultaneous representation of two or even three distinct but interlocking narratives on the stage.[8]

Jane Austen loved the theatre, wrote little playlets when she was young, took part in amateur dramatics, attended as many professional performances as she could in London and Bath, and learned a great deal from theatrical technique.[9] She succeeded in assimilating, transferring and modifying dramatic effects as she worked with the very different medium of the novel. In narrative fiction, the reader's immediate attention cannot be on two places, two dramas, at once, but Austen finds ways to generate the illusion of simultaneous occurrence through overhearing.[10] Especially in *Emma*, the threading of one dramatic line through the other, the apparently simultaneous presence of two or more different sites of action, is achieved as the heroine moves through a room and consequently, and apparently inevitably, hears others and catches their sequested or private talk. Subliminally the reader is introduced into spaces – the rooms that Austen declines to step back from and describe.

Overhearing in fact is even more ubiquitous in Jane Austen's novels than in the plays that she knew, though she employs it to very different effect. In contrast to the theatre, the person overhearing is her focus. Most importantly, overhearing in the novels is almost always an accidental occurrence: people don't hide under tables or dodge behind screens to listen to what others have to say. One counter example is when Anne Steele stands outside the door of the drawing-room so that she can listen to an exchange between the engaged couple, her sister Lucy and Edward Ferrars. This is roundly condemned as an egregious transgression of polite manners by Elinor Dashwood; it's a Burneyesque act of irredeemable vulgarity (*S&S* III: 2, 311). No one else actually plans or schemes to spy

on another (though Mr Knightley's interest in the silent letters of the
alphabet passing between Frank and Jane in the word game at Hartfield
(III: 5, 377) might be counted as the half-exception that proves this rule).
Overhearing is not usually planned or mischievous, as it so often is in the
theatre, and for these reasons what occurs in Jane Austen's novels is not
properly described as eavesdropping, which implies listening in with
deliberate, and even malicious, intent.[11] The whisper, or aside, another
common stage device which the young Jane Austen burlesqued to great
effect in 'The Mystery', her youthful 'unfinished comedy', is also not
uncommon in the novels (Mrs Elton is a great exponent of the whisper):
it is overhearing's match and complement.

But has overhearing any more significance in Jane Austen's novels than
as an incidental occurrence of everyday social life? The answer is yes and
no. The stage conventions of whispering and overhearing are in fact largely
naturalised, recognisable as unremarkable aspects of genteel sociability
among the tight-knit groups they represent. The accidental overhearing
that she writes of is only possible when her people are brought together in
small gatherings, such as evening parties and dances, so the phenomenon
evokes, if only by default, a 'confined and unvarying society' and the
comparative density of human presence. Quite often the listener, like
Mrs Jennings, catches only snatches of others' talk, especially when they
confer quietly together. Both the frequency and the casualness of overhearing, and the matching need to occasionally lower the voice, or to whisper,
evoke the actuality of domestic congregation, and hence omnipresent
challenges to the conduct of private dialogue. To be overheard is a constant
possibility. Enclaves or islets of privacy are precious, as when the sound of
the piano being played offers Elinor 'shelter' to confer with Brandon, and
more importantly – very importantly in *Pride and Prejudice* and *Emma* –
when a couple dances together. But in such company these opportunities
are snatched, brief, fragile at best, since comparatively quiet conversations
are still liable to be overheard. To speak freely, Austen's characters have
usually to be outdoors.

For even though interiors may be large, as the drawing-room at Rosings
undoubtedly is, a Lady Catherine can intrude on a conversation at the
piano and demand to know what her guests are talking of (*P&P* II: 8, 197).
The perhaps equally grand drawing-room at Mansfield Park is never
described, but when Fanny Price retires with a headache to a sofa at the
far end, away from the light of the work-candles, she can still be reached by
Mrs Norris' shrill, scolding voice. The seating is wide enough apart for her
aunt then to pretend not to hear Edmund when he bursts out in anger at

his mother and aunt's neglect of his cousin, though when he gets up and walks about, continuing to speak, she is 'unable to be longer deaf' (*MP* I: 7, 86). Later in the same drawing-room the conversation between Fanny and her brother William sitting together is observed by Henry Crawford, who turns his chair towards them, and their dialogue, being given in the novel, can readily be understood as overheard; meanwhile Sir Thomas observes Henry listening (*MP* II: 7, 289). In the smaller drawing-room at Hartfield, John Knightley and Jane Fairfax, old friends, enjoy a serious conversation together about her visits to the post office, reported to the reader as if it were taking place in seclusion from the rest of the party (II: 16, 316–17). But someone has heard Jane mention to John Knightley that she has been out walking by herself, because Mr Woodhouse comes up to her shortly and reprimands her for taking such a risk in the rain, and the result is a neighbourly inquisition. The reader is not informed who overhears, who spreads the word, though he or she might easily guess. Emma 'had heard and seen it all', one is later told (II: 16, 322).

As in these instances, then, overhearing is an important narrative tactic that represents the intermeshing lives of Jane Austen's characters. When what is overheard is boring or inconsequential, that is communicated to the reader by parodic or elliptical versions, but it is usually significant, and never just tiresome as it so often can be in real life in the age of the mobile or cell phone. Thus overhearing in Austen's novels, though more naturalistic, still retains a trace of its theatrical origins, and in *Persuasion* this residue of the theatrical can even bestow gravity on the scenes in which it resides. Moreover, the staging of overhearing moments throughout her novels allows Austen to thread other strands through a narrative that otherwise channels the consciousness of the main character, and might risk precluding or excluding any knowledge of the intimate lives of others. Momentarily, other 'centres of self' are located for the reader's attention, while the illusion of occupying the mind of the heroine is unviolated.

Overhearing is most ubiquitous in *Emma* and in *Persuasion*, Jane Austen's last two completed novels, but the consciousness of the heroine is quite differently rendered in each of them, and their overhearing has a quite distinct effect. It is employed with special dexterity in the second two volumes of *Emma*. With the arrival of Mrs Elton and Frank Churchill in Highbury a succession of semi-formal gatherings begins to occupy the narrative, including the 'rather large' evening party at the Coles (II: 8) and the smaller but still quite large formal dinner that Emma Woodhouse feels obliged to give at Hartfield for Mrs Elton. This takes up three whole chapters at the conclusion of the volume (II: 16–18). These occasions are of course presented from Emma's position. Her overhearing exists in different modalities: sometimes she casually or inadvertently hears others' talk, but on other occasions she actively focuses her attention and listens in to what is being said around her.

One cannot consider overhearing, then, without also thinking about attention.[12] There are dialogues in the novels, like the one between Jane and John Knightley, that are presented with no indication they are heard by the protagonists. More usually in *Emma*, the narrative tracks Emma's attention as it moves between different groups in the various Highbury drawing-rooms where the action is concentrated and presents their conversation as if heard or overheard by the heroine herself. As in all such gatherings, there are multiple centres of dialogue. No one can be present at more than one of these centres, but one can sometimes overhear. The reader is hostage to Emma's attention, sees, hears, understands things as if they were within her consciousness, but even Emma's attention cannot be equally everywhere at once. Using her as the vehicle, Austen takes the reader on a narrative itinerary of shifting aural attention that mimics the real-life phenomenon of a single person's shifting between different attentive sites in a room full of people, which is sometimes called the 'cocktail party effect' in the neurological literature.[13] Attention necessarily takes different forms: sometimes engaged in conversation, one sometimes overhears, then perhaps moves, and is engaged in another conversation, overhearing again; all these modalities are reproduced, serially, in Austen's narration of these evening dinner parties. The novel, being a sequential experience, cannot reproduce the condition of social life when, talking with one person, one is invariably aware of other people, other centres of interest in the room, but in representing these varieties of overhearing, Jane Austen certainly comes close to it.

If memory is critical in *Pride and Prejudice*, as I have suggested in Chapter 3, attention, memory's substrate and precursor, is as important a focus in *Emma*. Primitive creatures with minimal neuronal activity would perish if they did not attend to the ever-present dangers around them, and hence be able to retain something that may be defined as the 'memory' of threat.[14] In humans, attention (which need not mean alertness) is the foundation for much consequent psychological activity or elaboration. But perhaps because attention is so much the precondition for more sophisticated mental or emotional processes it is difficult to isolate and is rarely itself given much analytic attention. One way in which attentiveness is isolated and made accessible, dramatised and exposed in *Emma* is through the novel's recurrent narrations of overhearing. And in one scene in which memory does play a role Jane Austen offers in effect a little object lesson in the dependency of memory on prior attention. Harriet, at last freed from her infatuation with Mr Elton, comes to Emma with her 'Most precious treasures', including a piece of court plaister (an early band-aid) and the disused end of an old pencil. She tells Emma how she came by the bit of pencil, snatching it up on an occasion when Mr Elton and Mr Knightley were talking and Elton wanted to make a note about brewing spruce beer:

> 'I do remember it,' cried Emma; 'I perfectly remember it. – Talking about spruce beer. — Oh! yes. . .Stop; Mr Knightley was standing just here, was not he? — I have an idea he was standing just here.'
>
> 'Ah! I do not know. I cannot recollect. — It is very odd, but I cannot recollect. — Mr Elton was standing here, I remember, much about where I am now.' (III: 4, 368)

The room is not described (it is presumably the drawing-room) but made manifest, conjured up as a material condition, through the indicative gestures of 'just here' and 'where I am now'. Emma has always been conscious of where Mr Knightley stands. This is the obverse of that occasion in *Northanger Abbey* when Catherine has no memory of being in the same room with John Thorpe, let alone of his proposal, at all.

Emma is on her best behaviour in this scene, kindly hiding her amusement, trying to be judicious. Harriet casts the piece of sticking plaster into the fire, as the reader must gather from her speech, not from being shown the action: 'there is an end, thank Heaven! of Mr Elton'. But then Emma thinks, 'when will there be a beginning of Mr Churchill?', and that very dear part of Emma, her fancy, gets another outing. About a fortnight later,

> She merely said, in the course of some trivial chat, 'Well, Harriet, whenever you marry I would advise you to do so and so' — and thought no more of it, till after a minute's silence she heard Harriet say in a very serious tone, 'I shall never marry.'
>
> Emma then looked up, and immediately saw how it was; and after a moment's debate, as to whether it should pass unnoticed or not, replied, 'Never marry! — This is a new resolution.'
>
> 'It is one that I shall never change, however.' (III: 4, 369)

Attention can be addressed as a neurological phenomenon, but it can also be understood, importantly, within an ethical framework. The classic argument for the ethical primacy of attention is Iris Murdoch's essay 'The Idea of Perfection', which is framed as a critique of existentialist conceptions of moral choice. Borrowing from Simone Weil, Murdoch uses the notion of attention 'to express the idea of a just and loving gaze directed upon an individual reality'.[15] She introduces attention as the 'prior word' or precondition for an ethically valid action or choice. 'I can only choose within the world I can "see"', she writes, 'in the moral sense of "see" which implies that clear vision is the result of moral imagination and moral effort.'[16] It is evidently this sense of 'seeing' that is dramatised in the moment when 'Emma then looked up, and immediately saw how it was.' But the idea of attention, even here, cannot be legitimately circumscribed in the visual language or metaphors Murdoch employs. Emma is responding to Harriet's unusual silence and her subsequent 'very serious tone': the trigger for this moment of imaginative identification is aural, not visual. 'Seeing' in this sense is not a state but a movement of the senses, quick and immediate and (as the novel brings out) speedily liable to compromise and usurpation by other human promptings, here the occupation of Emma's mind by her belief in Harriet's attachment to Frank Churchill – which is to mislead her dreadfully. Her 'seeing' in fact, while still an admirable moment of intuitive sympathy, is also comically *not* seeing, because it entails this notion that Harriet must be thinking of Frank.

Another more critical moment of 'seeing' in the sense of focused attention occurs two chapters later at Donwell Abbey, when Emma is approached by Jane Fairfax to help her leave without fuss, and excuse her to the other members of the party. When Emma protests about the heat, Jane pleads, 'The greatest kindness you can show me, will be to let me have my own way, and only say that I am gone when it is necessary.'

> Emma had not another word to oppose. She saw it all; and entering into her feelings, promoted her quitting the house immediately, and watched her safely off with the zeal of a friend. Her parting look was grateful — and her parting words, 'Oh! Miss Woodhouse, the comfort of being sometimes alone!' — seemed to burst from an overcharged heart, and to describe somewhat of the continual endurance to be practised by her, even towards some of those who loved her best.
>
> 'Such a home, indeed! Such an aunt!' said Emma, as she turned back into the hall again. 'I do pity you. And the more sensibility you betray of their just horrors, the more I shall like you.' (III: 6, 394)

In this elevated moment Emma for once beams her whole intelligence towards another subject; for once, and for the crucial moment, relinquishes her prejudices. 'Seeing' Jane's predicament, she can immediately convert this into the benevolent and practical act of attentiveness. But how swiftly the milk of human kindness can curdle into spite, and Emma's feelings about Miss Bates take over. The reader's ensconsement within Emma's consciousness makes palpable the tremulous instability of even the best impulses of sympathetic identification with the other, that intuitive 'seeing it all'.[17] It is the intermittency of human attentiveness to another the novel understands (so that Murdoch's phrase about the 'gaze' would falsify the situation). But because the text itself is stable, re-reading it permits the possession of a mode of attention distinct from that of the heroine Jane Austen has created, a kind of heightened ethical consciousness, similar to the focused loving knowledge which the philosopher can name but not, within philosophic discourse, really describe.

The word is given ten definitions in Samuel Johnson's *Dictionary* of 1755, but two strands of meaning of this term and its cognates can be distinguished in *Emma*. The first has little to do with hearing. 'There is nobody half so attentive and civil as you are', Mr Woodhouse tells Emma. 'If any thing you are too attentive. The muffin last night — if it had been handed round once, I think it would have been enough' (II: 3, 183). Unlike gift-giving in *Mansfield Park*, discussed in the last chapter, such attention, though it is obviously a form of social patronage, is depicted in *Emma* as benign. To attend to someone – to send hind quarters of pork or baskets of apples, or to make your carriage available to the less well-off in the winter – is understood as the very stuff of civilised intercourse within this genteel community. Attention is clearly endued with ethical as well as psychological meaning in this register, for to attend to another person is to have had the moral imagination to anticipate their needs. Even Mr Elton attends to Mrs Bates, by ensuring she has a front pew in church. It is obvious, though, that social inequalities can be exploited in the guise of attentiveness, and it becomes for Mrs Elton an opportunity for domination. The Eltons apparently just forget to bring the Miss Bates and Jane to the ball (III: 2, 347). Emma thinks of this as a 'slight' mistake, but it is not one that any other genteel family in Highbury would be likely to make.

A variation on the term is the specific 'attention' of a lover, or would-be lover. 'His attentions were always — ' Fanny Price is forced to tell her uncle about Crawford, 'what I did not like' (*MP* III: 1, 365). In *Emma*, this meaning of attention is given a thorough workout in the chapters following the revelation of Frank and Jane's engagement. Emma at first tells Mrs Weston that 'no such effect has followed [Frank's] attentions to me, as you are apprehensive of', but soon allows herself to get indignant about his 'persevering attention', his 'repeated attentions' that, intended to pull the wool over everyone's eyes, might have made her fall for him

(III: 10, 431–2). Through this means Austen is suggesting that 'attention' is not necessarily an ethical act, or even an attentive one.

The more foundational meaning continually operates in *Emma*. This form of attention might be described as the focalisation of consciousness: it is the first sense Johnson gives, and he defines it as 'paying heed'. One can attend to a task, like 'deedily' fixing the rivet in an old lady's pair of spectacles. But paying heed, especially to another person, draws (as the idiom of 'paying' might suggest) on some form of energy, or mental concentration, which at the same time requires the neglect of other signals to which one does not pay heed. Attention, in this register, as William James long ago pointed out, is premised upon comparative inattention to other things, and is by definition selective: 'It implies withdrawal from some things in order to deal with others.'[18] Buzzing with ideas and schemes, 'Too eager and busy with her own preconceptions and views, to hear him impartially, or see him with clear vision' (I: 13, 118), Emma fails to notice what Mr Elton is about, just as her preoccupation with more ingenious conceptions leads her to miss her later opportunities to detect that something is going on between Jane Fairfax and Frank Churchill. But Jane Austen's phrases acknowledge that attention, in this register also, has a moral as well as a psychological implication. To attend to another person's demeanour or behaviour carefully requires the momentary suspension of ego-driven imagination or fancy.

At the Coles' 'rather large' dinner party, Emma finds Frank Churchill seated next to her, and the group being 'too numerous for any subject of conversation to be general', 'Emma could fairly surrender all her attention to the pleasantness of her neighbour'. But 'the first remote sound' she feels herself 'obliged to attend' to is when the name of Jane Fairfax is mentioned: although she is actively engaged in conversation with Frank, seated beside her, she cannot but respond to the signal, or stimulus, of Jane's name. A neurologist might classify this as 'exogenous orienting'.[19] Mrs Cole is talking of Miss Fairfax and the piano. Emma 'listened, and found it well worth listening to. That very dear part of Emma, her fancy, received an amusing supply' (II: 8, 231–2). In this instance, Emma does not passively overhear: she actively orients, or focuses, her alert mind on the 'remote' talk, and the text follows her, foregrounding and reporting Mrs Coles' gossip for a page and a half. What is supplied to Emma's fancy is supplied to the reader's fancy too, through the narrative's own shift of attention, and augmented in the next few pages in which Emma enjoys sharing her speculations about Jane Fairfax and the pianoforte with Frank and Frank enjoys leading her on.

Frank is discovering that Emma's suspicions about Mr Dixon are a useful way of deflecting this shrewd young woman's attention from the truth. His stay in Highbury has its dangers. He has come because he wants to see as much of Jane as possible, but this is difficult to achieve, and no one must suspect that they are engaged. In such a small community, privacy, even of the ordinary sort, is almost impossible (Miss Bates lets drop that she has heard about Miss Woodhouse's mistake over Mr Elton (II: 3, 188)), and made still more difficult in this instance because Emma has already deduced that something other than a resort to the healthy air of Highbury must be behind Jane's stay. In this setting where glances are noticed, and everything risks being overheard, Frank has to adopt some cunning manoeuvres. The word itself derived from the tactical or strategic movement of forces in battle or at sea. By 1815 it had acquired its more modern meaning of 'an ingenious expedient or artifice', as the OED puts it. Frank Churchill's adroit management of his opportunities unites both meanings of the word. These very often take the form of actual physical movement, the management of space to his advantage. Here as elsewhere the physical settings of the novel, the arrangements of rooms, and the characters' changing places within them become agents in its uncovering or display of the phenomenology and moral import of attending.

A few pages later, after dinner, Emma finds herself obliged to turn away from Frank and listen to Mr Cole. When 'her attention could be restored as before, she saw Frank Churchill looking intently across the room at Miss Fairfax, who was sitting exactly opposite'. Caught out, for once, Frank invents an excuse to go up to Jane, but conceals his conversation with her and her reactions, to Emma's annoyance, by standing 'exactly between them, exactly in front of Miss Fairfax', so that she can 'absolutely distinguish nothing' (II: 8, 240). The narrative shifts then to Emma's dialogue with Mrs Weston, who has got it into her head that Mr Knightley might be interested in Jane. They are interrupted by a 'little bustle in the room', the Coles' proud new possession, the grand pianoforte, is opened, and they then find

> at the same moment Mr Cole approaching to entreat Miss Woodhouse would do them the honour of trying it. Frank Churchill, of whom, in the eagerness of her conversation with Mrs Weston, she had been seeing nothing, except that he had found a seat by Miss Fairfax, followed Mr Cole, to add his very pressing entreaties; and as, in every respect, it suited Emma best to lead, she gave a very proper compliance. (II: 8, 245)

This miniature example demonstrates how the novel controls the reader's own perception. The bit of information that Frank 'had found a seat by

Miss Fairfax' (the formal and notional 'Miss Fairfax', not 'Jane') is slipped into a sentence shaped as if to appear to reaffirm Frank's courtship of Emma. It is Frank's movement across to her that the sentence follows and engages with, until it settles, with complacent satisfaction, on Emma. Her enjoyable egoism, her gratification in being the centre of attention, is offered as a readerly pleasure, in this instance of Austen's narrative dexterity, and thus actively diverts one from picking up a clue that has nevertheless been presented. The sentence itself is shaped to mimic what has been on the peripheries of Emma's visual field.

Having moved away from Jane to sing with Emma, knowing that she will be graciously flattered, Frank has neatly prepared the grounds for singing with Jane next, and after she has entertained the company, Emma moves 'at a little distance from the numbers round the instrument to listen' to them:

> But the sight of Mr Knightley among the most attentive, soon drew away half Emma's mind; and she fell into a train of thinking on the subject of Mrs Weston's suspicions, to which the sweet sounds of the united voices gave only momentary interruptions. Her objections to Mr Knightley's marrying did not in the least subside. She could see nothing but evil in it. (II: 8, 245–6)

Disturbed, she knows not why, by Mrs Weston's suggestion that Mr Knightley might be attracted to Jane, Emma does not attend to the singers, as she notices that Mr Knightley does. She is once again aware of Knightley's physical presence. Preoccupied with her own thoughts about him, she overhears only in snatches, though the 'united voices' gives a momentary hint of something beyond her ken. In such incidents Jane Austen thus stages the simultaneous co-presence of two romantic narratives, interlocking with each other. There are not two simultaneous exchanges, as in *Troilus*, but the focus on differing levels of attention, and its concomitant fragmentary overhearing in *Emma* enables Jane Austen not only to narrate the two strands of her plot concurrently, but also through syntactical means to evoke the physical setting in which such overhearing can plausibly take place. Dancing is next proposed ('originating nobody knew exactly where'!) which will allow Frank to dance with Jane, but (of course) he leads Emma into the first two dances. After this, though, Mr Knightley gets the whole thing called off. The chapter soon ends, with Frank assiduously attending Emma to her carriage and keeping up his deception: 'I must have asked Miss Fairfax, and her languid dancing would not have agreed with me after your's.' The novelist is manoeuvring too, using this conclusion to acknowledge, while disguising, the fact that he has missed out on the chance of a few minutes' private talk with Jane.

To say that someone is 'a reader of Jane Austen', or especially of *Emma*, is to imply a multiple personality. Such a reader incorporates the first-time reader, deceived about what is going on, and the second or umpteenth reader who with successive readings enjoys more of the pleasure of the text, which has much to do with detecting and knowing, and much with the pleasure of being deceived. This reader revisits the ignorance of their first reading and at the same time savours their subsequent enlightenment. The narrative excitement of *Emma* has much to do with this teasing of the reader's attention. One is invited both to perform deductive and inferential mental activity and at the same time to detect the narrative's blocking, or at least of waylaying, it. And at different readings the ratio between detection and enjoyment will alter. Chapter 9 in Volume II, which takes place the very next day after the party at the Coles, is a wonderful instance of the narrative clearly charting, but simultaneously disguising, what it offers, a virtuoso textual incident, or rather narrative coup, about overhearing.

Emma's attention is both coupled with and played against the reader's. The Bateses, mother and daughter, have come down in the world: they live 'in a very small way' (I: 3, 20) in rooms on the second floor of what is apparently an old house on the main street. Downstairs, the maid-of-all-work, Patty, answers the door and does the cooking. Emma and Harriet meet Mrs Weston and Frank Churchill, who are on their way to visit the Bateses, outside Ford's drapery. Harriet dilly-dallies in the shop, but it is not long before Miss Bates herself, accompanied by Mrs Weston, arrives to invite Emma to step in and see this new pianoforte that has so surprisingly arrived for Jane Fairfax. Miss Bates talks all the way there, until the party ascends the stairs to her dwelling, still 'pursued only by the sounds of her desultory good-will': 'Pray take care, Mrs Weston, there is a step at the turning. Pray take care, Miss Woodhouse, ours is rather a dark staircase — rather darker and narrower than one could wish. Miss Smith, pray take care. Miss Woodhouse, I am quite concerned, I am sure you hit your foot. Miss Smith, the step at the turning' (II: 9, 258). This is at the end of Chapter 9. Chapter 10, which opens on the next page in many editions, begins:

> THE appearance of the little sitting-room as they entered, was tranquillity itself; Mrs Bates, deprived of her usual employment, slumbering on one side of the fire, Frank Churchill, at a table near her, most deedily occupied about her spectacles, and Jane Fairfax, standing with her back to them, intent on her pianoforté. (II: 10, 259)

This tableau is designed to deceive Emma and the reader, who at this moment perceives the scene through Emma's eyes. But Frank and Jane have overheard the party coming up the stairs, and the sound of Miss Bates calling to her guests; they have heard also that Emma, twice mentioned, is among them. So they have just time to break away from each other and to take up these positions, though Jane's back being turned suggests that she needs a little more time than Frank to recover – perhaps from his embraces – or to deceive, as he does, with aplomb. Emma certainly senses that she is nervous.

The identification of the reader with Emma – even the reader who has enjoyed the scene more times than he or she remembers – is achieved by the mimicking of these small events through management of his or her attention. The little movement that is created by the shift of the reading eyes across from the end of one chapter, through the break, through the new chapter heading, to the resumption of the text, replicates the movement up the staircase, through the turn, and into the parlour where the characters are performing in that space. The brief time this takes also mimics in miniature the pause, the few moments of warning that gives the lovers time to adopt their apparently innocent positions. 'Till you were on the stairs,' Miss Bates declares to Emma later, when she pays her visit of contrition after Box Hill, 'we did not know any body was coming' (III: 8, 413). Here, thanks to her attentiveness to her guests, the lovers upstairs, Frank and Jane, who have been able to enjoy a few minutes together while old Mrs Bates is blinded and dozing, are warned. The reader, at once seeing through Emma's eyes, and hearing with her ears, partaking of her deception, partakes at the same time in the pleasure of her being deceived.

In this very scene, Frank manages to communicate to Jane a different meaning from the one Emma evidently hears. 'I believe you were glad we danced no longer', he says, referring to the previous evening, 'but I would have given worlds — all the worlds one ever has to give — for another half hour' (II: 10, 261). One must assume that Emma hears this, but she does not pay attention to it. Since Frank, on attending her to her carriage, has told her he is glad he didn't have to stand up with that languid Miss Fairfax, she has been plausibly deflected from understanding Frank's meaning, though he risks alerting her with his extravagant and lover-like phrasing. The subsequent two-word paragraph is: 'She played.' This gives Jane's answer, and a dialogue between lovers has taken place in Emma's presence without her being aware. Frank quickly resumes his deception with a mention of Weymouth that makes Jane blush: Emma knows what to think of *that*. Jane Austen's own exuberant skill in manipulating this interplay of hearing but not hearing, overhearing and not attending, is crowned when at the end of this short chapter she offers an instance of her motif to the reader on a plate. With everyone present in her parlour, Miss Bates withdraws into the next room to conduct a private conversation with Mr Knightley through the window, every word of which is narrated for the reader and – as Jane Fairfax tells her, perhaps bitterly – overheard by the party in the adjoining chamber (ii: 10, 265).

From a technical point of view, overhearing also enables Jane Austen to present at length Mrs Elton's remorseless harassment of Jane Fairfax without breaking the reader's assumption of Emma's viewpoint. In Emma's own drawing-room, Mrs Elton hogs Jane's attention and ignores her hostess:

> though much that passed between them was in a half-whisper, especially on Mrs Elton's side, there was no avoiding a knowledge of their principal subjects: — The post-office — catching cold — fetching letters — and friendship, were long under discussion; and to them succeeded one, which must be equally unpleasant to Jane — inquiries whether she had yet heard of any situation likely to suit her, and professions of Mrs Elton's meditated activity. (ii: 17, 323)

The comparatively restrained nature of these comments reflects Emma's sense of her duty as hostess, but they offer an excuse for the narrative to soon continue this overheard conversation in full over four pages. It includes Jane's firm rebuttal of Mrs Elton's offers to find her a job. 'When I am quite determined as to the time, I am not at all afraid of being long unemployed. There are places in town, where inquiry would soon produce something – offices for the sale — not quite of human flesh — but of human intellect.' Mrs Elton professes to be horrified at what she interprets as 'a fling at the slave trade' (coming from Bristol, which thrived on the trade, this is a sore spot). Jane's remarks suddenly increase the temperature of their communication. The violence that 'human flesh' brings into the conversation reads as a displaced expression of her exasperation and anguish at Mrs Elton's persistence in confronting her with a future she hopes to avoid. Mrs Elton's bullying is the exercise of power over a social inferior that is giving her a foretaste of the treatment she can look forward to as a governess (ii: 17, 325). Emma disappears from the narrative during this extended exchange. Austen has engaged the reader within Emma's consciousness for almost two volumes, so it's natural to assume that she overhears it.

Chapter 2 in the third volume relates events during another communal activity, the ball at the Crown Inn. Jane Austen carefully charts her characters' positions and movements relative to each other, with the consequent possibilities of overhearing. Frank, for instance, though 'by no means moving slowly' in his eagerness to meet the carriage carrying Jane, is compelled to overhear Mrs Elton's praise of his appearance (III: 2, 347). When Miss Bates finishes speaking, Emma is positioned again where 'she found herself necessarily overhearing the discourse of Mrs Elton and Miss Fairfax, who were standing a little way behind her. Whether [Frank] were overhearing too, she could not determine' (III: 2, 350). Mrs Elton's talk is then displayed in the text, and Frank, who evidently does hear Mrs Elton, begins talking vigorously to drown her out (though what he actually says is left out). 'How do you like Mrs Elton?' Emma says to him. Even more adroitly, as the ball proceeds, Emma 'half way up the set' of the dance finds herself in a spot from where the group in which Mr Elton stands is 'exactly behind her'. Although she does not allow herself to turn to watch 'any more of his display of contempt for Harriet, she can overhear 'every syllable' of Elton's conversation with Mrs Weston, and his rude refusal of her suggestion that he might dance with Harriet (III: 2, 354). Difficult to convey in a summary, the whole chapter is an extraordinarily choreographed evocation of figures in a crowded room moving in and out of each other's earshot. It generates a compelling sense of the pressure of different lives and preoccupations on each other, of a group of people interacting with each other within the confines of the not especially large public room of an inn.

Unusually for Jane Austen, the next two occasions on which her cast of figures is assembled take place out of doors – at Donwell Abbey (III: 6) and at Box Hill the very next day (III: 7). At the Crown Inn, the Highbury and neighbouring gentry arrive to share a rare treat, a dance; at Donwell, Austen's characters have come together for the purpose of gathering ripe strawberries, and the whole outing is under the aegis and management of Mr Knightley, while Frank Churchill is absent for most of the chapter. At Donwell, with Frank away, Emma is calm, gratified by her connection to the estate, and the bravura passage which represents Mrs Elton's discourse as a broken-up series of abbreviated and disconnected remarks may well represent, as with the earlier conversation with Jane, Emma's careless, perhaps contemptuous, inattention as she overhears snatches. Emma has that moment when she relinquishes her prejudice against Jane. But on the unhappy picnic excursion to Box Hill, nine main characters – Emma and Harriet, Miss Bates and Jane Fairfax, the Eltons, Frank Churchill, Mr Weston and Mr Knightley – are assembled, and the calming, ameliorative Mrs Weston stays behind. And there is no real reason for them to be there, or to be together.

As with Jane's unusually frank plea to Emma at Donwell, it is generally, as I have suggested, the outdoors that offers Austen's characters the opportunity for free and unfettered communication. It's in the garden that Elizabeth Bennet and Lady Catherine can speak frankly to each other, and lovers propose, without fear of being overheard. But the chapter about the picnic expedition to Box Hill offers a kind of perversion of these open-air scenes. Here both the pseudo-lovers, Frank and Emma, and the real lovers, Frank and Jane, converse outdoors with each other, but both exchanges in their different ways are distorted by being staged before a gathering so tight-knit that it might as well be a strange parody of the constraining conditions of Jane Austen's rooms. Frank and Emma's flirtation is performed; Frank and Jane's exchange is warped by the necessity of meeting two demands at once – urgent private converse and plausible public discourse. Frank's wild rebellion against Emma's caution ('lowering her voice'), 'Let every body on the Hill hear me if they can. Let my accents swell to Mickleham on one side, and Dorking on the other' (III: 7, 400), implicitly conjures up the walls of the invisible chamber that surrounds and holds them in.

What then happens at Box Hill is usefully illuminated by the psycho-analyst Wilfred Bion's now famous theory of group behaviour. Bion (1897–1979) argued that in many gatherings, two modes of grouping are present, that he called the 'work group' and the 'basic assumption group'.[20] People may come together to share a task or purpose (which could, for example, be a dance, or even strawberry-picking), and so long as that unites the personnel, rational levels or styles of conduct and co-operation predominate among them: this is the work group. But such rational and co-operative organisation, he argued, is continuously threatened with collapse into other styles of behaviour in which its members divide among themselves and revert to atavistic, childish modes. This is the basic assumption group, of which he distinguished three types. Bion was extrapolating from the Austrian analyst Melanie Klein's foundational theories of infant psychological development, in which the earliest state, which she eventually called the 'paranoid-schizoid position', evolved later into the 'depressive position'.[21] The 'paranoid-schizoid position' denotes the condition in which the infant being cannot recognise that others exist in their wholeness, and feels and acts as if nothing in the entire world exists but itself. The 'depressive position' was more helpfully called 'the capacity for concern' by the British analyst, Donald Winnicott.[22] This is the critical development during its first two years when the child becomes able to attend to the feelings of others as separate from itself. An important aspect of the theory is that both 'positions' remain within the normally functioning adult self, with the (more or less insane) paranoid-schizoid one latent and often threatening the other. Bion's 'basic assumptions' break down this earlier 'position' into different styles of behaviour in a dysfunctional adult group. It is dangerous for a number of persons to be brought together with no purpose, and no guide, to unite them, for this creates the conditions for reversion to childishness.

Where is the 'work' to be done at Box Hill? There is simply nothing much to do once the party has got there. Mrs Elton's ludicrous remark 'I am really tired of exploring so long on one spot' inadvertently hits the nail on the head. They have arrived at this famous tourist destination, and that's it. Besides, the group is full of hidden tensions: Miss Woodhouse and Mrs Elton dislike each other intensely; Frank and Jane have quarrelled the day before; Mr Knightley is suspicious and jealous of Frank; Frank hates Mrs Elton and resents Knightley, who has twice prevented him from talking to Jane. Most of them are unaware of the depth of these tensions. Mr Weston, Miss Bates and Harriet are simply out for a nice time. Emma quickly senses that there was 'a want of union, which could not be got over' (III: 7, 399).

In the absence of purpose or aim, or any form of task, nothing can bridge these divisions – nothing strong enough to hold the party's members to the level of sensible, adult functioning. And there is no one with the authority to lead or hold the group together; Mr Weston ought to be this person, but he has no particular purpose, assuming that they all like each other and that this is enough. So without work, without leadership, the party disintegrates and tends to revert to infantile modes, irrational, aberrant and almost crazy activities, almost, it seems, helplessly a prey to them. Frank and Emma flirt, or appear to, though neither of them believes in it: Emma is 'not gay and thoughtless from any real felicity'; she finds herself pretending to be gay because actually she is unhappy. Frank's fake high spirits reach a more or less hysterical pitch as they perform flirtatious dialogue in front of the others and he yells out 'I saw you first in February' to be heard all over the hillside. As if this wasn't childish enough, he then drops into conspiratorial whispering with Emma – whispering that the rest can hear and are meant to hear. Jane Fairfax's reactions to his behaviour are left to be guessed at. This leads to his proposal that the others entertain Emma with 'one thing very clever . . . or two things moderately clever — or three things very dull indeed', and poor Miss Bates falls into the trap (III: 7, 403).

When a gathering degenerates to this stage, Bion's types of 'basic assumption group' have come into play, and two of them are discernable in this chapter: those he called the 'pairing group' and the 'flight–fight' group. 'Pairing' denotes the splitting of the gathering into separate parties. Pairing is obvious enough in Emma and Frank's case, but also in the Eltons': these pairs assert themselves in opposition to the rest of the group. In 'fight–flight' the rational or sensible domain collapses into warfare, and individuals demonise others or, most commonly, seek out and verbally attack each other as scapegoats. Emma, herself a victim to the tensions crossing the group, finds herself picking on its weakest member: 'Emma could not resist.' Something other than her own adult conscious self is compelling her, and under the cover of polite demeanour she expresses her unhappiness and levels her charge at Miss Bates. 'Pardon me — but you will be limited as to number – only three at once.' Even when you have read the scene a dozen times, this still gives you a nasty shock. It seems as if a pit has opened beneath civilised manners, exposing something that has been hidden under the coherent kindly world the novel depicts. If anything, the ghastly, maladroit cover-up by Mr Weston and his son that follows makes it worse.

The effect of the four pages that culminate in this collapse of gentility into brutality is to relegate the narrative thread of Frank and Jane to the edge of the reader's attention. Thus the writer, who has tracked Emma's attention, at the same time controls the reader's. The Eltons stomp off, Jane declines to accompany them and now Frank Churchill's aberrant behaviour is resumed at an even higher pitch of disturbance. Frank has specialised in communicating privately to Jane within the exigent circumstances of crowded rooms and confined society. He has found many ingenious stratagems, including the gift of the piano, to mark his love, and even to display it, in ways that no one else but Jane Fairfax would understand. Often, as when he talked about dancing, he has spoken in a 'double-voiced' mode, or, in other words, he has communicated two distinct meanings within his speech: one for general consumption or hearing, and one for the object of his love, Jane. His display of false gallantry with Miss Woodhouse in this scene is a malign variation: he is pretending to be entertaining while at the same time doing his best to wound Jane. Like Emma, he has found a scapegoat for his frustration and accumulated tensions. With the Eltons gone, Frank again directs his speech to Jane while seeming to address the group. His blunt sarcasms about the Eltons ('Happy couple! ... How well they suit one another! Very lucky – marrying as they did, upon an acquaintance formed only in a public place!') are recklessly impolite, given that Miss Bates, Mr Knightley and Mr Weston are among his hearers, and equally recklessly pitched at Jane. 'How many a man has committed himself on a short acquaintance, and rued it all the rest of his life!' he tells her (III: 7, 405).

Though she has 'seldom rarely spoken before' (and not once in the textual record of events), Jane now answers him, but also as if she were continuing conversation in general terms. It must be understood that Emma, being close by, hears her speech, but there is no specific anchoring of the dramatised material to her overhearing. Emma is not interested, and that encourages a reader also to pass over the dialogue without much attention. 'Such things do occur undoubtedly', Jane begins, but is forced to stop by a cough. This acts as a punctuation device, which, together with Frank's 'grave' request to her to continue, hints at the meaningfulness of Jane's subsequent speech. For the first time in the novel, she breaks a rule, avails herself of Frank's stratagem and communicates a private meaning to him in a public setting. Their roles are here reversed, and in measured language she gives her response to his signals in terms that might pass over the heads of the others present. The narrator does not say so, but it is evident that she struggles for calm as she repudiates their engagement: 'I would be understood to mean, that it can be only weak, irresolute characters, (whose happiness must be always at the mercy of chance,) who will suffer an unfortunate acquaintance to be an inconvenience, an oppression for ever' (III: 7, 405–6). Frank greets this in silence, but he gets the message, and then defiantly resumes his hectic gallantry with Emma and talks of going abroad – claiming to resume the plan that was discarded when he first met and fell in love with Jane. Just to rub salt in Jane's wound, he commissions Emma to educate a wife for him. The narrative can then return for a brief paragraph to Emma with her comical assumption that he must mean Harriet. No one understands what is happening in front of their eyes, or rather what it is they are hearing.

The effect of the pages that display Emma and Frank's falsely happy dialogue and culminate in Emma's cruelty to Miss Bates ('How could she have been so brutal, so cruel to Miss Bates!' she is to wonder later (III: 7, 409)) is to obscure the conflict between the genuine lovers and the fact that Jane is suggesting that she wants to break off their engagement. Even though this is as dramatic a crisis as the novel holds, the resumption of Frank's strident gaiety and Emma's conceited reception of his remarks push the real lovers' dialogue once again into the background of the reader's attention. But more especially, the aftershock of Emma's nasty little joke at Miss Bates' expense is still reverberating. Mr Knightley's solemn and painful reprimand to Emma then picks up that dominant strand of the narrative, opens and cauterises the wound that Emma has inflicted on herself as much as on Miss Bates, and makes Emma cry, and the drama that climaxes Frank and Jane's own story still remains not fully acknowledged, or acknowledgeable, even, I think, by a re-reader. Emma's unprocessed hostility has erupted into such a gross transgression of polite demeanour that the debacle still remains in the reader's consciousness. Her slip speaks to the dread everyone has of the moments when what you have never allowed yourself to acknowledge somehow gets said.

Later, when the news of the engagement gets out, Emma takes herself to task for her behaviour on this occasion. Jane must have seen her 'as a perpetual enemy'. Frank, Jane and herself, she thinks, 'never could have been all three together, without her having stabbed Jane Fairfax's peace in a thousand instances; and on Box Hill, perhaps, it had been the agony of a mind that would bear no more' (III: 12, 459). Retrospectively, Emma understands that her flirtation with Frank has been the last straw that leads Jane to write her acceptance of the governess position to Mrs Suckling that very evening. But it is seemingly never disclosed to Emma that Jane's agony has resulted in her virtually breaking off the engagement in front of her. This scene set on a quiet hill in Surrey is a far cry from *Troilus and Cressida*, or from theatrical technique, but here Jane Austen again plaits together and simultaneously engages her reader with two distinct and equally compelling dramatic interchanges. Forced to congregate together, though wanting to be apart, everyone overhears everyone else, but the stabs and wounds pass unnoticed.

There are no further communal gatherings in *Emma*, and little need or opportunity for overhearing. Instead, the confinements of the indoors are given their dramatic apotheosis in this chapter (III: 12) in which Emma, boxed in with her complaining father on a blustery, cold, unseasonable and long evening in July, is left to work over her regrets. In the end, 'She was not able to refrain from a start, or a heavy sigh, or even from walking about the room for a few minutes' – tiny touches that register, that make palpable, the psychological tax of the confined room, the confined world, of which she now knows herself to be the denizen. Next day, in better spirits, she walks out and finds Mr Knightley unexpectedly passing through the 'garden door' and coming towards her (III: 13, 162). In the following scene, quiet tones of voice, and gestures, upon which so much here depends, are defined with an unusual precision for Jane Austen. This matches the tentative care with which, ambling through the undescribed garden, they approach each other. Emma now catches Knightley speaking 'in a tone of great sensibility', as he draws her arm within his, and then, 'speaking low', she overhears him 'in a more broken and subdued accent' murmuring his commiseration to her for the loss of Frank (III: 13, 464). The capacity of lovers to pick up the tones of each other's voice is an anticipation of a motif to become critical in *Persuasion*.

When Emma calls in at the Bateses to show her solidarity with Jane and offer her congratulations, and finds Mrs Elton already on the throne of Highbury, there is a moment when the tenuousness of privacy that has engrossed so much of *Emma* is given a last parodic twist in an instance of overhearing. Mrs Elton, not content with whispering to Miss Fairfax when Emma is also present in the tiny sitting-room, tells Jane that Mr Elton is shortly to arrive 'On a congratulatory visit, you know — Oh, yes, quite indispensible', Mr Elton supposedly now about to perform a last act of patronising attention. This is said by Mrs Elton while 'putting up her hand to screen her words from Emma'. The real queen of Highbury, who of course is in on the secret and filled now with her own happiness, is delighted at this spectacle, and Austen shares her delight with the reader: 'Miss Bates looked about her, so happily! — ' (III: 16, 497). Thus the motif of overhearing in *Emma* reaches its apogee in something very close to farce.

There can be few novels that dramatise intimate sociability so compellingly as *Emma*. At the same time, the novelist achieves this through the imitation of a single person's viewpoint, her experiential journey through social occasions, encounters and entertainments. The technical ligature between this sense of communal interaction and the experience of a single, busily preoccupied and imaginative individual is overhearing. *Emma* is not only about overhearing and attending: it is also a novel that manages the reader's own attention in extraordinary ways. Channelling the reader's focus through Emma, who both overhears, attends and inattends to so much that she hears, the reader too is impeded in their full attention, and not by their own thoughts and desires, but by the novelist's dexterity and ingenuity. The novel thus requires re-readings to discover – to attend to – what has been occluded through this rendering of solecism in the midst of social experience. *Emma* becomes an education in quite another mode of attention, one that in its ideal form is akin to the high ethical value of the 'seeing' of another individual in their difference. Attending to the thoughts and feelings of another is not a merely intellectual process, and neither is the attentive journey that this novel compels its re-reader to take.

The same device of overhearing plays a major role in *Persuasion*, but to very different effect and to a quite distinct end.

CHAPTER 7

Anne Elliot and the ambient world

'How eloquent could Anne Elliot have been, —' (II: 4, 32). As in these resonant words, *Persuasion* carries a freight of unspoken emotion and memories that remain unrevisited or unrecalled. This is a novel filled, too, with chance occasions, accidents and missed opportunities. But the emotional freight of the merely alluded to or implied, and these fortuitous events and moments, is undergirded by a structure that is strong, consistent and deliberate, and though it lies beneath the novel's obvious narrative, it is as compelling as in any other of Austen's works. While never for a moment relinquishing its commitment to the evocation of transient emotional reality, *Persuasion* has a persuasive agenda.

One of those chance, fortuitous events in *Persuasion* is its heroine's overhearing. This is almost as frequent in *Persuasion* as in *Emma*, but in this novel Jane Austen reveals that it has an aspect hardly touched on in the previous book. Emma Woodhouse's capacity to attend – in the sense of seeing and hearing what is going on about her – is interfered with because her consciousness is so often filled with fancies and schemes, animated by the immediate and the future. Anne Elliot's attention is equally contingent, but so often interfered with because her thoughts are saturated by the past. To put it more precisely, Anne's cognisance of the world about her is impaired for the first half of the novel because she is in that condition which we might now call chronic depression, the consequence of unresolved grief. The psychological motif of her half-hearing is crucial to the novel's implicit structure.

The author of *Persuasion* is interested in the way that depression interferes with the modalities of both hearing and sight. To use the novelist's own term, Anne is often 'self-occupied', without sufficient psychological energy to address or fully register the outside world. *Persuasion* is concerned with such states of self-absorption, internal reverie, introspective musing, half-absence and grieving, and then, in the course of the novel's action, with their gradual alleviation, the returning of the self to occupy the world.

From the very opening of the novel, Anne Elliot is positioned as 'nobody': 'her word had no weight . . . — she was only Anne' (1: 1, 6). Her speech is never listened to, her private feelings never find an auditor. Even conversation with her friend Lady Russell is inhibited by a veritable 'elephant in the room', the unspoken fact of Anne's broken engagement. And, as Ann Gaylin writes, 'The narrative style conspires with the fact that Anne has no listener or confidante except herself (and the reader).'[1] The novelist's technique mirrors the family's neglect. She is the unspeaking 'attentive listener' as the family's prospects are discussed; her contributions are often obliquely indicated, or taken for granted, as if they would be of as little account to the reader as to her sisters and father. When she seeks to make her views about Mrs Clay known, her words are not given, only her sister's long and angry repudiation of her right to make any contribution (1: 5, 37–8). Anne, far more intelligent and cultivated than the people in her imprisoning environment, has an inner life unknown to them.

Even when the story eventually turns towards her in Chapter 4, fully denoting her as the heroine, the writing does not allow her dramatic presence. Anne's point of view is represented, not like Elizabeth Bennet's, Fanny's or Emma's, as transcriptions of her thoughts, but veiled, held at a distance from the reader by the narrator's own sympathetic mediation. Anne might not speak of them, but 'how eloquent, at least, were her wishes on the side of early warm attachment, and a cheerful confidence in futurity, against that over-anxious caution which seems to insult exertion and distrust Providence! — She had been forced into prudence in her youth, she learned romance as she grew older — the natural sequel of an unnatural beginning' (1: 4, 32). Somewhere between character and narrator, these expressions subdue her even as they bring her forward. The Johnsonian echo signalled by 'that' ('that anxious inquietude which is justly chargeable with distrust of heaven')[2] lends an impersonal authority to statements which hover somewhere around the character but cannot be imputed to her. And this recession of Anne in the narrative plane continues in other forms throughout the first volume.

In *Emma*, overhearing implies proximity, but in *Persuasion* it evokes distance – not necessarily physical distance, but separation, emotional isolation intruded upon by others' talk. Anne often just hears patches or fragments of conversations, not only because the speakers are standing or walking a little away from her, but more importantly also because her own feelings impede or intercept the incoming communications. The often-cited moment in which Anne and Wentworth meet again is a telling illustration of this:

In two minutes after Charles's preparation, the others appeared; they were in the drawing-room. Her eye half met Captain Wentworth's; a bow, a curtsey passed; she heard his voice — he talked to Mary; said all that was right; said something to the Miss Musgroves, enough to mark an easy footing: the room seemed full — full of persons and voices — but a few minutes ended it. (1: 7, 64)

This is a convincing rendering of a reaction that might be named simply in Austen's earlier novels as 'confusion', meaning more or less what a modern reader would understand by the term 'embarrassment', though both words by themselves don't convey much. Elizabeth Bennet is herself embarrassed, 'astonished and confused' when she encounters Mr Darcy again so unexpectedly at Pemberley, and can scarcely lift her eyes to his face (*P&P* III: 1, 278). That reaction is telling enough, but in *Persuasion* the experience of confusion in all its uncannyness – the incapacity to respond normally, the disabling of avenues of attachment to the world, the failures of ordinary perception – is made palpable through small punctuation devices in a prose that otherwise employs only the simplest vocabulary. The recurrent semicolons enact the impeded flow of attention, the dashes mimic lapses of focus, the repetitions, the struggle to recuperate, to hold on to something palpable in the experienced world. In fact this is more than embarrassment: it is a plunge into the nether state of suppressed feelings, or what Mary Favret has called 'physiological vertigo'.[3] 'Mary talked, but she was unable to attend', the novelist writes of Anne a moment later, after Wentworth has gone. Anne may hear, she may see, but these avenues of perception are hostage to her nerves, and it is through the impeding itself that the reader is allowed some knowledge of these dormant aspects of her selfhood.

Though not in this instance, overhearing usually requires some small distance between speakers and overhearer, and through this trope Jane Austen conveys Anne's self-immolation. Anne has put up with the Musgrove family 'talking so much of Captain Wentworth, repeating his name so often' well before he actually appears in the narrative, her own memories, it is left to be understood, debarring her from the conversation (1: 6, 55). In the carefully choreographed interior scene in the Uppercross drawing-room (II: 8), among a larger than usual group, as it includes the Hayter sisters, and is a 'merry, joyous party', some way apart from the main cluster of folk, Anne is sitting on a sofa beside Mrs Musgrove. She comforts her in her revived grief for her son, and then must listen when, coming over and sitting down with them, Wentworth consoles the mother 'in a low voice'. She is so attuned to his inflections that she can hear and recognise how much consideration, 'sympathy and natural grace' he brings to the task of assuaging a grief that is surely less poignant than hers, but it is again left to the reader to make this reflection (1: 8, 73).

Anne Elliot is the most cultivated of Jane Austen's heroines, and the only one whose facility in a foreign language is mentioned. Austen is interested in *Persuasion* not merely in emphasising the importance of serious reading to an educated selfhood, as she implies in all her published novels, but in exploring, more explicitly than anywhere else, how far reading and memory, or music and musicianship, are an emotional safeguard. The novel's treatment of Anne's cultural capital amounts to the question: 'Yes, but how far do these resources stretch?' Perhaps they might cushion, or sublimate, the wounds of the world, the assaults of everyday life, but isn't this, when you come down to the wire, a pretty frail defence? So that within *Persuasion*, implicitly and on one occasion close to explicitly, Austen poses the question that was put by the young Prince to the stoic philosopher in Johnson's *Rasselas* (1759): 'Has wisdom no strength to arm the heart against calamity?'[4] The Prince is rebuking the philosopher for grieving so keenly over the loss of his daughter. But the older man has an irrefutable reply: 'What comfort, said the mourner, can truth and reason afford me?' This question, and its response, is one that the novel takes seriously enough for it to be addressed, and perhaps alluded to, in the conversation in which Anne advises Benwick about strategies to deal with grief, and then wonders whether she's taken her own advice (1: 11), and to reverberate even in the famous scene that is the novel's romantic resolution.

When this informal gathering at the Musgroves ends with dancing, Anne offers her services as pianist. Her role as accompanist within the family has already been established, amid 'the talking, laughing and singing of their daughters'. But Anne's ability to play the piano is more or less a poisoned fruit: it lends her occupation and independence – a role – but at the same time it isolates her with memories, which are glancingly evoked for one of the few times in the novel: 'excepting one short period of her life, she had never, since the age of fourteen, never since the loss of her dear mother, known the happiness of being listened to, or encouraged by any just appreciation or real taste' (1: 6, 50). 'One short period of her life' is slipped into the sentence, with the miniscule pause before the repeated 'never' (which a lesser writer might have written 'never, never') giving the reader a momentary glimpse of her past happiness with Wentworth, and suggesting the depressive process by which one re-experienced grief drags another in its train. And Anne's isolation is accompanied by feeling that she is, even at the Musgroves, within a family environment, however kindly, that can offer her no support, no outward venue through which to express or dissipate her grief.

Then when Wentworth reappears, Anne, again consigning herself to the bitter-sweet consolation of the pianist's role, becomes besieged by grief and self-wounding.[5] She is not saved or secured by the position she assumes, for the dancing around her, like the seasons that parodically 'revolve' about her elder sister in the novel's first chapter, only emphasise the hollowness of her isolation. Wentworth enjoys himself with the young ladies. They re-enact the delight that Anne herself had in his company. '*Once* she felt that he was looking at herself — observing her altered features, perhaps, trying to trace in them the ruins of the face which had once charmed him; and *once* she knew that he must have spoken of her; – she was hardly aware of it, till she heard the answer' (1: 8, 77–8). This is once again fragmented attention, hearing filtered not only by physical distance, but also by the listener's internal mood. Here is depression speaking: attributing to the external world that which most hurts and disables the self ('*once*'), and without the energy to find rescue in attending to its reality. But it suggests, in the most tentative way possible, that Wentworth might be more interested in her than either of them can allow.

Chapter 10 of the first volume of *Persuasion* is devoted to the walk to Winthrop, on a very fine November day. Everyone comes along: the Musgrove sisters, Anne and Mary, Charles Musgrove and Captain Wentworth. 'Anne's object was not to be in the way of any body': this is diplomacy, yes, but also self-abasement. She tries to occupy her mind by repeating to herself fragments of poetry, 'but it was not possible, that when within reach of Captain Wentworth's conversation with either of the Miss Musgroves, she should not try to hear it', and what she overhears is a dialogue in which Wentworth praises Louisa's enthusiastic pledge that 'if she really loved a man' she would always stay with him, whatever befell them. They are enjoying the pleasures of reciprocal feeling and shared views:

> 'Had you?' cried he, catching the same tone; 'I honour you!' And there was silence between them for a little while.
>
> Anne could not immediately fall into a quotation again. The sweet scenes of autumn were for a while put by — unless some tender sonnet, fraught with the apt analogy of the declining year, with declining happiness, and the images of youth and hope, and spring, all gone together, blessed her memory. (1: 10, 91)

This can sound like indulgence on the narrator's part, collusion with her imagined character's self-pity.[6] But there is more to this narrative tactic than that, for, as Anne lapses into a condition of withdrawal from her own feelings, the writing itself withdraws from any claim to transcribe that inner condition and instead offers its own analogy or synecdoche, its own devolution into cadences of lament and sorrow. 'Blessed', which might sound sentimental, means in effect that remembering poetry might impersonalise Anne's sadness, offer it an anchor somewhere in a shared world. Perhaps 'blessed' also touches the tragic fact that it cannot. Anne indeed 'rouses' herself from the depths to speak, but her isolation is offered back to her when no one answers.

There follows, after an interval, the well-known passage in which Anne, sitting on a stile and hidden from them by the hedgerow, again overhears Wentworth and Louisa talking as they amble about matters that deeply, if indirectly, concern her. Emma Woodhouse never overhears herself spoken of, but in *Persuasion* it is Anne Elliot's fate, and the novelist's contrivance, to overhear herself mentioned all the time. In *Emma* Austen's metamorphosis of the theatrical device of overhearing turned it into the plausible rendering of a natural occurrence of indoor social occasions. This outdoor sequence, with its extended dialogue overheard by a concealed listener, is a reversion to those lime walks and screens behind which eavesdroppers hide on the stage. Later, after Louisa's impetuous jump and fall, 'Anne coming quietly down from Louisa's room, could not but hear what followed, for the parlour door was open', and – waiting on the stairs, it seems – she overhears Wentworth (who speaks of Mary as 'Mrs Charles Musgrove') speak of her fondly as 'Anne' (1: 12, 123). Similarly, coming down to breakfast at Bath she catches Elizabeth whispering to Mrs Clay that she 'is nothing to me, compared with you' (II: 4, 157). These are both more convincing moments than the display of Wentworth and Louisa's dialogue, but that scene certainly embeds the trope of a sitting listener's overhearing within the novel's structure.

It is interesting, though, that while Wentworth later feels that his behaviour to Louisa has in honour committed himself to her, there is nothing in his conversation here that could count as flirting. His remarks, though readily understood as prompted by his personal experience (so that for Anne they carry a sting) are more friendly, even avuncular, than insinuating. Overhearing the dialogue between them, which culminates in Louisa telling Wentworth that Anne refused a proposal from Charles Musgrove (and attributing this to Anne's being too much under the influence of Lady Russell), Anne's emotions are once again left to be guessed at by the reader. She has 'much to recover from', but that is all that is said. As on other occasions, Anne's keeping her thoughts to herself, and the narrator's keeping them from the reader, contributes to a kind of bank, or freight, of painful, unexpressed experience and emotion that the novel accumulates around the character. Jane Austen will not allow Anne inner soliloquies dwelling upon her loss. This is not only because Anne is conceived as a strong and self-controlled figure, but because such long-enduring grief is by its nature inexpressible, a mere everyday burden of sorrow, and because depression is so entrammelled with lassitude that allowing the character to articulate it even to herself would tend to betray the condition. Instead, the narrative finds other means, one of which is Anne's impaired overhearing, together with understatement and indirection, to convey her plight. Anne might have been eloquent, but she never is; Mrs Musgrove can unburden her heart, and receive Wentworth's attention and consolation.

As the isolated, helpless, dependent listener, Anne Elliot is enacting an aspect of her conventional gender position as the superfluous, unentitled spinster. She might also be read as an egregious version of the early nineteenth-century ideal of genteel femininity propagated by pre-Victorian arbiters of social ideals.[7] Her circumstances have assigned to her the usual spinster roles, depicted serially: Anne is by turns confidante, adviser, piano accompanist, baby-sitter and nurse; most frequently of all, the listener, whether preoccupied or attentive. She is powerless, and assumed to be sexless. After all, she is still single at 27. She sits, listening. In contrast – a contrast more marked than in any other of Austen's novels – the hero Wentworth incarnates or models both the masculine role and virility itself. Like all the gentlemen, he travels around on horseback or by carriage, able to go where he pleases, whereas ladies, like Jane Austen herself, must wait until a suitable lift in another's vehicle (or in this book, a passage in his ship) presents itself. Like the other men of his class, too, Wentworth is a sportsman, keen to be taken out shooting with Charles Musgrove. More importantly, he is the bearer of professional identity. Wentworth is the embodiment of that amalgam of the personal life with professional role that Nietzsche defined as a nineteenth-century masculine phenomenon.[8] This tendency for men to take their sense of selfhood from their occupation can be seen in the other novels, from Darcy's acute consciousness of his 'character' as powerful landlord to Edmund Bertram's utter commitment to his vocation as clergyman. The difference between Wentworth and the other men is that his profession, effectively, is his whole life; it provides him not only with a livelihood, but with a circle of male friends and acquaintances, like those that Admiral Croft constantly acknowledges as he walks the streets of Bath, life-long comrades such as

Captain Harville and Benwick, men who have shared the excitements and dangers of his career. And his own professional courage and skill (and in addition, as he candidly acknowledges, good luck) honourably earn him the fortune that creates him a gentleman.

The gender antithesis is made even sharper. Wentworth is the able raconteur, able to set the table on a roar, witty, daring (he does not spare the Admiralty, his employer) and fascinating to his audience. In *Mansfield Park*, William Price's naval adventures were summed in generalities – 'every variety of danger which sea and war together could offer' (*MP* II: 6, 275), but Wentworth's are brought to life through his vivid, expressive narration. Anne's 'shudderings were to herself alone', as Wentworth cheerfully recounts his escapades and lucky breaks. If Anne rarely speaks, he is outspoken. Nor does he hesitate to step in where her relative Charles Hayter is negligent and lift the imperious 2-year-old from Anne's back: in contrast, when her feelings are narrated, they are so confused and embarrassed that she cannot even express her thanks. Physically, too, he is fit, imagined as capable and free as no other of the heroes is, quick to act when needed; at the end of the Winthrop walk, when his sister offers a lift in the gig, he clears the hedge 'in a moment' to mention Anne's name to her (1: 10, 97). His agility and athleticism contrast here with Anne's physical exhaustion, which, like Jane Fairfax's at Donwell Abbey, is of the body but also of the spirit.

This unforeseen kindness from Wentworth agitates Anne so much that when she finds herself in the gig, she cannot focus on the Crofts' conversation, though when she does she is overhearing his name, 'Frederick' (1: 10, 98). Once again, a conversation near her is used to register Anne's incapacity to fully attend, and her responses are 'unconsciously given'. But then her thoughts, for once, are articulated as inner speech: 'Yes – he had done it. She was in the carriage, and felt that he had placed her there, that his will and his hands had done it' (1: 10, 98). The repetition of the three simple words signals Anne's recognition that something very significant has happened, both in his action and her feelings. There are other moments in this novel when knowledge is transmitted through the body, in what Anne has 'felt'.

Anne's relation to the ambient world, then, is shown to be impeded both by her depression and by her marginal status. This is actualised in spatial terms by moments in which she is partly present, and partly not: when she stands just outside doors, or on the stairs adjacent to a room, or sits apart overhearing what others are talking of, able only to partially attend to, or guess, what they are saying. Where people are standing or

sitting, how much distance there is between them, when the men get up
and move: all these are indicators of the novelist's capacity to make
domestic space play a key role in her story. During and after the critical
scene of Louisa's fall at Lyme, and into the second volume, away from her
immediate family, Anne gains more authority and prominence, is shown
to speak more and is given more capacity to take her own life into her
hands. When she defies her father's disapproval and visits her sick friend,
Mrs Smith, in Bath, for example, she is shown as an independent agent,
taking an action that, on a more domestic scale, parallels Wentworth's
decision to visit his disabled and poor comrade, Harville, at Lyme. Most
crucially, she begins to be recognised in different ways, by Wentworth, by
William Elliot, by the Musgroves: she has become no longer merely a
cypher as she is within her own family.

If hearing is often blurred or incapacitated by self-absorption, the
opposite is true, that hearing's acuteness can be amplified by happiness,
emotional arousal or, as the novel has already shown, familiarity with a
speaker's quiet tones. Certainly it is this other aspect of the phenomenology of hearing that begins to be elucidated and presented in the novel's
second half. If receptivity to others is dependent on our emotional state, if
depression and anxiety dampen our hearing, Jane Austen now registers the
way that increased self-esteem and cheerful feelings heighten her heroine's
receptive capacities. A telling example occurs in the octagon rooms at Bath.
Here, amid the crowd but standing next to Wentworth, 'a whispering
between her father and Elizabeth caught her ear' (11: 8, 197), and she
guesses that they are agreeing to acknowledge him. This improves her
spirits, and soon Wentworth begins an intimate conversation with her.
Speaking of Benwick's seeming inconstancy to Fanny Harville, he declares
feelingly, 'A man does not recover from such a devotion of the heart to
such a woman! — He ought not — he does not.' Anne, 'in spite of all the
various noises of the room, the almost ceaseless slam of the door, and
ceaseless buzz of persons walking through, had distinguished every word'
(11: 8, 199). Within a crowded assembly, then, her attentiveness charged by
love, she can pick up everything. 'My ears have not yet drunk a hundred
words/ Of thy tongue's uttering, yet I know the sound', Juliet declares to
Romeo from the balcony, despite the drop below and the darkness that
hides him in the garden.[9] But this is a public room in Bath, and increasingly *Persuasion* threads her estranged lovers' attempts to communicate
privately though the social hubbub of other people's competing lives and
purposes. There is one proleptic moment when the narrative, which,
except for a brief excursion into Wentworth's angry and resentful memory

of Anne Elliot in the seventh chapter, has kept close to her viewpoint, inserts a dialogue that must be overheard, as Ann Gaylin points out, by Wentworth.[10] The ladies of his party in Bath comment on the attractiveness of Mr Elliot and then talk about how much they like Anne, leaving the reader to judge the effect of this exchange on its silent, undenoted, auditor (II: 7, 193). In its painfulness for Wentworth, it would mirror the effect of his own exchange with Louisa on Anne.

This reflection of one character's position in the other's becomes crucial in the novel's final scenes. When Jane Austen wrote her first version of *Persuasion*'s concluding chapters, she presented an episode in which the reiterated trope of Anne's unhappy and partial overhearing is given climactic and even extreme form. In this draft, later discarded, Anne overhears through a door. Because the listening behind a door seems quasi-theatrical, and because Jane Austen, rather than rewriting the chapter, abandoned it altogether, the passage can be more readily dismissed than it deserves. But this first attempt throws considerable light on the determinants of the novel's underlying structure. In the Chapter 10 later cancelled, Anne, on her way to the White Hart, is waylaid by Admiral Croft, who insists that she drop by for a moment to see his wife. She gives in, protesting that she can stay only a few minutes, and he ushers her into the drawing-room saying, 'you will find nobody to disturb you – there is nobody but Frederick here'. He insists on Anne's sitting down. Both Wentworth and Anne are taken aback, though it seems that Anne begins after a few moments to feel that this might be the opportunity they need. This hope is cut short when the Admiral calls Frederick out of the room:

> Here the door was very firmly closed; she could guess by which of the two; and she lost entirely what immediately followed; but it was impossible for her not to hear parts of the rest, for the Adml. on the strength of the Door's being shut was speaking without management of voice, tho' she cd. hear his companion trying in an undertone to check him. – She could not doubt their being speaking of her. She heard her own name & *Kellynch* repeatedly – it agitated her very much. She knew not what to do, or what to expect –.[11]

The text given here is a transcription of Austen's very first thoughts as they appear in the surviving manuscript. 'Hear' was quickly replaced by 'distinguish' and 'in an undertone' deleted. 'It agitated her very much' was crossed out and replaced by 'she was very much distressed'. These small changes may indicate that the author was concerned to get the dynamics of this moment exactly right: 'distinguish' improves on the simple 'hear' because it confirms the filtered, partial aspect of Anne's attention; 'in an undertone' is crossed out because if Wentworth were speaking softly Anne might not be able to catch any of his words. Anne's agitation is replaced by distress, leaving the more intense word for a later description of her reactions.

She is stuck, sitting trapped in the room, made to become the unwilling witness of a dialogue that, despite Wentworth's keeping his voice down, and trying to restrain Admiral Croft's, evidently becomes an altercation between the two men about something to do with her. She fears that Wentworth will go away, leaving her on her own. In the transcription of the Cambridge editors, the next passage reads:

> Then, in a lower tone, Capt. W — seemed remonstrating — wanting to be excused — wanting to put something off. 'Phoo, Phoo — answered the Admiral, now is the time. If *you* will not speak, I will stop & speak myself.' — 'Very well, Sir, very well Sir,' followed with some impatience from his companion, opening the door as he spoke. — 'You will then — you promise you will?' replied the Admiral, in all the power of his natural voice, unbroken even by one thin door. — 'Yes — Sir — Yes.' And the Adm^l was hastily left, the door was closed, and the moment arrived in which Anne was alone with Capt. W—.[12]

The manuscript facsimile now available on the internet shows that Jane Austen also made several small changes to this passage as she wrote.[13] Most interestingly the phrase 'replied the Admiral' is written above cancelled words that read 'met her eye ear'. 'Eye' was apparently cancelled before 'ear' was substituted, and then the whole phrase was struck through and replaced.[14] The phrase 'met her eye' entailed the antecedent subject 'his companion, who opening the door as he spoke', in which 'who' was subsequently cancelled. So the phrase might have run 'his companion, who opening the door as he spoke, met her eye'.

It is as if Austen's incipient idea was that Anne should see Captain Wentworth at this point. But the speech 'You will then – you promise you will?', continuing the Admiral's impatience and insistently laying an obligation on Wentworth, seems to have overridden this in her conception of the drama, and she reshaped the sentences as she wrote, improving a phrase originally written as 'all the strength of his voice' into 'all the power of his natural voice' to heighten the wit and paradox of the addition 'unbroken even by one thin door' which returns attention to the listening Anne. Perhaps the writer quickly realised that the shift to the visual with 'who . . . met her eye' was a slip, that she must keep attention on the aural, not the visual, that the comedy as well as Anne's anxiety would be heightened by delaying the moment when she actually sees

Wentworth.[15] Anne's not looking at Wentworth then becomes a key aspect of the scene she now shapes. Wentworth replies:

> 'Yes — Sir — Yes.' And the Adm[l] was hastily left, the door was closed, and the moment arrived in which Anne was alone with Captain W—. She could not attempt to see how he looked; but he walked immediately to a window.

As before in *Persuasion*, Anne Elliot hears herself spoken of, again only in snatches, but in this scene it is even in a context she cannot understand. Her powerlessness is graphically represented by the door: a 'thin', permeable barrier, so that her hearing through it becomes an acute representation in physical terms of her marginal social status – being both inside and outside – that the novel has found so many ways to define. The very forcefulness of the men, with the impatient Wentworth almost losing his temper, seems to underline the fact that she has no power to govern her own life. This carefully staged scene thus recapitulates the novel's contrast between genders, representing it, again, in material terms.

When the door opens and Wentworth comes in, and then first walks to the window away from Anne, his speech lasts a page in the Cambridge edition, and conveys by Austen's usual means his embarrassment and distress at the commission he has to undertake:

> 'The Adm[l], Madam, was this morning confidently informed that you were — upon my word, I am quite at a loss — ashamed, — (breathing and speaking quick) — the awkwardness of giving Information of this sort to one of the parties — You can be at no loss to understand me — It was very confidently said that Mr Elliot — that every thing was settled in the family for an Union between Mr Elliot – & yourself.'[16]

The address 'Madam' is repeated five times throughout the speech to demonstrate that he is attempting to gain control of his feelings and now to set a proper distance between them, even if what they must discuss is highly personal to both. Anne has taken a newspaper in her hand, Wentworth moves towards the table where she is sitting, but through the whole of his speech no visual contact between them is recorded. This is reserved for the climax. Though as overwhelmed as Wentworth is, Anne manages to make clear that 'there is no Truth in any such report', able to represent herself and her wishes only through a denial, although she does it firmly enough. What then follows in this cancelled chapter is 'a silent, but a very powerful Dialogue' between the lovers, now face to face alone, which brings about their union. The scene is vividly imagined: 'She turned her eyes towards him for the first time since his re-entering the room. His colour was varying — & he was looking at her with all the Power &

Keenness, which she beleived no other eyes than his, possessed'. Their reconciliation is rather more than 'a creditable piece of theatre', more intimate and more subtle than this suggests, though the 'Dialogue' is left to be imagined by the reader. Yet, as Kathryn Sutherland writes, this first reconciliation 'does not resolve the novel thematically nor accord with its deeper logic'.[17] One might feel, as Austen evidently felt, that there is something foreclosed, some business unfinished here. There is no resolution or redemption of Anne's dependent position in which her emotions have been suppressed and her speech, her self-expression, baffled or curtailed. A reader of this scene is left thinking, once again, 'How eloquent could Anne Elliot have been –' . . . More than the romantic drama needs to be resolved.

It is known that Jane Austen was unhappy with this conclusion to her lovers' story. She wrote 'Finis' on the manuscript on 18 July 1816, but, according to her nephew, 'she thought it tame and flat', and one night 'retired to rest in very low spirits' after signing it off.[18] Because the two endings of *Persuasion* are so different, and because it seems astonishing that the novelist should not have worked out how her lovers were to be reunited, even before she began her work, one is inevitably led to some biographical, or rather bioliterary, speculation. Austen knows, then, as she approaches the end of the novel in July 1816 that the final scene must be the culmination of the situations she has imagined throughout the novel. It should be another scene of overhearing, it should again rehearse in some form those impediments that have so far prevented the lovers from understanding each other, and it must be a scene in which the contrasting roles, or even natures, of ladies and gentlemen, of men and women, are somehow again the subject. And as a skilled writer she knows this climactic scene must be a scene of heightened drama, of emotional tension. But how to bring off all these requirements? She could imagine a scene in which Wentworth simply avows his love and is accepted. But she has already written one in which he comes very near to this, only to be interrupted by the man who he thinks is his rival. This has effectively achieved one of her fundamental aims – to reiterate the contingent, continually besieged nature of their communication, now made even more difficult by the jealousy Mr Elliot's attentions have aroused and the continual interference of other people's affairs. Through Anne, she has even declared the problem that confronts her: 'How was the truth to reach [Wentworth]? How, in all the peculiar disadvantages of their respective situations, would he ever learn her real sentiments?' (II: 8, 207). As a woman in the early nineteenth century, Anne can hardly confess her love to him. How could a scene of Wentworth avowing his undying love be made convincing? She has to imagine them coming together through some mode of silent communication.

And so the scene she writes meets these co-ordinates of her imagination. It is a good scene, half comic, half dramatic. It presents two men quarrelling about how to act, but each able to act, to take charge; and it shows Anne in an extreme condition of contingency, a lonely prisoner in the next room, a prisoner, now literally, of the female role. Her fate is again apparently being decided by men. But if Jane Austen goes to bed depressed after writing this scene, isn't it because – to use a modern phrase – the novel now makes no statement? She has left her heroine in a powerless, an actually silenced, condition. Perhaps unwell herself, she may have reflected her own depression by returning her heroine to the position that her narrative has shown her gradually escaping. She has written a scene that intensifies, that climaxes many of the earlier situations she has worked with, but there is something crucial missing. Isn't the problem that there is no overturning in the silent if 'very powerful Dialogue' of Anne's self-suppression, of that miserable abeyance she has constructed her sentences throughout the novel so carefully to both replicate and hide? Is the problem that she has not allowed Anne to express and recover something of her own personal history, never allowed Anne to be fully present to the reader? And hasn't the minor theme she has worked at, the way Anne's consciousness is imbued with her reading, been left behind? But soon she begins to feel herself less ill, and, moreover, 'feeling new strength',[19] she imagines a completely new scene.

Over the next fortnight, according to her sister's record,[20] Jane Austen radically revised the conclusion of her novel, inventing in the course of it two new chapters in which the cast of characters is reassembled at the White Hart inn, Bath (Chapters 10 and 11 of volume 11). But she retained, and reworked, the central trope of this earlier version: overhearing and, specifically, the partial overhearing of the marginalised subject. In both scenes the interior setting plays a critical role; in the first Anne sits in a drawing-room, listening anxiously to a dialogue in the next room or stairwell which she hears only through a door; in the revised and rethought scene, the domestic geography of the apartment at the White Hart as it emerges in the new chapter is even more important, and the physical conditions – the window and the tables – play a key role in the human transactions that take place within it. As Brian Southam wrote, 'In contrast to the confusion and excitement of events that threw them together in the admiral's lodgings, at the White Hart there is an air of outward calm and spaciousness. The five people are carefully arranged about the room.'[21]

Anne enters, sits down and, since she sees that Wentworth is one of the party, is 'deep in the happiness of such misery, or the misery of such happiness, instantly'. Wentworth gets up and goes to a separate table some distance away to write a letter on behalf of his friend Harville. Near where Anne is sitting, Mrs Musgrove and Mrs Croft begin a conversation about Henrietta's engagement, Mrs Musgrove speaking 'just in that inconvenient tone of voice which was perfectly audible while it pretended to be a whisper' (II: II, 250). This grounds the events of the occasion in the valencies of the aural dimension. Anne hopes that the gentlemen 'might each be too self-occupied to hear', a phrase that recovers and reminds the reader of all the previous moments in the novel when for similar reasons Anne herself has been incapable of attending. Soon the ladies, now speaking more emphatically, touch on the subject of long engagements; both Anne and Wentworth, who stops writing and looks up, recognise its relevance to their own history. Wentworth gives Anne 'one quick, conscious look'. Anne herself becomes self-occupied, aware only of a buzz of words in the background of her thought. Thus the physical relationships between the figures in the room are configured as aural relations, and the complexities of hearing, the trope of overhearing, are set once more in play.

When Captain Harville gets up and moves to a window, he invites Anne to join him, and not for the first time she 'rouses' herself from an absent state of mind, gets up and crosses the room to join him. (Her movement mirrors Wentworth's movement to the window in the earlier version.) Now the geography of this interior is made more specific: 'The window at which he stood, was at the other end of the room from where the two ladies were sitting, and though nearer to Captain Wentworth's table, not very near' (II: II, 252). Thus the 'thin door' that once kept Anne apart from Wentworth and Admiral Croft is re-created as a space that should preserve, and yet does not quite preserve, privacy, but with the positions of speakers and listener reversed.

Rather than rehearsing once again the polarisation of genders, like the first version of the novel's resolution, the conversation between Harville and Anne that Austen now conceives is an explicit debate about gender difference, and it is one in which both speakers take equal roles. Anne Elliot now achieves textual being as an intellectual woman, who, like Elizabeth Bennet and Emma Woodhouse, enjoys an argument and has lawyer-like logic at her command. Their exchange is about grief, and the different ways in which a man and a gentlewoman experience and deal with it. Unknown to Captain Harville, this is a topic that touches on

Anne's private experience, and the phrases that describe the tones of her voice convey this to the reader. Harville is himself grieving for his sister, as he speaks to Anne 'with a quivering lip' of the speed with which Benwick has forgotten her: 'Poor Fanny! She would not have forgotten him so soon!' Anne reciprocates 'in a low feeling voice: "That, I can easily believe"' (11: 11, 252). There is great delicacy in the way in which Austen now evokes the unresolved sorrow of Anne's own life, so that for the reader this little initial response is like a flag on the deep stream that has run through the novel. It indicates how in the ensuing contest, though conducted in the dignified, almost abstract terms becoming an amicable argument between two people who have not known each other long, Anne is at last allowed to speak in effect of what she has long been forced to withhold. The depth of her experience emerges when she speaks of the feelings that 'prey' upon a woman who has no outlet for her emotional energies, or when, after an escalating series of sentences, she finds herself speaking 'with a faltering voice' (though still in general terms) about what her tremor admits are her personal feelings.

Both enjoy their debate, but they are talking quietly so as not to disturb Wentworth's writing at the desk, till they hear a noise from his 'perfectly quiet division of the room'. ('Division' suggests both contiguity and separation: he is equally present in the same space, and cut off.) It is at the precise moment when Anne speaks 'with a faltering voice' that Wentworth drops his pen. Anne is 'startled at finding him nearer than she had supposed; and half inclined to suspect that the pen had only fallen, because he had been occupied by them, striving to catch sounds, which yet she did not think he could have caught' (1: 11, 254).

Anne has herself caught fragments of speech, throughout the novel, but at this moment the phenomena, or the word, repeated draws on another register of meaning. One might be reminded of that earlier occasion when Anne, sitting hidden nearby, overheard Wentworth 'catching the same tone' from Louisa Musgrove (1: 10, 91). But here, finding the words 'catch' and 'caught' in such proximity with the word 'fallen', might not a re-reader also recall, if only subliminally, that crucial event in the novel's action when he failed to catch Louisa, she fell, and he, too late, 'caught her up'? Both the moment at Lyme and the sequence in the White Hart are a test of one person's attunement to the emotions of the other. Jane Austen has thus made the word 'caught' reveal itself as the repository of a spectrum of meanings, with the verbal drawing the physical one into its aura. This apparently coincidental recurrence of language is a sign that the novelist's imagination is now in full poetic command of the inner meaning of the narrative that she has worked on so far. Everything in this reconceived scene now takes its themes, its situations, to another level. In this rewriting, to put it another way, the various components of the novel's inner structure are finally brought and clasped together.

The dialogue between Harville and Anne is broken off by a brief exchange between the two men. When they resume their conversation, the emotional pitch rises. "'Ah!" cried Captain Harville, in a tone of strong feeling', as he responds to Anne. As in their earlier dialogue about his sister's death (1: 12, 116–17), it is Harville whose speech becomes eloquent, and here even florid, with phrases like 'the glow of his soul', 'as if Heaven had given them wings', 'the treasures of his existence' registering the force of his desire to convince her. For all his toughness, this naval captain is a man of sensibility. He suits actions to the words as 'with emotion' he presses his hand to his heart. His histrionic intensity communicates itself to Anne, who responds to him with a fervour that increases as she speaks. "'Oh!" cried Anne eagerly ... God forbid that I should undervalue the warm and faithful feelings of any of my fellow-creatures.' What some readers feel is that the rhetoric of her speech (which certainly builds up in a series of escalating sentences) is thus grounded in the communicated emotion between a man and a woman. Anne's response is, however, tempered by the sadness of recollection and some hesitation as she draws once again obliquely, not directly, on her experience of life:

> 'I hope I do justice to all that is felt by you, and by those who resemble you. God forbid that I should undervalue the warm and faithful feelings of any of my fellow-creatures. I should deserve utter contempt if I dared to suppose that true attachment and constancy were known only by woman. No, I believe you capable of every thing great and good in your married lives. I believe you equal to every important exertion, and to every domestic forbearance, so long as — if I may be allowed the expression, so long as you have an object. I mean, while the woman you love lives, and lives for you. All the privilege I claim for my own sex (it is not a very enviable one, you need not covet it) is that of loving longest, when existence or when hope is gone.'
> She could not immediately have uttered another sentence; her heart was too full, her breath too much oppressed. (11: 11, 256)

"'You are a good soul," cried Captain Harville.' He detects the pain and sincerity behind Anne's speech, even if he does not know what lies behind that. Her careful qualifications, even the touch of humour or self-irony in her speeches, suggest the metamorphosis of grief into something like mourning. If grief is the suffering of loss, mourning is its commemoration;

rather than the self retracting inwards, mourning allows one to express bereavement or regret outwards in the world. Anne's speech here, even more than her earlier exchanges with Harville, is at once energetic in argument and a lament, not for her own history, her own mistake, but for the condition she shares with all gentlewomen. This final eloquent assertion of human equality is picked up by Wentworth's ears as he writes his last sentences to Anne in his 'division of the room'. 'You sink your voice, but I can distinguish the tones of that voice, when they would be lost on others. — Too good, too excellent creature! You do us justice indeed. You do believe that there is true attachment and constancy among men' (ii: 11, 258). He is repeating the phrase he has just overheard Anne speak, which in its turn mirrors what he himself said to Anne when he spoke about Benwick's love for Fanny Harville: 'his attachment to her was indeed attachment. A man does not recover from such a devotion of the heart to such a woman!' (ii: 8, 199). The 'silent, but a very powerful Dialogue' of the first draft's resolution is now recreated in different terms, and precisely dramatised, as the writing Wentworth responds silently, single phrase by single phrase, in a time-lapse duet, to the more audible emotional moments of Anne's quiet speech. And it is a recreation that recuperates and refashions the novel's structural antithesis between genders.

It may be a mistake, though, to suggest, as some distinguished critics do, that Anne is implicitly addressing her speeches, and especially the last one, to Wentworth.[22] This reading assumes that she has not concluded he is too far away to catch her words. If her speech, as Tony Tanner put it, has a 'double target and dual purpose', this implies a certain insincerity in her avowals to Harville, as if she were not aroused and stimulated by Harville's own strong feeling, and makes much less telling the response in Wentworth's letter. It is the purity of Anne's feelings here, not their doublings, that is moving. Jocelyn Harris writes that 'like Desdemona to Othello [Anne] is half the wooer', and moreover that 'Anne declares her love within Wentworth's hearing'.[23] Anne and Harville are talking about the different accommodations of men and women to grief: it may sound to a reader that Anne is affirming the enduring power of her own feelings, but this is implicit, and what is implicit is not a declaration. The truth is that the scene is more subtle and more subtly conceived: that Austen makes it difficult to be sure of how much Anne's awareness of Wentworth's presence in the room is transmuted into the emotional force of her eloquence. 'All the privilege I claim for my own sex (it is not a very enviable one, you need not covet it) is that of loving longest, when existence or when hope is gone': this is hardly a declaration of love, but the expression of feelings long withheld in silence, and now at last put into words, an eloquence at last achieved, and the more convincing for its wryly ironic retrospective sadness.

At Box Hill, Jane Fairfax communicates to Frank Churchill through a speech that can pass as a general comment on hasty engagements. Reserved as she has been throughout the novel, Jane now employs his technique of double meanings in an exchange that brings their drama (whose inner activity has been more or less kept from the reader) to a critical point. If this is quite different from the authority and independence of Anne Elliot here in *Persuasion*, a similar, but more fundamental, reversal does occur. Anne has been the dependent listener; Wentworth by contrast has been shown as the confident, attention-commanding, textually dominant speaker. The subordinate role assigned to her, even in that first draft of their romance's conclusion, is now assigned to him. Their positions (as before, literally) are reversed. She has been forced to sit, catching fragments of discourse, listening in to conversations that – whether they wound or elevate her – cause her consciousness to cloud or her heart to beat faster. Her emotional life has often been lived and displayed to the reader only through these overhearings. Now it is Wentworth, the energetic male raconteur, who is the passive partner, sitting at the table, held there by his task, while she stands at the window, he overhearing sounds that bear upon his life, his prospects, his feelings, unable wholly to possess what he overhears. Through the novel's trope of filtered hearing, the conventional attributes of their gender are exchanged.

Jane Austen's first version of her finale climaxed many of the situations that her previous chapters had displayed. But it had failed to engage with the crucial issue of Anne's reticence: her silences not only within the action, but within her own text. *Persuasion* repeatedly presented Anne as 'only Anne', the despised, marginal, unregarded spinster. At the same time it allowed the reader to know what a fund of intelligence and feeling lay beneath her quietness, to accumulate a sense of her hidden passionate life, intimated by the novelist in many, but oblique, ways. In the finale as it now stands Anne Elliot commands the textual stage. She defines and laments the life of the gentlewoman, a life of severely restricted opportunities. But at this moment she has an opportunity, and she is now prepared to seize it.[24] When she tells Harville 'if you please, no reference to examples in books', her authority is augmented by the clear, extra-diegetic implication that now in this volume, the book in which she is now speaking, the text her reader is now reading, a different story is being told.

It has been argued that Jane Austen's first published novel began 'an open revision of gender norms', but 'of the five [other] novels, *Persuasion* is perhaps the least aggressive about fictionally remodeling its protagonists' gender'.[25] Anne's character in this chapter is certainly not aggressively remodelled; she is still mild, kind, sympathetic, attentive, though if she represents the dependent life of women, and reflects on her own life, she is at the same time surely lamenting it. The novel's reversal of gender positions in this scene is not at the service of one gender or the other but a crowning statement of complementarity between them. The exchange of attributes that is represented here does not involve a remaking of womanhood; instead, it is a moment of equality. Anne's speech is emancipated from rhetoric, and Wentworth's response from sentimentality, because the exchange is prepared for and underwritten by the novel's structure, which is a way of saying that the attentive reader needs, wants, requires this resolution. This is a balance and harmony achieved not by explicit, characterological means, but through narrative means. The impediments to their communication here recapitulate all the other barriers that the novel has erected between them, but because they are overcome here, what is conveyed is a transcendence of the mundane. And so this interior scene is followed by a paragraph in which Anne and Wentworth are wholly liberated within a space of their own, even as they walk through the noisy crowded streets of Bath.

Jane Austen naturalised the stage convention of overhearing, making it seem an incidental and common event of ordinary communal life. As I have shown, however, overhearing in *Emma* and *Persuasion* is a structural component of their narration. It is thus at the same time almost as artificial, as much of a convention, as it is on the stage. When one asks what makes this rewritten chapter of *Persuasion* attain its elevation, one might reply that Jane Austen's carefully particularised positioning of the various players in her setting carries a trace of the theatre, and that this trace of artifice, along with the near-rhetoric of her principals, is what fosters its almost operatic grandeur. Behind this scene may certainly lie Viola's oblique description of her helpless love to Orsino in *Twelfth Night*, and Sir Peter Teazel's avowal of respect and care for his wife, overheard from her hiding-place in the closet, and even Romeo and Juliet catching each other's voices 'bescreened in night'.[26] Perhaps I might say, though, that these scenes were all written by men. Jane Austen takes over from them, disposes her three sets of figures in everyday, plausibly different sites in the room and then orchestrates their aural relations to each other so convincingly that the reader is issued into the presence of an art greater than her predecessors'.

The painter Lily Briscoe in *To the Lighthouse* describes what she wants to achieve with her painting: 'Beautiful and bright it should be on the surface, feathery and evanescent, one colour melting into the other like the colours on a butterfly's wing; but underneath the fabric must be clamped together with bolts of iron.'[27] There is nothing in *Persuasion* or in Austen's art even remotely akin to the post-impressionist style that Lily espouses, but Virginia Woolf's description (plausibly read as a reference to her own novelistic practice) does have a bearing on Austen's. As has been long understood, this is a novel in which luck and contingency make up much of the substance of the narrative: the injury to the little boy, the fall from the Cobb, the chance meeting with Mr Elliot on the steps at Lyme, above all perhaps the necessarily adventitious nature of overhearing.[28] The narrative draws its suspense from these chance events, as well as from the unpredictable interruptions of the conversations that might lead Anne and Wentworth to reconciliation. But undergirding the story of these events, their interrupted and contingent dialogues and final reconciliation, is an intellectual framework of steel.

The world assumes that Austen is a romantic novelist and that all 'Jane Austen novels' are alike. But they are all distinct, and equally serious, and, as her re-readers know, there certainly is a hidden Jane Austen.

The novels do all obey the demands of the marriage plot. The convention was necessary to the market she hoped to reach. Yet each of her works, while presenting the reader, and certainly the first-time reader, with a romance and a romantic resolution, bend that plot to her own ends. Each of them has its own distinct and pervasive intention – a quality that I have described in the shorthand of their different 'worlds'. *Northanger Abbey* is an apparently light-hearted satire of the Gothic novel, but in all of its aspects – plot, characterisation, narrative style – it is a vindication of clarity and honesty in opposition to concealment, and devoted to the exposure of the Gothic romance. *Sense and Sensibility* is the story of two young women finding their marriage partners, but at the same time, indivisible from this concern, it is an examination of the rigours and compulsions of concealment that the social world demands. *Pride and Prejudice* is always thought of as the romantic novel par excellence, but besides including three marriages that certainly cast a shadow over romance, as many critics have noted, it offers a concerted enquiry into the formation of memories, a matter quite distinct, and ultimately argues that respecting one's memories is essential to the hero and heroine's union. *Mansfield Park*, most remarkably and challengingly, turns the romantic narrative against itself, and presents a central character whose love is understood by herself to be taboo, illegitimate, disobedient. At the same time it treats sexual desire in a range of other characters in a distinctively non-romantic manner – as an agent of impaired if not ruined happiness. *Emma* threads one concealed story of love at first sight through a comedy of errors, while engaging the reader in a small, congested community, and uses overhearing, at once defining independence and engagement, to bring that experience home. The love it eventually celebrates turns not on romance but on mutual familiarity and respect. Of all the novels, *Persuasion* is the most obviously a love story. It opens with a tale of love thwarted, its action details the impediments to that love's renewal, and it ultimately brings about the return and retrieval of that love, become perhaps deeper and truer than at first. But Austen's genius was to turn this romantic narrative into a vindication of the right to self-expression, and thus to make her fiction a statement of her own professional and personal identity. As in all of Jane Austen's novels, it is this unromantic intelligence that leads her readers to re-read, again and again.

Notes

Introduction

1 Lorna J. Clark, *The Letters of Sarah Harriet Burney*, Athens, GA and London: The University of Georgia Press, 1998, p. 176.

2 Kathryn Sutherland, 'Jane Austen's Dealings with John Murray and his Firm', *Review of English Studies*, 64, 263 (March 2012), p.17. In Samuel Smiles' *A Publisher and his Friends: Memoir and Correspondence of the Late John Murray*, London: John Murray, 1891, vol. 1, p. 282, 'again' is italicised, as if to remark its significance.

3 Clark, *The Letters of Sarah Harriet Burney*, p. 420. Janet Todd, 'Criticism', in Janet Todd, ed., *The Cambridge Companion to Pride and Prejudice*, Cambridge University Press, 2013, p. 139.

4 Susannah Fullerton, *Happily Ever After*, London: Frances Lincoln, 2013, p. 23.

5 [Lewes:] 'The Great Appraisal 1859', in B. C. Southam, ed., *Jane Austen: The Critical Heritage*, London: Routledge and Kegan Paul, 1968, pp, 148–66, p. 151, first published in *Blackwood's Edinburgh Magazine*, July 1859.

6 B. C. Southam, ed., *Jane Austen: The Critical Heritage Volume II 1870–1940*, London and New York: Routledge and Kegan Paul, 1987, pp. 209, 251.

7 A. C. Bradley, 'Jane Austen', in *A Miscellany*, London: Macmillan, 1929, pp. 32–72, p. 32.

8 'Jane Austen's Novels: Form and Structure', in J. David Grey, ed., *The Jane Austen Handbook*, London: Athlone, 1986, pp. 165–78, p. 167.

9 Richard Cronin and Dorothy McMillan, eds., Jane Austen, *Emma*, The Cambridge Edition of the Works of Jane Austen, Cambridge University Press, 2005, Introduction, p. lvii.

10 See also Deidre Shauna Lynch, *The Economy of Character, Novels, Market Culture and the Business of Inner Meaning*, University of Chicago Press, 1998, to which I am more generally indebted.

11 John Mullan, *What Matters in Jane Austen? Twenty Crucial Puzzles Solved*, London: Bloomsbury, 2012, p. 4.

12 Peter Knox-Shaw, *Jane Austen and the Enlightenment*, Cambridge University Press, 2004, p. 179.

13 Katie Trumpener, 'The Virago Jane Austen', in Deidre Lynch, ed., *Janeites: Austen's Disciples and Devotees*, Princeton and Oxford: Princeton University Press, 2000, pp. 140–65, p. 154.

14 Mary A. Favret, *War at a Distance: Romanticism and the Making of Modern Wartime*, Princeton and London: Princeton University Press, 2009.

15 Moira Ferguson writes that 'contemporaries could have amplified Sir Thomas's character . . . Planters were infamous for taking slave mistresses and fathering children', in 'Mansfield Park, *Slavery, Colonialism and Gender*', *Oxford Literary Review*, 3 (1991) pp. 118–39, p. 128; Brian Southam, in an even more influential piece, 'The Silence of the Bertrams: Slavery and the Chronology of *Mansfield Park*', first published in the *TLS*, 17 February 1995, writes that Sir Thomas, 'one of the West Indian lobby', 'would have voted for the trade's continuation' in the abolition debates in Parliament; 'When in Jane Austen's *Emma* young Frank Churchill deserts the ladies on the excuse that he has to go to London to have his hair cut (in fact to buy a gift for his secret fiancée), knowing male readers, if they read the novel at all, might have at once assumed that, hair once cut and away from those chaste and watchful females, Frank would have drifted towards club, brothel or bagnio, and had a bit on the side, as everyone else did.' Vic Gatrell, *City of Laughter: Sex and Satire in Eighteenth-Century London*, London: Atlantic Books, 2006, pp. 118–19. There is no evidence for any of these propositions in the novels. Second-guessing what contemporary readers might have assumed can become an excuse for treating characters as if they were real persons, existing outside the text. However, in 'The Politics of Silence: *Mansfield Park* and the Amelioration of Slavery', George E. Boulukos presents arguments from the text for seeing Sir Thomas Bertram as a Christian ameliorist planter, concerned to improve the conditions of slaves (*Novel: A Forum for Fiction* (Summer 2006) pp. 362–83).

16 Brandon: 'Little did Mr Willoughby imagine, I suppose, when his looks censured me for incivility in breaking up the party, that I was called away to the relief of one, whom he had made poor and miserable' (*S&S* ii: 9, 237).

17 'You are but *now* coming to the heart & beauty of your book', JA to Anna Austen, 9 September 1814, *Letters*, p. 275.

18 'Serious reading . . . is a recreation in which, by a considering attentiveness, we ensure a more than ordinary faithfulness and fulness', F. R. Leavis, 'Valuation in Criticism' (1966), in G. Singh, ed., *Valuation in Criticism and Other Essays*, Cambridge University Press, 1986, pp. 276–84, p. 278.

19 Ariane Hudelet, 'Beyond Words, Beyond Images: Jane Austen and the Art of Mise en Scène', in Ariane Hudelet, David Monagham and John Wiltshire, *The Cinematic Jane Austen: Essays on the Filmic Sensibility of the Novels*, Jefferson, NC and London: McFarland and Company, 2009, p. 57.

20 This difficult and controversial matter is extensively discussed in Kathryn Sutherland, *Jane Austen's Textual Lives: From Aeschylus to Bollywood*, Chapter 5 'Speaking Commas', Oxford University Press, 2005, pp. 266–313.

21 Linda Bree, Peter Sabor and Janet Todd, eds., *Jane Austen's Manuscript Works*, Peterborough, Ontario: Broadview Literary Texts, 2013, p. 323. The published rewriting is on p. 272.

22 *Jane Austen's Lady Susan: A Facsimile of the Manuscript in the Pierpont Morgan Library and the 1925 Printed Edition*, New York and London: Garland, 1989.

23 *Jane Austen's Manuscript Works*, Introduction, p. 15.

24 The manuscript shows that 'Carefulness – Discretion' is written above 'The Caution.' 'Appendix A: Transcription of "The Watsons"', Janet Todd and Linda Bree, eds., *Later Manuscripts*, The Cambridge Edition of the Works of Jane Austen, Cambridge University Press, 2008, p. 287.

25 *Later Manuscripts*, p. 93.

26 Chapter 11 of the MS of *Persuasion* became Chapter 12 of the published novel. In the first twenty lines of the MS chapter in the transcription of the Cambridge edition there are four dashes (p. 322). One of these appears in the printed text. The last ('– Sir Walter indeed') was taken to be a paragraph marker, and is replaced by indentation in the printed text (p. 270). In this second paragraph of the published version there are no dashes, but there are three in the equivalent material of the MS.

27 Valérie Cossy, *Jane Austen in Switzerland: A Study of the Early French Translations*, Geneva: Editions Slatkine, 2006, p. 111.

28 Southam, *Critical Heritage*, p. 125.

Chapter 1: Into the open with Catherine Morland

1 D. W. Harding, *Regulated Hatred and Other Essays on Jane Austen*, ed. Monica Lawlor, London: Athlone Press, 1998, p. 134.

2 Joe Bray, *The Female Reader in the English Novel: From Burney to Austen*, New York and London: Routledge, 2009, Chapter 5 'Absorbed Attention', pp. 144–56, p. 148.

3 Ann Radcliffe, *The Romance of the Forest*, ed. Chloe Chard, World's Classics, Oxford University Press, 1986, p. 114.

4 Ibid. p. 114.

5 Ibid. p. 109.

6 In the publishing process an Austenian dash following 'might have yielded to her hand — ' might have been changed into a colon.

7 *Romance of the Forest*, pp. 127–8.

8 Barbara M. Benedict and Deirdre Le Faye, eds., Jane Austen, *Northanger Abbey*, The Cambridge Edition of the Works of Jane Austen, Cambridge University Press, 2006, Introduction, p. xlviii.

9 Elie Halévy, *England in 1815* [1913, 1924], trans. E. I. Watkin and D. A. Barker, London: Ernest Benn, 1961. Tony Tanner, drawing on Warren Roberts, who asserts in *Jane Austen and the French Revolution* (1979) that 'Austen was referring to actual spies' (p. 29) describes Henry as trying 'to evoke a kind of phantasm of peaceful life from which the possibility of horror and violence has

been eradicated.' *Jane Austen*, [1986] reissued edition, Basingstoke: Palgrave Macmillan, 2007, pp. 70, 71.

10 Deirdre Le Faye, *Jane Austen: A Family Record*, 2nd edn. Cambridge University Press, 2004, p. 260.

11 There is perhaps a parody of Johnson's *Journey to the Western Islands of Scotland* in 'Love and Freindship', as R. W. Chapman suggested (*The Works of Jane Austen*, vol. VI. *Minor Works*, Oxford University Press, 1954, p. 458), but this is found unconvincing by Peter Sabor, *Juvenilia*, The Cambridge Edition of the Works of Jane Austen. Cambridge University Press, 2006, p. 438, note 77.

12 Isobel Grundy, 'Jane Austen and Literary Tradition', Edward Copeland and Juliet McMaster, eds., in *The Cambridge Companion to Jane Austen*, Cambridge University Press, 1997, p. 198.

13 In the Preface to his translation of Father Lobo's *Voyage to Abyssinia* (1735) Johnson wrote that the reader would find in the book none of the 'romantick absurdities' of other travel writers, 'nor are the nations here described either devoid of all sense of humanity, or consummate in all private or social virtues ... he will discover ... that wherever human nature is to be found, there is a mixture of vice and virtue, a contest of passion and reason'. This passage was singled out from Johnson's first prose publication by Burke and reprinted by Boswell as an early example of Johnson's 'brilliant and energetick statement'. James Boswell, *Boswell's Life of Johnson*, ed. G. B. Hill, rev. L. F. Powell, Oxford: Clarendon Press, 1934, vol. I, pp. 88–9. Jane Austen wrote to Cassandra in November 1798 that they 'are to have [Boswell's] "Life of Johnson"', *Letters*, p. 22.

14 Tanner, *Jane Austen*, p.73.

15 Jocelyn Harris, *Jane Austen's Art of Memory*, Cambridge University Press, 1989, pp. 9–10.

16 Ibid. p. 25.

17 *Letters*, p. 333.

Chapter 2: Elinor Dashwood and concealment

1 Shawn Lisa Maurer, 'At Seventeen: Adolescence in *Sense and Sensibility*', *Eighteenth-Century Fiction*, 25, 4 (Summer 2013) pp. 721–50.

2 The Regency began in 1811, the year *Sense and Sensibility* was published, but the Prince of Wales had intermittently acted as the king's regent for several years before this. I am using 'Regency' in the accepted broader sense, to include the period before the official Regency began.

3 Paula Byrne, *Jane Austen and the Theatre*, London: Hambledon and London, 2002, p. 118. Byrne usefully compares Lucy and Elinor's dialogues with the first exchange in Congreve's *The Way of the World*.

4 Bree, Sabor and Todd, *Jane Austen's Manuscript Works*, p. 21.

5 'Instead of having the narrator reveal Lucy's true intentions, Austen makes us directly see these motivations in her look, in the tone of her voice. We do not know ... the exact place where they are walking, and yet we feel we are direct,

physical witnesses to the scene thanks to this interplay of looks and to these perfidious nuances in Lucy's voice.' Hudelet, 'Beyond Words, Beyond Images', pp. 57–75, p. 66.

6 Janet Todd, *The Cambridge Introduction to Jane Austen*, Cambridge University Press, 2006, p. 50; Sandra M. Gilbert and Susan Gubar, *The Madwoman in the Attic: The Woman Writer and the Nineteenth-Century Literary Imagination*, New Haven: Yale University Press, 1979, p. 120.

7 'A sign of the animal in the human' is a remark of Marcia Poynton's, cited by Jill Heydt-Stevenson, *Austen's Unbecoming Conjunctions*, New York: Palgrave Macmillan, 2005, p. 36. Heydt-Stevenson discusses the exchange of hair and other tokens fully, pp. 34–44.

8 Byrne, *Theatre*, p. 121.

9 Edward Copeland, ed., Jane Austen, *Sense and Sensibility*, The Cambridge Edition of the Works of Jane Austen, Cambridge University Press, 2006, p. 466, note 9.

10 D. A. Miller, *Jane Austen, or The Secret of Style*, Princeton and Oxford: Princeton University Press, 2003, p. 20.

11 James Gillray, 'A Voluptuary under the Horrors of Digestion' (1792): British Museum.

12 The London Stock Books of Erard, the principal and most fashionable manufacturer of harps in London, now held at the Centre for Performance History at the Royal College of Music, show that sales were at a peak in 1808–9, the years in which *Mansfield Park* is set. Ann Griffiths, 'Sébastien Erard, A Dynasty of Harp Makers', www.dlaismusicpublishers.co.uk/pages/harpists/erard.htm. Accessed 26 January 2013.

13 Marcia McClintock Folsom, 'The Narrator's Voice and the Sense of *Sense and Sensibility*', *Persuasions*, 33 (2011) pp. 29–39.

14 Penny Gay, *Jane Austen and the Theatre*, Cambridge University Press, 2002, p. 46.

15 Claudia L. Johnson, *Jane Austen: Women, Politics, and the Novel*, Chicago University Press, p. 50.

16 Godfrey Cass in *Silas Marner* is an example of Eliot's portrayal of figures tormenting themselves over their own past conduct, but trapped by it: 'If Godfrey could have felt himself simply a victim, the iron bit that destiny had put into his mouth would have chafed him less intolerably ... But he had something else to curse – his own vicious folly, which now seemed as mad and unaccountable to him as almost all our follies and vices do when their promptings have long passed away' (*Silas Marner*, in *The Novels of George Eliot*, vol. III, Edinburgh and London: Blackwood and Sons, n. d., Chapter 3, pp. 24–5).

17 On this difficult passage, see Claudia L. Johnson, 'A "Sweet Face as White as Death", Jane Austen and the Politics of Female Sensibility', *Novel: A Forum on Fiction*, 22 (1989) pp. 159–74.

18 Johnson, *Jane Austen*, p. 50.

19 D. W. Harding, 'Regulated Hatred: An Aspect of the Work of Jane Austen', in his *Regulated Hatred*, pp. 5–26.

Chapter 3: Elizabeth's memory and Mr Darcy's smile

1 Todd, *The Cambridge Introduction to Jane Austen*, p. 66.

2 Cited in Endel Tulving, 'Coding and Representation: Searching for a Home in the Brain', in Henry L. Roediger III, Yadin Dudai, and Susan M. Fitzpatrick, eds., *Science of Memory: Concepts*, New York: Oxford University Press, 2007, pp. 65–8, p. 65.

3 John Locke, *An Essay Concerning Human Understanding* [1689], ed. Peter Nidditch, Oxford: Clarendon Press, 1975, Book II, Chapter x, 'Of Retention', p. 150.

4 Paul John Eakin, 'Autobiography, Identity and the Fictions of Memory', in Daniel L. Schacter and Elaine Scarry, eds., *Memory, Brain, and Belief*, Cambridge, MA and London: Harvard University Press, 2000, pp. 290–306, p. 293.

5 Alison Winter, *Memory: Fragments of a Modern History*, Chicago and London: University of Chicago Press, 2012, p. 198.

6 Ibid., Chapter 9 'Frederic Bartlett and the Social Psychology of Remembering', passim and p. 202.

7 Daniel L. Schacter, *The Seven Sins of Memory*, Boston and New York: Houghton Mifflin Company, 2001, p. 26.

8 Paul Ekman and Wallace V. Friesen, *Unmasking the Face*, Engelwood Cliffs, NJ: Prentice Hall [1975]; Cambridge, MA: Major Books, 2003, pp. 142, 143.

9 In *Jane Austen and the Didactic Novel*, London: Macmillan, 1983, Jan Fergus noted that though Elizabeth says here that Darcy allows 'nothing for the influence of friendship and affection', 'Elizabeth herself has been allowing nothing for the friendship and affection of Bingley and Darcy in her response to their dialogue ... She is not the judge she thinks herself' p. 114.

10 Mary Poovey, 'From Politics to Silence: Jane Austen's Nonreferential Aesthetic', in Claudia L. Johnson and Clara Tuite, eds., *A Companion to Jane Austen*, Oxford: Wiley–Blackwell, 2009, pp. 251–60, p. 253.

11 'So oft it chances in particular men / That for some vicious mole of nature in them ... Carrying, I say, the stamp of one defect... (*Hamlet*, I, 4, ll. 24–5, 31 (Q2)).

12 Ekman and Friesen, *Unmasking*, p. 102.

13 The term was invented by the social psychologist Martin Orne in 1962: Winter, *Memory*, p. 149.

14 Locke, *An Essay Concerning Human Understanding*, pp. 152–3. The word 'affection' may have the pathological colouring it acquired in the sixteenth century, as a state of the body (OED, sense 2). In its modern sense, Locke's remark might apply to Elizabeth's interest in Wickham.

15   Alertness and attention depend on physiological processes such as blood flow and hormonal level. Memory involves emotion as well as cognition, and hormones produced outside the brain, notably adrenaline and its neurotransmitter relative noradrenaline, are engaged in determining what is remembered ... learning and remembering – memory – is a property not of individual synapses or nerve cells or brains, but of the entire organism, the person

Steven Rose, 'Memories are Made of This', in A. S. Byatt and H. H. Wood, eds., *Memory: An Anthology*, London: Vintage Books, 2009, pp. 54–76, p. 65.

16 'Confabulation was a psychological term dating back to the early years of psychoanalysis, referring to a process that knitted memories of past experiences together with fantasies or suggestions to form an imaginative construction that appeared to be a memory.' Winter, *Memory*, p. 153.

17 Schacter, *Seven Sins*, p. 101.

18 Winter, *Memory*, p. 202.

19 Marcia McClintock Folsom persuasively argues that 'he misses the analogy, replying to her literal comment on piano playing, not to the implied criticism of himself', and that his failure to notice her criticism is another example of his well-established arrogance and conceit: his inattention to her here is akin to his assumption that, if he proposes, she will naturally accept. '"Taking Different Positions": Knowing and Feeling in *Pride and Prejudice*', in Marcia McClintock Folsom ed., *Approaches to Teaching Jane Austen's Pride and Prejudice*, New York: Modern Language Association, 1993, pp. 100–14, p. 104.

20 Howard S. Babb, *Jane Austen's Novels: The Fabric of Dialogue*, Columbus: Ohio State University Press, 1962, emphasises 'performance' in these dialogues. Babb's thoughtful account of Darcy's speech illustrates how difficult it is to reach a firm interpretation. 'Perhaps, as a gallant gesture, he is straining to use "perform" in Elizabeth's narrow sense', he writes (p. 144).

21 Reuben A. Brower, 'The Controlling Hand: Jane Austen and *Pride and Prejudice*', *Scrutiny*, 13, 2 (1945) pp. 99–111.

22 Darcy starts again, for instance, when the door opens on Elizabeth's 'pale face and impetuous manner' at Lambton (III: 4, 304).

23 Henry James, *The Bostonians* [1886], London: John Lehmann, 1952, p. 351.

24 Joseph Conrad, Author's Note, *The Shadow-Line, A Confession*, London: John Grant, 1923, p. xi.

25 Ignês Sodré, 'Where the Lights and Shadows Fall: On Not Being Able to Remember and Not Being Able to Forget', in A. S. Byatt and H. H. Wood, eds., *Memory: An Anthology*, London: Vintage Books, 2009, pp. 40–53, p. 41.

26 In Chapter 11 of Volume 11, following this scene, Wentworth and Anne do go over the past, and explain their conduct to each other.

27 On this moment, see Robert M. Polhemus, 'The Fortunate Fall: Jane Austen's *Pride and Prejudice*', in his *Erotic Faith, Being in Love from Jane Austen to D. H. Lawrence*, Chicago and London: University of Chicago Press, 1990, pp. 28–54, pp. 37–40.

Chapter 4: The religion of Aunt Norris

1 In neither the 1814 nor the 1816 edition is 'them' italicised, but the sense seems to require it.

2 Boswell, *Boswell's Life of Johnson*, vol. 1, p. 394.

3 Kathryn Sutherland, 'Jane Austen and the invention of the serious modern novel', in Thomas Keymer and Jon Mee, eds., *The Cambridge Companion to English Literature*, Cambridge University Press, 2004, pp. 244–62, p. 254.

4 James Wood, 'Jane Austen's heroic consciousness', in his *The Broken Estate, Essays on Literature and Belief*, New York: The Modern Library, 2000, pp. 32–41, p. 35. Wood also comments that there is a 'distinctly Protestant, even Evangelical bent' to the 'hermeneutical task' of Austen's heroines.

5 Knox-Shaw, *Jane Austen and the Enlightenment*, p. 70.

6 Francis Bacon, *Novum Organum* [1620], trans. R. Ellis and James Spedding, in Edwin A. Burtt eds., *The English Philosophers from Bacon to Mill*, New York: The Modern Library, 1939.

7 J. C. D. Clark, *English Society 1660–1832*, Cambridge University Press, 2000, p. 28.

8 *Letters*, p. 245.

9 Ibid., p. 215.

10 Todd and Bree, *Later Manuscripts*, p. 573.

11 Brian Southam, *Jane Austen: A Students' Guide to the Later Manuscript Works*, London: Concord Books, 2007, pp. 83–96, p. 86.

12 The Cambridge editors, after considering all the evidence, doubt whether these prayers are by Jane Austen herself, and consign them to an Appendix. Introduction, Todd and Bree, *Later Manuscripts*, pp. cxviii–cxxvi. Southam, on the other hand, expresses no doubt as to their authorship.

13 Apart from being better written than the other two, this prayer includes five of Jane Austen's signature long dashes as well as one of the most important words in her lexicon, 'comfort'. My argument here, though, does not depend on the prayer being by Jane Austen: it is used as an example of the way an Anglican prayer can employ a dramatic mode that is akin to the dramatic mode of the novels.

14 A. S. Byatt and Ignês Sodré, *Imagining Characters: Six Conversations about Women Writers*, London: Vintage, 1995, p. 41.

15 Todd and Bree, *Later Manuscripts*, p. 573.

16 Laura Mooneyham White, in *Jane Austen's Anglicanism*, New York and Farnham, Surrey: Ashgate, 2011, comments on 'the spirit of Evangelical self-examination' in this question (p. 133).

17 Sir Thomas has had a bad press during the past decades, especially from critics who foreground the 'Antiguan connection' in their interpretation of the novel. Susan Fraiman, for example, remarks that 'slavery' is 'a trope Austen introduces to argue the essential depravity of Sir Thomas's relations to other people'. 'Jane Austen and Edward Said: Gender, Culture and Imperialism', in D. Lynch, ed., *Janeities: Austen's Disciples and Devotees*, Princeton and Oxford: Princeton University Press, 2000, pp. 206–23, p. 213. An important correction is A. J. Downie, 'Rehabilitating Sir Thomas Bertram', *SEL*, 50, 4 (2010), pp. 739–58.

18 'Mrs Transome, whose imperious will had availed little to ward off the great evils of her life, found the opiate for her discontent in the exertion of her will about smaller things . . . she liked every little sign of power her lot had left her.' George Eliot, *Felix Holt the Radical*, ed. Fred C. Thomson, Oxford: Clarendon Press, 1980, Chapter 1, p. 28.

19 Kay Souter, '*Mansfield Park* and Families', in Marcia McClintock Folsom and John Wiltshire, eds., *Approaches to Teaching Jane Austen's 'Mansfield Park'*, New York: MLA, 2014.

20 Bree, Sabor and Todd, *Jane Austen's Manuscript Works*, p. 21.

21 Souter, '*Mansfield Park* and Families'.

22 Todd, *The Cambridge Introduction to Jane Austen*, p. 77.

23 Janet Malcolm, 'What Maisie Didn't Know', in her *The Purloined Clinic*, New York: Vintage Books, 1993, pp. 92–102, p. 102.

Chapter 5: The story of Fanny Price

1 Among many distinguished recent fictions concerning displaced children are W. G. Sebald's *Austerlitz* (2001) and Richard Ford's *Canada* (2012).

2 Andrew Smith, 'Migrancy, Hybridity, and Post-Colonial Literary Studies', in Neil Lazarus, ed., *The Cambridge Companion to Post-Colonial Studies*, Cambridge University Press, 2004, pp. 241–61, p. 247.

3 Frances Burney was trapped in France by the abrupt renewal of the Napoleonic wars in 1802, and then forced to flee from Paris by Napoleon's escape from Elba and triumphant progress towards the city in 1815. In her 'Waterloo Journal' (1823) she gives an account of the terrors of her journey across France to Brussels that anticipates such accounts by refugees published since. 'What dreadful & afflicting scenes and vicissitudes have I witnessed and experienced', she wrote in a letter from Tornay in March 1815. *The Journals and Letters of Fanny Burney (Madame d'Arblay)*, vol. VIII, ed. Peter Hughes et al., Oxford: Clarendon Press, 1980, p. 71.

4 Kay Souter, 'Jane Austen and the Reconsigned Child: The True Identity of Fanny Price', *Persuasions: The Jane Austen Journal*, 23 (2002), pp. 205–14. I am indebted to this important article.

5 Margaret Humphreys, *Oranges and Sunshine* (originally published as *Empty Cradles* in 1994), London: Corgi Books, 2011. 'The child-migrant schemes were motivated by a desire to "rescue" children from the destitution, poverty and moral danger they were exposed to as part of the lower orders of British society', writes David Hill (himself one of the children) in the Preface to *The Forgotten Children, Fairbridge Farm School and its Betrayal of Australia's Child Migrants*, Sydney: Random House Australia, 2007, p. iii.

6 Humphreys, *Oranges and Sunshine*, pp. 164, 345. Aboriginal children of the 'stolen generations' were sometimes literally torn from their mothers and grandmothers: see, for example, Rita Huggins and Jackie Huggins, *Aunty Rita*, Sydney: Aboriginal Studies Press, 1994.

7 Fanny Price, a fictional figure, has been the target of extraordinary amounts of critical abuse, from Reginald Farrer in the *Quarterly Review*, July 1917 ('fiction holds no heroine more repulsive in her cast-iron self-righteousness and steely rigidity of prejudice'); to D. W. Harding in the 1970s ('Fanny is a dreary, debilitated, priggish goody-goody' (*Regulated Hatred*, p. 122)), to William H. Galperin, who, in *The Historical Jane Austen*, Philadephia: University of Pennsylvania Press, 2003, calls Fanny Price 'an especially odious figure' (p. 156).

8 'Southey's Life of Nelson; – I am tired of Lives of Nelson, being that I never read any. I will read this however, if Frank is mentioned in it.' Letter of 11–12 October 1813, *Letters*, p. 235.

9 Robert Southey, *The Life of Nelson* [1813], ed. E. R. H. Harvey, London: Macdonald, 1953, p. 4.

10 William Deresiewicz's account of *Mansfield Park* in terms of 'substitution' is one of the most perceptive the novel has received (*Jane Austen and the Romantic Poets*, New York: Columbia University Press, 2004, Chapter 3). I am indebted to his work. However, I understand substitution as a means, if not of self-healing, then of self-soothing that enables Fanny to attain some measure of independence and stability. Edmund is more to Fanny than a substitute for William.

11 'A geopolitical scaffolding surrounds the central construction of *Mansfield Park*', Knox-Shaw, *Jane Austen and the Enlightenment*, p. 186.

12 Lionel Trilling, 'Jane Austen and *Mansfield Park*', in Boris Ford, ed., *From Blake to Byron*, Harmondsworth: Penguin Books, 1957, pp. 112–29, p. 117; Tanner, *Jane Austen*, pp. 143, 171; Marilyn Butler, *Jane Austen and the War of Ideas*, Oxford: Clarendon Press, 1975, p. 248.

13 Nina Auerbach, 'Jane Austen's Dangerous Charm', in Judy Simons, ed., *Mansfield Park and Persuasion*, New Casebooks, London: Macmillan, 1997, pp. 49–66, p. 51; reprinted from Janet Todd, ed., *Jane Austen: New Perspectives*, New York and London: Holmes and Meier, 1983.

14 Gilbert and Gubar, *The Madwoman in the Attic*, p. 165; Galperin, *The Historical Jane Austen*, p. 170. The OED reserves 'metastatic' for the spread of a disease from its original site.

15 Eva Hoffman, *Lost in Translation* [1989], London: Minerva, 1991, p. 110.

16 The dating of the novel's action has been a subject of controversy. The dating of 1808–9, argued for by Chapman, and confirmed in the Cambridge edition, is shown on new evidence to be correct by A. J. Downie, 'The Chronology of *Mansfield Park*', *Modern Philology*, forthcoming. See also Knox-Shaw, *Jane Austen and the Enlightenment*, pp. 180–1.

17 Monica Cohen, 'The Price of a Maxim: Plausibility in Fanny's Happy Ending', in McClintock Folsom and Wiltshire, *Approaches to Teaching Jane Austen's Mansfield Park*; 2014.

18 Bharat Tandon writes of 'Fanny's righteous occupancy of the sofa' in *Jane Austen and the Morality of Conversation*, London: Anthem Press, 2003, p. 214. William H. Galperin writes that Fanny's 'headaches and somatic complaints' are means to gain attention, 'and, by turns, her way', in 'The Missed

Opportunities of *Mansfield Park*', in Claudia L. Johnson and Clara Tuite, eds., *A Companion to Jane Austen*, Oxford: Wiley–Blackwell, 2009, pp. 123–42, p. 131.

19 See especially Arthur Kleinman, *Social Origins of Distress and Disease: Depression, Neurasthenia and Pain in Modern China*, New Haven: Yale University Press, 1986, and Byron J. Good, *Medicine, Rationality and Experience: An Anthropological Perspective*, Cambridge University Press, 1994.

20 'The Quiet Thing: *Mansfield Park*' in Tanner, *Jane Austen*, p. 143. Tanner's 1986 essay, originally written as an Introduction to the Penguin edition of *Mansfield Park* in 1966, is also included, with Kathryn Sutherland's modern Introduction, in the most recent Penguin issue of the novel.

21 Marcia McClintock Folsom, 'Power in *Mansfield Park*: Austen's Study of Domination and Resistance', *Persuasions*, 34 (2012) pp. 83–98.

22 Richard Whateley, unsigned review, *Quarterly Review*, 24, 48 (January 1821) pp. 352–76, p. 367.

23 A reader need not know *Lovers' Vows* to feel for Fanny's anguish in this scene. Knowing the play's text may in fact deflect one's attention away from the novel's already understated focus on her responses.

24 The paragraphs that describe it in Chapter 16 of *Mansfield Park* have received much perceptive critical attention in recent years. An especially interesting discussion can be found in Julia Prewitt Brown, *The Bourgeois Interior*, Charlottesville and London: University of Virginia Press, 2008, pp. 48–52; 'Questions of Interiority: From *Pride and Prejudice* to *Mansfield Park*', in McClintock Folsom and Wiltshire, *Approaches to Teaching Jane Austen's Mansfield Park*, 2014; Deresiewitz, *Romantic Poets*, pp. 57–62; Claudia L. Johnson, 'Jane Austen's Relics and the Treasures of the East Room', *Persuasions* 28 (2006) pp. 217–20.

25 Gaston Bachelard, *The Poetics of Space* [1964], trans. Maria Jolas, Boston: Beacon Press, 1994. Chapter 4, 'Nests', p. 102.

26 Deresiewitz, *Romantic Poets*, p. 60.

27 Byatt and Sodré, *Imagining Characters*, p. 37.

28 This is what Bharat Tandon calls 'implicature': the switch to another subject implies everything that Fanny cannot say. *Morality of Conversation*, p. 96.

29 In the nineteenth century, the onset of puberty was around 15 for girls. Fanny's early ill-nourishment is unlikely to have made it earlier.

30 Dorice Williams Elliot, 'Gifts Always Come with Strings Attached: Teaching *Mansfield Park* in the Context of Gift Theory', in McClintock Folsom and Wiltshire, *Approaches to Teaching Jane Austen's Mansfield Park*, forthcoming. This essay uses Maus' work on gift relations to throw considerable light on the interpersonal dynamics in the novel, and I am indebted to it here.

31 Mary Hays, *Memoirs of Emma Courtney*, ed. Marilyn L. Brooks, Peterborough, Ontario: Broadview Press, 2000, p. 131.

32 Most sophisticatedly in Ellen Pollack, 'Incest and Liberty: *Mansfield Park*', in her *Incest and the English Novel 1684–1814*, Baltimore and London: Johns Hopkins University Press, 2003, pp. 162–99.

33 See Ruth Perry's authoritative discussion in 'Family Matters', in Clandia L. Johnson and Clara Tuite, eds., *A Companion to Jane Austen*, Oxford: Wiley–Blackwell, 2009, pp. 323–31, pp. 328–9. One example is Colonel Brandon's love for his cousin Eliza and their proposed elopement: Eliza is married off to his brother, also her cousin (*S&S* II: 9, 231).

34 Richard Cronin, 'The Literary Scene', in Janet Todd, ed., *Jane Austen in Context*, Cambridge University Press, 2005, pp. 289–96, p. 294.

35 Mary Waldron usefully diagnoses and is severe on this and other examples of Fanny's conduct: 'though without "guile"' Fanny is not harmless, representing as she does, not open-minded Christian charity, but an inflexible moral system which has little room for generosity and which gives her every opportunity for self-deception'. *Jane Austen and the Fiction of her Time*, Cambridge University Press, 1999, Chapter 4, 'The Frailties of Fanny' p. 109.

36 Byatt and Sodré, *Imagining Characters*, p. 39.

37 Frances Burney, *Evelina, or The History of a Young Lady's Entrance into the World* [1778], ed. F. D. MacKinnon, Oxford: Clarendon Press, 1930, vol. III, Letter XIX, pp. 476–85.

38 Lionel Trilling's 1954 article, which threw a long shadow over the criticism of *Mansfield Park*, is a pertinent example. He cites the final sentence: 'Fanny thinks that all that comes "within the view and patronage of Mansfield Park" as "dear to her heart and thoroughly perfect in her eyes,"' and adds that 'The judgment is not ironical. For the author as well as the heroine Mansfield Park is the good place – it is the Great Good Place.' He goes on to quote Yeats' praise of the country house in 'A Prayer for My Daughter' ('Jane Austen and "Mansfield Park", pp. 112–29, p. 127). Edward Said, following Trilling and Raymond Williams many years later, wrote that Mansfield Park is 'the very embodiment of all that is benign and actively good in England' ('Invention, Memory and Place', *Critical Inquiry* 26, 2 (2000) pp. 175–92, p. 182). The celebration of the house was also a celebration of Fanny's return. Trilling suggested that 'by reason of her virtue, the terrified little stranger in Mansfield Park grows up to be virtually its mistress'. Alistair Duckworth followed, with Fanny becoming 'effective mistress of the Mansfield estate' (*The Improvement of the Estate* [1971], rev. edn, Baltimore and London: Johns Hopkins University Press, 1994, p. 72). Soon critics were describing Fanny's position at the end of the novel as the estate's 'final spiritual mistress' (Edward W. Said, *Culture and Imperialism*, London: Vintage, 1993, p. 110) or, in a more recent variation, as the 'redeemer' of its fallen state (Michael Giffin, *Jane Austen and Religion: Salvation and Society in Georgian England*, London: Palgrave Macmillan, 2002, p. 138).

39 *Brideshead Revisited: The Sacred and Profane Memoirs of Captain Charles Ryder* [1945], rev. edn, London: Chapman and Hall, 1960, Preface, p. ii.

40 Peter Gay, ed., *The Freud Reader*, London: Vintage, 1995, pp. 297–300. Gay points out that '"Roman" is a broader designation than "romance"' (p. 297). Freud notices that children often imagine that they are a step-child or adopted, and that their real parents are of much higher social status. (This

common fantasy is visible in many fairy tales, but also informs the novels and plays mentioned.)

41 Said, *Culture and Imperialism*, p. 106.

Chapter 6: Emma's overhearing

1 Henry James, *The Portrait of a Lady* [1881], Oxford: World's Classics, 1958, p. 56.

2 Southam, *Critical Heritage*; [Lewes:] 'The Great Appraisal 1859', pp. 148–66, pp. 158, 159. Lewes' statements need qualification. But Pemberley and Donwell Abbey, which seem to be described, are in fact appraised as commodities: Pemberley for its picturesque values, and Donwell for its productivity as a working estate. Neither house's external appearance is particularised. The estate at Sotherton is not described, although its various divisions and the boundaries between them are important signifiers in the ethical action of the sequence in *Mansfield Park*. For an alternative view, see Barbara Britton Wenner, *Prospect and Refuge in the Landscape of Jane Austen*, Aldershot: Ashgate, 2006.

3 John Wiltshire, 'By Candlelight: Jane Austen, Technology and the Heritage Film', in Ariane Hudelet, David Monagham and John Wiltshire, *The Cinematic Jane Austen: Essays on the Filmic Sensibility of the Novels*, McFarland: Jefferson, NC and London: McFarland and Company, 2009, pp. 38–56, p. 45.

4 Andrew Elfenbein, 'Austen's Minimalism', Janet Todd, ed., in *The Cambridge Companion to Pride and Prejudice*, Cambridge University Press, 2013, pp. 109–21.

5 Byrne, *Theatre* discusses this incident and writes that here Austen 'taps into a long theatrical tradition of such overhearings' (pp. 126–7).

6 *The School for Scandal*, Act IV, scene 3; *Much Ado About Nothing*, Act III, scene 1, l. 30.

7 I know of no evidence that Jane Austen knew *Troilus*: my argument is that complex effects of multiple overhearing on the stage are replicated by other means in the novels.

8 I am grateful to Ann Blake for helping me identify occasions of overhearing in the theatre, and especially for alerting me to this scene.

9 Byrne, *Theatre*, note 5 above, and Gay, *Jane Austen and the Theatre*.

10 Reading – a matter of visual attention – is in fact similar to auditory attention since one cannot read (that is, focus on) two objects of perception, or passages of text, at the same time.

11 See Ann Gaylin, *Eavesdropping in the Novel from Austen to Proust*, Cambridge University Press, 2002. Though I give a different emphasis to overhearing in *Emma* and *Persuasion*, I am indebted to Gaylin's work.

12 A useful overview of research into attention is Elizabeth A. Styles, *The Psychology of Attention*, 2nd edn, Hove and New York: Psychology Press, 2006. In Chapter 5, 'Auditory and crossmodal attention', Styles writes that 'Much less is known about auditory attention than visual attention' (p. 120).

13 On the 'cocktail party effect' or 'problem', Styles writes that 'Somehow internal processes can allow one set of auditory information to gain precedence over the rest', ibid., p. 8.

14 Eric R. Kandel, *In Search of Memory: The Emergence of a New Science of Mind*, New York: Norton and Co., 2006, passim.

15 Iris Murdoch, *Existentialists and Mystics: Writings on Philosophy and Literature*, ed. Peter Conradi, London: Chatto and Windus, 1997, 'The Idea of Perfection', pp. 299–336, p. 327. I owe my knowledge of this work to June Sturrock's General Introduction to *Jane Austen's Families*, London and New York: Anthem Press, 2013, and have profited by her account.

16 Murdoch, *Existentialists and Mystics*, p. 329.

17 Emma assumes that Jane means Miss Bates, but it becomes clear later that it is Mrs Elton who has been harassing Jane that afternoon (III: 8, 414). Thus Emma's 'seeing' is once again woven together with misunderstanding.

18 William James, *The Principles of Psychology*, New York: Henry Holt, 1890, vol. I, pp. 403–4: 'Every one knows what attention is. It is the taking possession by the mind, in clear and vivid form, of one out of what seem several simultaneously possible objects or trains of thought. Focalization, concentration, of consciousness are of its essence. It implies withdrawal from some things in order to deal with others.'

19 Most neuroscience to date has concentrated on visual orienting or attention shifts. Richard Wright and Lawrence Ward, *Orienting of Attention*, New York: Oxford University Press, 2008; Michael I. Posner, *Cognitive Neuroscience of Attention*, 2nd edn, New York: Guildford Press, 2012.

20 W. R. Bion, *Experiences in Groups and Other Papers*, London: Tavistock, 1961, passim.

21 Melanie Klein, *Envy and Gratitude and Other Works 1946–1963*, London: Hogarth Press and the Institute of Psycho-Analysis, 1973, 'Notes on Some Schozoid Mechanisms' (1946).

22 D. W. Winnicott, *The Maturational Process and the Facilitating Environment*, Madison, CT: International Universities Press, 1991, 'The development of the capacity for concern' (1963), pp. 170–81. A succinct account of the capacity for concern is given in Winnicott's *The Family and Individual Development*, London: Tavistock, 1965, p. 13.

Chapter 7: Anne Elliot and the ambient world

1 Gaylin, *Eavesdropping*, p. 44.

2 Samuel Johnson, *The Yale Edition of the Works of Samuel Johnson*, vol. III, *The Rambler*, ed. W. J. Bate and Albrecht R. Strauss, New Haven and London: Yale University Press, 1969, p. 11.

3 Mary Favret, *Romantic Correspondence: Women, Politics and the Fiction of Letters*, Cambridge University Press, 1993, p. 169.

4 Samuel Johnson, *The History of Rasselas, Prince of Abisinnia* [1759], ed. J. P. Hardy, Oxford University Press, 1968, Chapter 18: 'The Prince finds a wise and

happy man', pp. 46–8, p. 48. Johnson's phrasing is more present in this novel even than in *Mansfield Park*. When Anne reflects on her attempt to persuade Benwick to read improving books 'that like many other moralists and preachers, she had been eloquent on a point in which her own conduct would ill bear examination' (1: 11, 109) Austen may well be remembering Johnson: '"Be not too hasty, said Imlac, to trust or to admire, the teachers of morality: they discourse like angels, but they live like men"' (*Rasselas*, 18, p. 47).

5 Linda Bree, Introduction, *Persuasion*, Peterborough, Ontario: Broadview Literary Texts, 1998, remarks on 'something very like masochism' in Anne Elliot's struggles to control her grief (p. 24).

6 D. A. Miller treats *Persuasion* as 'the great sentimental favorite in the Austen canon' in *Jane Austen, or The Secret of Style*, p. 68.

7 'This modesty, which I think so essential in your sex, will naturally dispose you to be rather silent in company', John Gregory, for example, advised his daughters: *A Father's Legacy to his Daughters* [1761], London: John Sharpe, 1822, p. 26. Mr Elliot, conventional in all things but his amours, 'thought her a most extraordinary young woman; in her temper, manners, mind, a model of female excellence' (11: 5, 172).

8 Friedrich Nietzsche, *The Gay Science*, ed. Bernard Williams, Cambridge University Press, 2001, p. 215. Lionel Trilling comments that 'In nineteenth-century England the ideal of professional commitment inherits a large part of the moral prestige of the gentleman' ('Jane Austen and *Mansfield Park*', p. 119).

9 *Romeo and Juliet*, Act 11, scene 1, ll. 100–1.

10 Gaylin, *Eavesdropping*, p. 47.

11 This extract is based on my interpretation of the reproduction of the manuscript (held at the British Library) in Appendix 1, 'Cancelled Chapters of *Persuasion*' in the Cambridge edition of the novel, edited by Janet Todd and Antje Blank, Appendix 1, p. 286, Cambridge University Press, 2006, together with the editors' transcription on p. 316.

12 'Cancelled Chapters of *Persuasion*' in the Cambridge edition, Appendix 1, p. 316.

13 'Jane Austen's Fiction Manuscripts: Two Chapters of Persuasion' at www. janeausten.ac.uk (accessed 21 January 2013).

14 I am indebted to, and am relying on, note 2 on page 7 of the 'Two Chapters of *Persuasion*: Diplomatic Display' in 'Jane Austen's Fiction Manuscripts'.

15 Jocelyn Harris discusses in full Jane Austen's cancellations and their significance in the chapter 'The Reviser at Work' in her *A Revolution beyond Expression: Jane Austen's Persuasion*, Delaware: University of Newark Press, 2007, pp. 43–8. I am indebted to her astringent commentary.

16 'Cancelled Chapters of *Persuasion*' in the Cambridge edition, Appendix 1, p. 317.

17 Sutherland, *Jane Austen's Textual Lives*, p. 166.

18 J. E. Austen-Leigh, *A Memoir of Jane Austen* [1870], ed. Kathryn Sutherland, Oxford: World's Classics, 2002, p. 125.

19 Beethoven's note on the MS of the Adagio movement of String Quartet 132, '*Neue Kraft fühlend*' (1825). 'The sense of power revived' is Austen's nephew's phrase, Austen-Leigh, *Memoir*, p. 125.

20 Cassandra recorded that the novel was 'finished' on 6 August 1816, Austen-Leigh, *Memoir*, pp. 253–4.

21 Brian Southam, '*Persuasion*: The Cancelled Chapters', in J. David Grey, ed., *The Jane Austen Handbook*, London: Athlone Press, 1986, pp. 322–3, p. 323. Mary Favret writes that 'As our attention switches from one spot to another in the salon, we feel the mounting force of an unarticulated undercurrent. Each phrase in the air is transformed by Anne's consciousness into a message or phrasal signal to herself', *Romantic Correspondence*, p. 167.

22 'As she is arguing with Harville – and of course her words have a double target and dual purpose, as she hopes that the nearby Wentworth, seated and writing, will hear them and detect the personal message contained in the general statements' (Tanner, *Jane Austen*, p. 241); 'The rhetorical speeches to Harville form the heroine's declaration of love to the listening Wentworth, to whom she has tried to speak clearly over several interrupted encounters' (Introduction, *Persuasion*, in the Cambridge edition, p. lxxxii); 'While Anne converses with Harville, she deliberately addresses Wentworth' (Gaylin, *Eavesdropping*, p. 49).

23 Harris, *A Revolution beyond Expression*, pp. 47, 190.

24 Sutherland writes that 'we sense a linked thematic and somatic recovery of rhythm' in the writing of this scene, *Jane Austen's Textual Lives*, p. 167.

25 Moreland Perkins, *Reshaping the Sexes in Sense and Sensibility*, Charlottesville, VA and London: University Press of Virginia, 1998, p. 5.

26 Richard Simpson in the *North British Review* of April 1870 was the first to suggest that 'the chapters which she wrote during the last months of her life are directly founded upon Shakespeare' and that the exchange between Anne and Wentworth resembles Viola's oblique recounting of her own love in *Twelfth Night* (Act II, scene 4, ll. 102–20); Southam, *Critical Heritage*, pp. 256–7. Orsino's claim in this scene that women's hearts 'lack retention' is answered earlier in the novel: 'Alas! . . . she found, that to retentive feelings, eight years may be little more than nothing' (1: 7, 65).

27 Virginia Woolf, *To the Lighthouse* [1927], ed. Stella McNichol, London: Penguin Books, 2000, p. 186: 'She saw the colour burning on a framework of steel' p. 54.

28 Paul N. Zietlow, 'Luck and Fortuitous Circumstance in *Persuasion*: Two Interpretations', *ELH*, 32 (1965) pp. 179–95.

Bibliography

Primary texts

Benedict, Barbara M., and Le Faye, Deidre, eds., Jane Austen, *Northanger Abbey*, The Cambridge Edition of the Works of Jane Austen, Cambridge University Press, 2006.

R. W. Chapman, ed., *The Works of Jane Austen*, vol. vi, *Minor Works*, Oxford University Press, 1954.

Copeland, Edward, ed., Jane Austen, *Sense and Sensibility*, The Cambridge Edition of the Works of Jane Austen, Cambridge University Press, 2006.

Cronin, Richard and McMillan, Dorothy, eds., Jane Austen, *Emma*, The Cambridge Edition of the Works of Jane Austen, Cambridge University Press, 2005.

Le Faye, Deidre, ed., *Jane Austen's Letters*, 3rd edn, Oxford University Press, 1995.

Rogers, Pat, ed., Jane Austen, *Pride and Prejudice*, The Cambridge Edition of the Works of Jane Austen, Cambridge University Press, 2006.

Sabor, Peter, ed., Jane Austen, *Juvenilia*, The Cambridge Edition of the Works of Jane Austen, Cambridge University Press, 2006.

Todd, Janet, and Blank, Antje, eds., Jane Austen, *Persuasion*, The Cambridge Edition of the Works of Jane Austen, Cambridge University Press, 2006.

Todd, Janet, and Bree, Linda, eds., Jane Austen, *Later Manuscripts*, The Cambridge Edition of the Works of Jane Austen, Cambridge University Press, 2008.

Wiltshire, John, ed., Jane Austen, *Mansfield Park*, The Cambridge Edition of the Works of Jane Austen, Cambridge University Press, 2005.

Secondary texts

Auerbach, Nina, 'Jane Austen's Dangerous Charm', in Judy Simons, ed., *Mansfield Park and Persuasion*, London: Macmillan, 1997, pp. 49–66.

Austen-Leigh, J. E., *A Memoir of Jane Austen* [1870], ed. Kathryn Sutherland, Oxford: World's Classics, 2002.

Babb, Howard S., *Jane Austen's Novels: The Fabric of Dialogue*, Columbus: Ohio State University Press, 1962.

Bachelard, Gaston, *The Poetics of Space* [1964], trans. Maria Jolas, Boston: Beacon Press, 1994.

Bacon, Francis, *Novum Organum* [1620], trans. R. Ellis and James Spedding, in Edwin A. Burtt, ed., *The English Philosophers from Bacon to Mill*, New York: The Modern Library, 1939.

Bion, W. R., *Experiences in Groups and Other Papers*, London: Tavistock, 1961.

Boswell, James, *Boswell's Life of Johnson*, ed. G. B. Hill, rev. L. F. Powell, 5 vols., Oxford: Clarendon Press [1934–] 2nd edn 1964.

Boulukos, George E., 'The Politics of Silence: *Mansfield Park* and the Amelioration of Slavery', *Novel: A Forum for Fiction* (Summer 2006) pp. 362–83.

Bradley, A. C., 'Jane Austen', in his *A Miscellany*, London: Macmillan, 1929, pp. 32–72.

Bray, Joe, *The Female Reader in the English Novel: From Burney to Austen*, New York and London: Routledge, 2009.

Bree, Linda, 'Introduction', *Persuasion*, Peterborough, Ontario: Broadview Literary Texts, 1998.

Bree, Linda, Sabor, Peter and Todd, Janet, eds., *Jane Austen's Manuscript Works*, Peterborough, Ontario: Broadview Literary Texts, 2013.

Brower, Reuben A., 'The Controlling Hand: Jane Austen and *Pride and Prejudice*', *Scrutiny*, 13, 2 (1945) pp. 99–111.

Brown, Julia Prewitt, *The Bourgeois Interior*, Charlottesville and London: University of Virginia Press, 2008.

   'Questions of Interiority: From *Pride and Prejudice* to *Mansfield Park*', in Marcia McClintock Folsom and John Wiltshire, eds., *Approaches to Teaching Jane Austen's Mansfield Park*, New York: Modern Language Association, 2014.

Burney, Frances, *Evelina, or The History of a Young Lady's Entrance into the World*, ed. F. D. MacKinnon, Oxford: Clarendon Press, 1930.

   The Journals and Letters of Fanny Burney (Madame d'Arblay), vol. VIII, ed. Peter Hughes et al., Oxford: Clarendon Press, 1980.

Butler, Marilyn, *Jane Austen and the War of Ideas*, Oxford: Clarendon Press, 1975.

Byatt, A. S. and Sodré, Ignês, *Imagining Characters: Six Conversations about Women Writers*, London: Vintage, 1995.

Byrne, Paula, *Jane Austen and the Theatre*, London: Hambledon and London, 2002.

Clark, J. C. D., *English Society 1660–1832*, Cambridge University Press, 2000.

Clark, Lorna J., *The Letters of Sarah Harriet Burney*, Athens, GA and London: University of Georgia Press, 1998.

Cohen, Monica, 'The Price of a Maxim: Plausibility in Fanny's Happy Ending', in Marcia McClintock Folsom and John Wiltshire, eds., *Approaches to Teaching Jane Austen's Mansfield Park*, New York: Modern Language Association, 2014.

Conrad, Joseph, *The Shadow-Line, A Confession*, London: John Grant, 1923.

Cossy, Valérie, *Jane Austen in Switzerland: A Study of the Early French Translations*, Geneva: Editions Slatkine, 2006.

Cronin, Richard, 'The Literary Scene', in Janet Todd, ed., *Jane Austen in Context*, Cambridge University Press, 2005, pp. 289–96.

Deresiewicz, William, *Jane Austen and the Romantic Poets*, New York: Columbia University Press, 2004.

Downie, A. J., 'The Chronology of *Mansfield Park*', *Modern Philology*, forthcoming.

'Rehabilitating Sir Thomas Bertram', *SEL*, 50, 4 (2010) pp. 739–58.

Duckworth, Alistair, *The Improvement of the Estate* [1971], rev. edn, Baltimore and London: Johns Hopkins University Press, 1994.

Eakin, Paul John, 'Autobiography, Identity and the Fictions of Memory', in Daniel L. Schacter and Elaine Scarry, eds., *Memory, Brain, and Belief*, Cambridge, MA and London: Harvard University Press, 2000, pp. 290–306.

Ekman, Paul, and Friesen, Wallace V., *Unmasking the Face*, Engelwood Cliffs, NJ: Prentice Hall [1975]; Cambridge, MA: Major Books, 2003.

Elfenbein, Andrew, 'Austen's Minimalism', in Janet Todd, ed., *The Cambridge Companion to Pride and Prejudice*, Cambridge University Press, 2013, pp. 109–21.

Elliot, Dorice Williams, 'Gifts Always Come with Strings Attached: Teaching *Mansfield Park* in the Context of Gift Theory', in Marcia McClintock Folsom and John Wiltshire, eds., *Approaches to Teaching Jane Austen's Mansfield Park*, New York: Modern Language Association, 2014.

Eliot, George, *Felix Holt the Radical*, ed. Fred C. Thomson, Oxford: Clarendon Press, 1980.

Silas Marner, in *The Novels of George Eliot*, vol. III, Edinburgh and London: Blackwood and Sons, n. d., Chapter 3, pp. 24–5.

Favret, Mary, *Romantic Correspondence: Women, Politics and the Fiction of Letters*, Cambridge University Press, 1993.

War at a Distance: Romanticism and the Making of Modern Wartime, Princeton and London: Princeton University Press, 2009.

Fergus, Jan, *Jane Austen and the Didactic Novel*, London: Macmillan, 1983.

Ferguson, Moira, '*Mansfield Park*, Slavery, Colonialism and Gender', *Oxford Literary Review*, 3 (1991) pp. 118–39.

Folsom, Marcia McClintock, 'Power in *Mansfield Park*: Austen's Study of Domination and Resistance', *Persuasions*, 34 (2012) pp. 83–98.

'The Narrator's Voice and the Sense of *Sense and Sensibility*, *Persuasions*, 33 (2011) pp. 29–39.

'"Taking Different Positions": Knowing and Feeling in *Pride and Prejudice*', in Marcia McClintock Folsom, ed., *Approaches to Teaching Jane Austen's Pride and Prejudice*, New York: Modern Language Association, 1993, pp. 100–14.

Folsom, Marcia McClintock, and Wiltshire, John, eds., *Approaches to Teaching Jane Austen's Mansfield Park*, New York: Modern Language Association, 2014.

Fraiman, Susan, 'Jane Austen and Edward Said: Gender, Culture and Imperialism', in D. Lynch, ed., *Janeities: Austen's Disciples and Devotees*, Princeton and Oxford: Princeton University Press, 2000, pp. 206–23.

Fullerton, Susannah, *Happily Ever After*, London: Frances Lincoln, 2013.
Galperin, William H., *The Historical Jane Austen*, Philadephia: University of Pennsylvania Press, 2003.
'The Missed Opportunities of *Mansfield Park*', in Claudia L. Johnson and Clara Tuite, eds. *A Companion to Jane Austen*, Oxford: Wiley–Blackwell, 2009, pp. 123–42.
Gatrell, Vic, *City of Laughter: Sex and Satire in Eighteenth-Century London*, London: Atlantic Books, 2006.
Gay, Penny, *Jane Austen and the Theatre*, Cambridge University Press, 2002.
Gay, Peter, ed., *The Freud Reader*, London: Vintage, 1995.
Gaylin, Ann, *Eavesdropping in the Novel from Austen to Proust*, Cambridge University Press, 2002.
Giffin, Michael, *Jane Austen and Religion: Salvation and Society in Georgian England*, London: Palgrave Macmillan, 2002.
Gilbert, Sandra M. and Gubar, Susan, *The Madwoman in the Attic: The Woman Writer and the Nineteenth-Century Literary Imagination*, New Haven: Yale University Press, 1979.
Good, Byron J., *Medicine, Rationality and Experience: An Anthropological Perspective*, Cambridge University Press, 1994.
Gregory, John, *A Father's Legacy to his Daughters* [1761], London: John Sharpe, 1822.
Griffiths, Ann, 'Sébastien Erard, A Dynasty of Harp Makers', www.dlaismusicpublishers.co.uk/pages/harpists/erard.htm. Accessed 26 January 2013.
Grundy, Isobel, 'Jane Austen and Literary Traditions', in Edward Copeland and Juliet McMaster, eds., *The Cambridge Companion to Jane Austen*, Cambridge University Press, 1997, pp. 189–210.
Halévy, Elie, *England in 1815* [1913, 1924], trans. E. I. Watkin and D. A. Barker, London: Ernest Benn, 1961.
Harding, D. W., *Regulated Hatred and Other Essays on Jane Austen*, ed. Monica Lawlor, London: Athlone Press, 1998.
Harris, Jocelyn, *Jane Austen's Art of Memory*, Cambridge University Press, 1989.
A Revolution beyond Expression: Jane Austen's Persuasion, Delaware: University of Newark Press, 2007.
Hays, Mary, *Memoirs of Emma Courtney*, ed. Marilyn L. Brooks, Peterborough, Ontario: Broadview Press, 2000.
Heydt-Stevenson, Jill, *Austen's Unbecoming Conjunctions*, New York: Palgrave Macmillan, 2005.
Hill, David, *The Forgotten Children, Fairbridge Farm School and its Betrayal of Australia's Child Migrants*, Sydney: Random House Australia, 2007.
Hoffman, Eva, *Lost in Translation* [1989], London: Minerva, 1991.
Hudelet, Ariane, 'Beyond Words, Beyond Images: Jane Austen and the Art of Mise en Scène', in Ariane Hudelet, David Monagham and John Wiltshire, eds., *The Cinematic Jane Austen: Essays on the Filmic Sensibility of the Novels*, Jefferson, NC and London: McFarland and Company, 2009, pp. 57–75.

Huggins, Rita and Huggins, Jackie, *Aunty Rita*, Sydney: Aboriginal Studies Press, 1994.

Humphreys, Margaret, *Oranges and Sunshine* (originally published as *Empty Cradles* in 1994), London: Corgi Books, 2011.

James, Henry, *The Bostonians* [1886] London: John Lehmann, 1952.

The Portrait of a Lady [1881], Oxford: World's Classics, 1958.

James, William, *The Principles of Psychology*, New York: Henry Holt, 1890.

'Jane Austen's Fiction Manuscripts: Two Chapters of *Persuasion*' at www.janeausten.ac.uk

Jane Austen's Lady Susan: A Facsimile of the Manuscript in the Pierpont Morgan Library and the 1925 Printed Edition, New York and London: Garland, 1989.

Johnson, Claudia L., *Jane Austen: Women, Politics, and the Novel*, Chicago University Press, 1988.

'A "Sweet Face as White as Death", Jane Austen and the Politics of Female Sensibility', *Novel: A Forum on Fiction*, 22 (1989) pp. 159–74.

Johnson Samuel *The History of Rasselas, Prince of Abisinnia* [1759], ed. J. P. Hardy, Oxford University Press, 1968.

A Journey to the Western Islands of Scotland, ed. Mary Lascelles, New Haven and London: Yale University Press, 1971.

The Yale Edition of the Works of Samuel Johnson, vol. II, *The Idler* and *The Adventurer*, ed. W. J. Bate *et al.* 1963; vol. III, *The Rambler*, ed. W. J. Bate and Albrecht R. Strauss, New Haven and London: Yale University Press, 1969.

Kandel, Eric R., *In Search of Memory: The Emergence of a New Science of Mind*, New York: Norton and Co., 2006.

Klein, Melanie, *Envy and Gratitude and Other Works 1946–1963*, London: Hogarth Press and the Institute of Psycho-Analysis, 1973.

Kleinman, Arthur, *Social Origins of Distress and Disease: Depression, Neurasthenia and Pain in Modern China*, New Haven: Yale University Press, 1986.

Knox-Shaw, Peter, *Jane Austen and the Enlightenment*, Cambridge University Press, 2004.

Le Faye, Deirdre, *Jane Austen: A Family Record*, 2nd edn, Cambridge University Press, 2004.

Leavis, F. R., in *Valuation in Criticism and Other Essays*, ed. G. Singh, Cambridge University Press, 1986.

[Lewes, George:] 'The Great Appraisal 1859', in B. C. Southam, ed., *Jane Austen: The Critical Heritage*, London: Routledge and Kegan Paul, 1968, pp, 148–66, first published in *Blackwood's Edinburgh Magazine*, July 1859.

'G. H. Lewes on Jane Austen 1847'; 'The Great Appraisal 1859', first published in *Blackwood's Edinburgh Magazine*, July 1859), in B. C. Southam, ed., *Jane Austen: The Critical Heritage*, London: Routledge and Kegan Paul, 1968, pp. 124–5, 148–66.

Locke, John, *An Essay Concerning Human Understanding* [1689], ed. Peter Nidditch, Oxford: Clarendon Press, 1975.

Lodge, David, 'Jane Austen's Novels: Form and Structure', in J. David Grey, ed., *The Jane Austen Handbook*, London: Athlone, 1986, pp. 165–78.

Lynch, Deidre Shauna, *The Economy of Character, Novels, Market Culture and the Business of Inner Meaning*, University of Chicago Press, 1998.

Malcolm, Janet, 'What Maisie Didn't Know', in her *The Purloined Clinic*, New York: Vintage Books, 1993, pp. 92–102.

Maurer, Shawn Lisa. 'At Seventeen: Adolescence in *Sense and Sensibility*', *Eighteenth-Century Fiction*, 25, 4 Summer (2013) pp. 721–50.

Miller, D. A., *Jane Austen, or The Secret of Style*, Princeton and Oxford: Princeton University Press, 2003.

Mullan, John, *What Matters in Jane Austen? Twenty Crucial Puzzles Solved*, London: Bloomsbury, 2012.

Murdoch, Iris, *Existentialists and Mystics: Writings on Philosophy and Literature*, ed. Peter Conradi, London: Chatto and Windus, 1997.

Nietzsche, Friedrich, *The Gay Science*, ed. Bernard Williams, Cambridge University Press, 2001.

Perkins, Moreland, *Reshaping the Sexes in Sense and Sensibility*, Charlottesville, VA and London: University Press of Virginia, 1998.

Perry, Ruth, 'Family Matters', in Claudia L. Johnson and Clara Tuite, eds., *A Companion to Jane Austen*, Oxford: Wiley–Blackwell, 2009, pp. 323–31.

Polhemus, Robert M., *Erotic Faith, Being in Love from Jane Austen to D. H. Lawrence*, Chicago and London: University of Chicago Press, 1990.

Pollack, Ellen, *Incest and the English Novel 1684–1814*, Baltimore and London: Johns Hopkins University Press, 2003.

Poovey, Mary, 'From Politics to Silence: Jane Austen's Nonreferential Aesthetic', in Claudia L. Johnson and Clara Tuite, eds., *A Companion to Jane Austen*, Oxford: Wiley–Blackwell, 2009, pp. 251–60.

Posner, Michael I., *Cognitive Neuroscience of Attention*, 2nd edn, New York: Guildford Press, 2012.

Radcliffe, Ann, *The Romance of the Forest*, ed. Chloe Chard, World's Classics, Oxford University Press, 1986.

Roberts, Warren, *Jane Austen and the French Revolution*, London: Macmillan, 1979.

Rose, Steven, 'Memories are Made of This', in A. S. Byatt and H. H. Wood, eds., *Memory: An Anthology*, London: Vintage Books, 2009, pp. 54–76.

Said, Edward W., *Culture and Imperialism*, London: Vintage, 1993.
    'Invention, Memory and Place', *Critical Inquiry* 26, 2 (2000) pp. 175–92.

Schacter, Daniel L., *The Seven Sins of Memory*, Boston and New York: Houghton Mifflin Company, 2001.

Smiles, Samuel, *A Publisher and his Friends: Memoir and Correspondence of the Late John Murray*, London: John Murray, 1891.

Smith, Andrew, 'Migrancy, Hybridity, and Post-Colonial Literary Studies', in Neil Lazarus, ed., *The Cambridge Companion to Post-Colonial Studies*, Cambridge University Press, 2004, pp. 241–61.

Sodré, Ignês, 'Where the Lights and Shadows Fall: On Not Being Able to Remember and Not Being Able to Forget', in A. S. Byatt and H. H. Wood, eds., *Memory: An Anthology*, London: Vintage Books, 2009, pp. 40–53.

Souter, Kay, 'Jane Austen and the Reconsigned Child: The True Identity of Fanny Price', *Persuasions: The Jane Austen Journal*, 23 (2002) pp. 205–14.

'*Mansfield Park* and Families', in Marcia McClintock Folsom and John Wiltshire, eds., *Approaches to Teaching Jane Austen's Mansfield Park*, New York: MLA, 2014.

Southam, B. C. *Jane Austen: A Students' Guide to the Later Manuscript Works*, London: Concord Books, 2007.

ed., *Jane Austen: The Critical Heritage*, London: Routledge and Kegan Paul, 1968.

ed., *Jane Austen: The Critical Heritage Volume II 1870–1940*, London and New York: Routledge and Kegan Paul, 1987.

'*Persuasion*: The Cancelled Chapters', in J. David Grey, ed., *The Jane Austen Handbook*, London: Athlone Press, 1986, pp. 322–3.

'The Silence of the Bertrams: Slavery and the Chronology of *Mansfield Park*', *TLS*, 17 February 1995.

Southey, Robert, *The Life of Nelson* [1813], ed. E. R. H. Harvey, London: Macdonald, 1953.

Sturrock, June, *Jane Austen's Families*, London and New York: Anthem Press, 2013.

Styles, Elizabeth A., *The Psychology of Attention*, 2nd edn, Hove and New York: Psychology Press, 2006.

Sutherland, Kathryn. 'Jane Austen and the Invention of the Serious Modern Novel', in Thomas Keymer and Jon Mee, eds., *The Cambridge Companion to English Literature*, Cambridge University Press, 2004, pp. 244–62.

'Jane Austen's Dealings with John Murray and his Firm', *Review of English Studies*, 64, 263 (March 2012), pp. 105–26.

Jane Austen's Textual Lives: From Aeschylus to Bollywood, Oxford University Press, 2005.

Tanner, Tony, *Jane Austen* [1986], reissued edition, Basingstoke: Palgrave Macmillan, 2007.

Tandon, Bharat, *Jane Austen and the Morality of Conversation*, London: Anthem Press, 2003.

Todd, Janet, ed., *The Cambridge Companion to Pride and Prejudice*, Cambridge University Press, 2013.

The Cambridge Introduction to Jane Austen, Cambridge University Press, 2006.

Trilling, Lionel, 'Jane Austen and *Mansfield Park*', originally published in *Encounter*, 3, 3, (1954) pp. 9–19, cited from Boris Ford, ed., *From Blake to Byron*, Harmondsworth: Penguin Books, 1957, pp. 112–29.

Trumpener, Katie, 'The Virago Jane Austen', in Deidre Lynch, ed., *Janeites: Austen's Disciples and Devotees*, Princeton and Oxford: Princeton University Press, 2000, pp. 140–65.

Tulving, Endel, 'Coding and Representation: Searching for a Home in the Brain', in Henry L. Roediger III, Yadin Dudai and Susan M. Fitzpatrick, *Science of Memory: Concepts*, New York: Oxford University Press, 2007, pp. 65–8.

Waldron, Mary, *Jane Austen and the Fiction of her Time*, Cambridge University Press, 1999.

Waugh, Evelyn, *Brideshead Revisited: The Sacred and Profane Memoirs of Captain Charles Ryder* [1945], rev. edn, London: Chapman and Hall, 1960.

Wenner, Barbara Britton, *Prospect and Refuge in the Landscape of Jane Austen*, Aldershot: Ashgate, 2006.

[Whateley, Richard], unsigned review, *Quarterly Review*, 24, 48 (January 1821) pp. 352–76.

White, Laura Mooneyham, *Jane Austen's Anglicanism*, New York and Farnham, Surrey: Ashgate, 2011.

Wiltshire, John, 'By Candlelight: Jane Austen, Technology and the Heritage Film', in Ariane Hudelet, David Monagham and John Wiltshire, eds., *The Cinematic Jane Austen: Essays on the Filmic Sensibility of the Novels*, McFarland: Jefferson, NC and London: McFarland and Company, 2009, pp. 38–56.

Winnicott, D. W., *The Family and Individual Development*, London: Tavistock, 1965.

The Maturational Process and the Facilitating Environment, Madison, CT: International Universities Press, 1991.

Winter, Alison, *Memory: Fragments of a Modern History*, Chicago and London: University of Chicago Press, 2012.

Wood, James, *The Broken Estate, Essays on Literature and Belief*, New York: The Modern Library, 2000.

Woolf, Virginia, *To the Lighthouse* [1927], ed. Stella McNichol, London: Penguin Books, 2000.

Wright, Richard, and Ward, Lawrence, *Orienting of Attention*, New York: Oxford University Press, 2008.

Zietlow, Paul N., 'Luck and Fortuitous Circumstance in *Persuasion*: Two Interpretations', *ELH*, 32 (1965) pp. 179–95.

Index

Austen's novels are listed alphabetically with chapters and their notes in bold.